iPhone
For Seniors

FOR
DUMMIES
A Wiley Brand

5th Edition

by Nancy C. Muir

FOR
DUMMIES
A Wiley Brand

iPhone For Seniors For Dummies®, 5th Edition

Published by: **John Wiley & Sons, Inc.,** 111 River Street, Hoboken, NJ 07030-5774, www.wiley.com

Copyright © 2016 by John Wiley & Sons, Inc., Hoboken, New Jersey

Published simultaneously in Canada

No part of this publication may be reproduced, stored in a retrieval system, or transmitted in any form or by any means, electronic, mechanical, photocopying, recording, scanning or otherwise, except as permitted under Sections 107 or 108 of the 1976 United States Copyright Act, without the prior written permission of the Publisher. Requests to the Publisher for permission should be addressed to the Permissions Department, John Wiley & Sons, Inc., 111 River Street, Hoboken, NJ 07030, (201) 748-6011, fax (201) 748-6008, or online at http://www.wiley.com/go/permissions.

Trademarks: Wiley, For Dummies, the Dummies Man logo, Dummies.com, Making Everything Easier, and related trade dress are trademarks or registered trademarks of John Wiley & Sons, Inc., and may not be used without written permission. iPhone is a registered trademark of Apple. All other trademarks are the property of their respective owners. John Wiley & Sons, Inc., is not associated with any product or vendor mentioned in this book.

For general information on our other products and services, please contact our Customer Care Department within the U.S. at 877-762-2974, outside the U.S. at 317-572-3993, or fax 317-572-4002. For technical support, please visit www.wiley.com/techsupport.

Wiley publishes in a variety of print and electronic formats and by print-on-demand. Some material included with standard print versions of this book may not be included in e-books or in print-on-demand. If this book refers to media such as a CD or DVD that is not included in the version you purchased, you may download this material at http://booksupport.wiley.com. For more information about Wiley products, visit www.wiley.com.

Library of Congress Control Number: 2015954370

ISBN 978-1-119-13776-4 (pbk); ISBN 978-1-119-14136-5 (ebk); ISBN 978-1-119-14137-2 (ebk)

Manufactured in the United States of America

10 9 8 7 6 5 4 3 2 1

Contents at a Glance

Table of Contents

Introduction

*I*f you bought this book (or are even thinking about buying it), you've probably already made the decision to buy an iPhone. The iPhone is designed to be easy to use, but still you can spend hours exploring the preinstalled apps, finding out how to change settings, and figuring out how to sync the device to your computer or through iCloud. I've invested those hours so that you don't have to — and I've added advice and tips for getting the most out of your iPhone.

This book helps you get going with the iPhone quickly and painlessly so that you can move directly to the fun part.

About This Book

This book is specifically written for mature people like you, folks who may be relatively new to using a smartphone and want to discover the basics of buying an iPhone 6s or 6s Plus, making and receiving phone calls, working with its preinstalled apps, and getting on the Internet. In writing this book, I've tried to consider the types of activities that might interest someone who is 50 years old or older and picking up an iPhone for the first time.

Foolish Assumptions

This book is organized by sets of tasks. These tasks start from the beginning, assuming that you've never laid your hands on an iPhone, and guide you through basic steps using nontechnical language.

This book covers going online using either a Wi-Fi or 3G/4G connection. I'm also assuming that you'll want to use the iBooks e-reader app, so I cover its features in Chapter 14. I also assume that you might be interested in the Health app, so I give you an overview of it in Chapter 20.

Icons Used in This Book

Icons are tiny pictures in the margin of pages that call your attention to special advice or information, such as:

 These brief pieces of advice help you to take a skill further or provide alternate ways of getting things done.

 New icons indicate a feature new with iOS 9 or new iPhone 6s phones.

Beyond the Book

Extra online content supplements this book to help you go further. Go online to take advantage of these features:

Cheat Sheet (www.dummies.com/cheatsheet/iphoneforseniors): This book's Cheat Sheet offers a list of General settings, Mail, Contacts, and Calendar settings to be aware of, and the settings you can control for browsing in Safari.

Dummies.com online articles: The Parts Pages of this book provide links to helpful articles on Dummies.com. These articles are listed on the book's Extras page at www.dummies.com/extras/iphonesforseniors. Topics include commands to use when talking to Siri, some News, Weather, and Stocks apps you might want to check out, and a rundown of Apple Music.

Where to Go from Here

You can work through this book from beginning to end or simply open a chapter to solve a problem or acquire a specific new skill whenever you need it. The steps in every task quickly get you to where you want to go, without a lot of technical explanation.

Note: At the time I wrote this book, all the information it contained was accurate for the iPhone 4s, 5, 5s, and 5c, 6 and 6 Plus, 6s and 6s Plus and version 9 of the iOS (operating system) used by the iPhone, and version 12/2/2 of iTunes. Apple is likely to introduce new iPhone models and new versions of iOS and iTunes between book editions. If you've bought a new iPhone and found that its hardware, user interface, or the version of iTunes on your computer looks a little different, be sure to check out what Apple has to say at www.apple. com/iphone. You'll no doubt find updates there on the company's latest releases.

Part I
Making the iPhone Work for You

Buying Your iPhone

You've read about it. You've seen on the news the lines at Apple Stores on the day a new version of the iPhone is released. You're so intrigued that you've decided to get your own iPhone to have a smartphone that offers much more than the ability to make and receive calls. iPhone also offers lots of fun apps, such as games and exercise trackers; allows you to explore the online world; lets you read e-books, magazines, and other periodicals; allows you to take and organize photos; plays music and videos, and a lot more.

Trust me: You've made a good decision, because the iPhone redefines the mobile phone experience in an exciting way. It's also an absolutely perfect fit for many seniors.

In this chapter, you learn about the advantages of the iPhone, as well as where to buy this little gem and associated data plans from providers. After you have one in your hands, I help you explore what's in the box and get an overview of the little buttons and slots you'll encounter — luckily, the iPhone has very few of them.

Discover What's New in iPhone 6s and 6s Plus, and iOS 9

Apple's iPhone gets its features from a combination of hardware and its software operating system (called *iOS*; the term is short for iPhone operating system. The most current operating system is iOS 9. It's helpful to understand which new features the iPhone 6s and 6s Plus phones and iOS 9 bring to the table (all of which are covered in more detail in this book). New features in iPhone 6s and 6s Plus include

➡ **Improved display:** Apple says that the iPhone 6s and 6s Plus have a stronger glass face, but also a better touch sensor to accommodate their new 3D Touch feature.

➡ **An A9 chip:** This 64-bit chip is 70 percent faster handling basic processing functions and 90 percent faster handling graphics tasks.

➡ **An M9 coprocessor:** This updated motion sensing coprocessor makes it possible for your iPhone to detect and monitor data that provides information about your motion even more efficiently than its predecessor does. This capability supports lots of interesting fitness apps, including the Health app from Apple.

➡ **The case and charging docks:** Both new iPhones are offered in gold, silver, rose gold, and space gray with the new 2000 series aluminum case. Additionally, Apple has come out new charging dock accessories for your phone.

➡ **A 12mp iSight camera:** The camera in iPhone 6s and 6s Plus offers such features as a True Tone Flash sensor that knows when flash is needed for a shot and a new display chip that lights up three times brighter than previous flash features.

➡ **Camera frames per second:** The camera offers 4K video quality with 8 million pixels in every frame (that means your photos are super clear). For FaceTime calls, you can take advantage of the 5MP FaceTime HD camera.

➡ **3D Touch and Quick Actions:** This new feature for iPhone 6s Plus allows you to use three levels of pressure on the iPhone screen to select, preview, or view an item such as an email or map. Additionally, Quick Actions allow you to press an app on the Home screen and get shortcut options for things like messaging a favorite contact or quickly open the camera app for taking a selfie (a picture of yourself).

➡ **Apple Pay:** This feature offers the ability to pay at selected retailers using the Apple Pay feature and Touch ID feature built into the Home button. With iOS 9, even more credit and store cards are compatible with Apple Pay. You can also double-tap the Home button from the lock screen to make a payment. Set up Apple Pay from the Wallet & Apple Pay settings on your iPhone, or visit Apple's website for more about setting up and using Wallet.

➡ **Improved battery life:** The iPhone 6s supports up to 24 hours of talk and up to 14 hours of video viewing. The 6s Plus can give you as many as 14 hours of talk and 11 hours of video. With iOS 9 comes a Lower Power mode, which stops power-draining features such as updating and downloading emails automatically to save power. Also, there's a sensor that detects when you place your iPhone face down and goes to the lock screen to save power.

Throughout this book, I highlight features that are relevant only in using the iPhone 5s and/or iPhone 5c, as well as 6 and 6 Plus and 6s and 6s Plus, so you can use the majority of this book no matter which version of the iPhone you own as long as you have iOS 9 installed.

Any iPhone device from the iPhone 4s forward can make use of most features of iOS 9 if you update the operating system (discussed in detail in Chapter 2); this book is based on version 9 of iOS. This update to the operating system adds many new features, including

➡ **The News App:** This new app is an intelligent news aggregator, which means that it gathers news stories from various sources in one place. It's intelligent because it "learns" to present you with stories that are similar to other content you've viewed.

➡ **More integrated Notes:** The Notes app gets a facelift with iOS 9, with the ability to add photos, maps, and URLs to notes. In addition, you can create instant checklists, and even sketch in your notes. You can also share items to Notes using the Share feature in apps such as Photos. See Chapter 23 for more about Notes.

➡ **Improvements to the Maps app:** With iOS 9, Maps gets a Transit view for finding information about public transit in select cities around the world. Also, the Nearby feature provides suggestions of nearby businesses and services, such as restaurants, bank ATMs, and gas stations.

➡ **Improved Siri suggestions and search:** Siri, iPhone's personal assistant feature, can now offer suggestions of items you might be interested in even before you ask. For example, if you read a newspaper the same time every morning, Siri might suggest the publication to you. Siri can even search for a photo or video based on the date and location where you took the photo. See Chapter 8 for details about using Siri.

➡ **Move from Android to iOS:** If you have an Android phone and are moving to iPhone, you can download the Move to iOS app and use it to transfer contacts, message history, photos, mail accounts, calendars, and more to iPhone easily.

➡ **Stronger passcodes and 2-factor authentication:** With iOS 9, longer passcodes provide more security, while 2-factor authentication helps your iPhone make sure you're you. With this feature, when you try to access any accounts or information from a new device, you're asked to retrieve a code from an email to sign in, in addition to your account information.

➡ **Car Play:** Car Play is a new feature that is largely still on the drawing board because car manufacturers are only now planning to build it into their car models. If you buy a car down the road with Car Play, it will allow you to control several features and use apps and play content from your iPhone from a graphical screen built into the dashboard.

Choose the Right iPhone for You

iPhone 6s, measuring 4.7" diagonally and 7.1 mm thick, is bigger and thinner than some previous iPhones with their 4" screen (see **Figure 1-1**). iPhone 6s Plus is even bigger at 5.5" and only slightly thicker than iPhone 6s, at 7.3 mm thick. You can get iPhone 6s or 6s Plus in gold, silver, rose gold, or space gray. Other differences between iPhone models come primarily from the current iOS, iOS 9.

Figure 1-1

iPhone 6s and 6s Plus models have a few variations:

➡ 3G talk time of up to 24 hours on 6s Plus and 14 hours on 6s.

➡ Amount of built-in storage, ranging from 16GB to 128GB.

➡ Screen resolution (the higher the resolution, the crisper and brighter the phone display). The iPhone 6s provides 1334 x 750 resolution (more than 1 million pixels) and 6s Plus provides 1920 x 1080 (more than 2 million pixels).

Read on as I explain these variations in more detail in the following sections.

Table 1-1 gives you a quick comparison of iPhone 5s, 5c, 6, 6 Plus, and 6s and 6s Plus. All costs are as of the time this book was written. Note that a few carriers such as Verizon were also coming out with non-contract terms at the time of this writing.

Table 1-1		iPhone Model Comparison	
Model	**Storage**	**Cost (with a Two-Year Contract)**	**Carriers**
5s	16, 32, and 64GB	Free with contract.	AT&T, Verizon, Sprint, contract free with T-Mobile
6	16, 64, and 128GB	$99, $199, $299 with contract; from $649 with contract).	AT&T, Verizon, Sprint, contract free with T-Mobile
6 Plus	16, 64, and 128GB	$199, $299, $399 with contract.	AT&T, Verizon, Sprint, contract free with T-Mobile
6s	16, 64, and 128GB	$199, $299, and $399 with contract.	AT&T, Verizon, Sprint, contract free with T-Mobile
6s Plus	16, 64, and 128GB	$299, $399, and $499 with contract.	AT&T, Verizon, Sprint, contract free with T-Mobile

 One exciting new pricing option is the iPhone Upgrade Program. You choose your carrier, get an unlocked phone so you can change carriers, and receive Apple Care + to cover you in case your phone has problems, all at a cost of $32 a month. Data usage from your carrier will come on top of that.

Decide How Much Storage Is Enough

Storage is a measure of how much information — for example, movies, photos, and software applications (apps) — you can store on a computing device. Storage can also affect your iPhone's performance when handling tasks such as streaming favorite TV shows from the World Wide Web or downloading music.

Streaming refers to playing video or music content from the web (or from other devices) rather than playing a file stored on your iPhone. You can enjoy a lot of material online without ever downloading its full content to your phone — and given that the most storage endowed iPhone model has a relatively small amount of storage, that's not a bad idea. See Chapters 15 and 17 for more about getting your music and movies online.

Your storage options with an iPhone 6s and 6s Plus are 16, 64, or 128 gigabytes (GB). You must choose the right amount of storage because you can't open the unit and add as you usually can with a desktop computer. However, Apple has thoughtfully provided iCloud, a service you can use to back up content to the Internet (you can read more about that in Chapter 3).

So how much storage is enough for your iPhone? Here's a rule of thumb: If you like lots of media, such as movies or TV shows, you might need 128GB. For most people who manage a reasonable number of photos, download some music, and watch heavy-duty media such as movies online, 64GB is probably sufficient. If you simply want to check email, browse the web, and write short notes to yourself, 16GB *might* be enough.

 Do you have a clue how big a gigabyte (GB) is? Consider this: Just about any computer you buy today comes with a minimum of 500GB of storage. Computers have to tackle larger tasks than iPhones do, so that number makes sense. The iPhone, which uses a technology called *flash storage* for data storage, is meant (to a great extent) to help you experience online media and email; it doesn't have to store much and in fact pulls lots of content from online. In the world of storage, 16GB for any kind of storage is puny if you keep lots of content and graphics on the device.

What's the price for larger storage? For the iPhone 6s, a 16GB unit costs $199 with a two-year contract; 64GB jumps the price to $299; and 128GB adds another $100, setting you back a pricey $399. iPhone 6s Plus tops out at $499 for a 128GB model. Note that prices may vary by carrier and by where you buy your phone.

Understand What You Need to Use Your iPhone

Before you head off to buy your iPhone, you should know what other connections and accounts you'll need to work with it optimally.

At a bare minimum, to make standard cellular phone calls, you need to have a service plan with a cellular carrier such as AT&T, as well as a data plan that supports iPhone. The data plan allows you to exchange data over the Internet, such as emails and text messages and to download content. Try to verify the strength of coverage in your area, as well as how much data your plan provides each month before you sign up.

You also need to be able to update the iPhone operating system and share media such as music among Apple devices. Though these things can be done without a phone carrier service plan, you have to plug your phone into your computer to update the iOS or update wirelessly over a network. You need to use a local Wi-Fi network to go online and make calls using an Internet service such as Skype. Given the cost and hi-tech nature of the iPhone, having to jury-rig these basic functions doesn't make much sense, so trust me: Get an account and data plan with your phone service provider.

You should open a free iCloud account, Apple's online storage and syncing service, to store and share content online among your Apple devices. You can also use a computer to download photos, music, or applications from non-Apple online sources, such as stores or sharing sites like your local library, and transfer them to your iPhone through a process called *syncing*.

Apple has set up its iTunes software and the iCloud service to give you two ways to manage content for your iPhone — including apps, music, or photos you've downloaded — and specify how to sync your calendar and contact information.

There are a lot of tech terms to absorb here (iCloud, iTunes, syncing, and so on). Don't worry: Chapter 3 covers those settings in more detail.

Know Where to Buy Your iPhone

You can't buy an iPhone from every major retail store. You can buy an iPhone at the brick-and-mortar or online Apple Store and from the mobile phone providers AT&T, Sprint, T-Mobile, and Verizon. You can also find an iPhone at major retailers such as Best Buy and Walmart, through which you have to buy a two-year service contract for the phone carrier of your choice. You can also find iPhones at several online retailers such as Amazon.com and Newegg.com, and through smaller, local service providers, which you can find by visiting `https://support.apple.com/en-us/HT204039`.

 Apple offers unlocked iPhones. Essentially, these phones aren't tied into a particular provider, so you can use them with any of the four iPhone cellular service providers. Though you save a lot by avoiding a service commitment, these phones without accompanying phone plans can be pricey. That said, there's a trend for providers offering cheaper plans and installment payments on the hardware.

Explore What's in the Box

When you fork over your hard-earned money for your iPhone, you'll be left holding one box about the size of a deck of tarot cards. Here's a rundown of what you'll find when you take off the shrink-wrap and open the box:

⇒ **iPhone:** Your iPhone is covered in a thick, plastic-sleeve thingy that you can take off and toss (unless you think there's a chance you'll return the phone, in which case you might want to keep all packaging for 14 days — Apple's standard return period).

⇒ **Apple EarPods with Remote and Mic:** Plug the EarPods into your iPhone 6s or 6s Plus for a free headset experience.

⇒ **Documentation (and I use the term loosely):** Notice, under the iPhone itself, a small, white envelope about the size of a half-dozen index cards. Open it and you'll find:

  • A *tiny pamphlet:* This pamphlet, named *Important Product Information Guide,* is essentially small print (that you mostly don't need to read) from folks like the FCC.

  • A *label sheet:* This sheet has two white Apple logos on it. (I'm not sure what they're for, but my husband and I use one sticker to differentiate my iPhone from his.)

  • A *small foldout card:* This card provides panels containing photos of the major features of iPhone 6s or 6s Plus and information about where to find out more.

⇒ **Lightning to USB Cable:** Use this cable (see **Figure 1-2**) to connect the iPhone to your computer, or use it with the last item in the box, the USB power adapter. If you own an iPhone 4s or earlier, you have the Dock Connector to USB Cable, a larger, bulkier, 30-pin connector.

Lightning to USB Cable   Apple USB power adapter

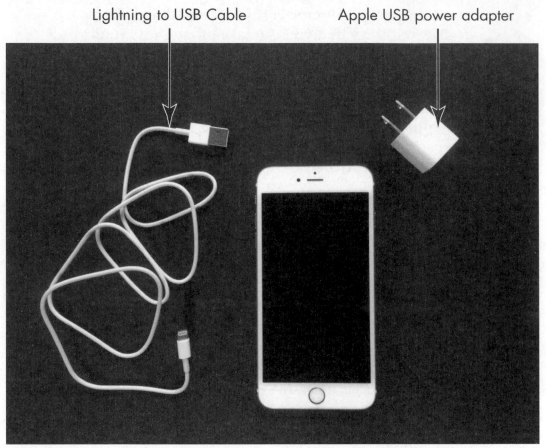

Figure 1-2

➠ **Apple USB power adapter:** The power adapter (refer to Figure 1-2) attaches to the Lightning to USB Cable so that you can plug it into the wall and charge the battery.

➠ **SIM Eject Tool:** Some carriers such as AT&T and T-Mobile use a SIM card in their phones that contains all the information your phone needs to operate. This tool, which you can use to eject a SIM card from any phone that uses this technology, is provided with iPhones in some areas.

That's it. That's all there is in the box. It's kind of a study in Zen-like simplicity.

 Try searching for iPhone accessories online. You'll find iPhone cases, ranging from leather to silicone, car chargers, and screen guards to protect your phone's screen.

Take a First Look at the Gadget

The little card contained in the documentation (see the preceding section) gives you a picture of the iPhone with callouts to the buttons you'll find on it. In this section, I give you a bit more information about those buttons and other physical features of the iPhone 6s and 6s Plus. **Figure 1-3** shows you where each of these items is located.

Here's the rundown on what the various hardware features are and what they do:

➡ **(The all-important) Home button:** On the iPhone, you can press this button to go back to the Home screen to find just about anything. The Home screen(s) displays all your installed and preinstalled apps and gives you access to your iPhone settings. No matter where you are or what you're doing, press the Home button and you're back at home base. You can also press the Home button twice to pull up a scrolling list of apps so that you can quickly move from one to another (Apple refers to this capability as multitasking). If you press and hold the Home button, you open Siri, the iPhone voice assistant. Finally, with iPhone 5s and later, the Home button contains a fingerprint reader used with the Touch ID feature.

➡ **Sleep/Wake button:** You can use this button (whose functionality I cover in more detail in Chapter 2) to power up your iPhone, put it in Sleep mode, wake it up, or power it down.

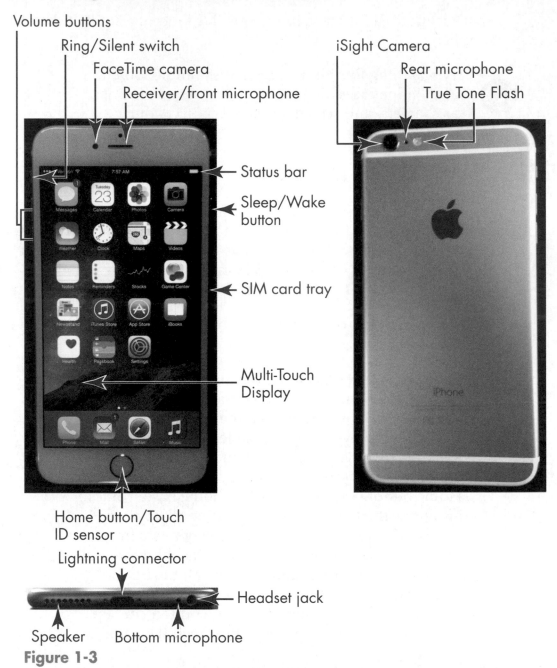

Volume buttons

Ring/Silent switch

FaceTime camera

Receiver/front microphone

iSight Camera

Rear microphone

True Tone Flash

Status bar

Sleep/Wake button

SIM card tray

Multi-Touch Display

Home button/Touch ID sensor

Lightning connector

Headset jack

Speaker   Bottom microphone

Figure 1-3

➠ **Lightning connector:** Plug in the Lightning connector at one end of the Lightning to USB Cable that came with your iPhone to charge your battery or sync your iPhone with your computer (which you find out more about in Chapter 3).

➠ **FaceTime/iSight Cameras:** iPhone 4 and later models offer a FaceTime camera (on the front of the phone) and an iSight camera (on the back of the phone) that you can use to make video calls and shoot photos or video. Make note of the location of the iSight camera on the back of the phone — you need to be careful not to put your thumb over it when taking shots. (I have several very nice photos of my thumb already.)

➠ **Ring/Silent switch:** Slide this little switch to mute or unmute the sound on your iPhone.

➠ **(A tiny, mighty) Speaker:** One nice surprise when I got my first iPhone was hearing what a nice little sound system it has and how much sound can come from this tiny speaker. The speaker is located on the bottom edge of the phone, to the right of the Home button.

➠ **Volume buttons:** Tap the volume up button for more volume and the volume down button for less. You can use the volume up button as a camera shutter button when the camera is activated.

➠ **Headset jack and microphones:** If you want to listen to your music in private, you can plug in the EarPods (which give you bidirectional sound) or 3.5mm minijack headphones. Three microphones (one on the front of the phone — this is also the Receiver — and one on the bottom of the phone, as well as one on the back of the phone) make it possible to speak into your iPhone to deliver commands or content. This feature allows you to do things such as make phone calls using the Internet, use video calling services such as Skype, or work with other apps that accept audio input such as the Siri built-in assistant.

➡ **Receiver:** The rectangular spot on the top front of the device that you hear through.

➡ **SIM card tray:** The little slot for placing your phone carrier's SIM card, which allows your phone to connect to the carrier and stores data such as contacts in storage. Note that iPhones have a smaller SIM card (called a nano-card) than several other phones.

➡ **True Tone flash:** The flash device for the built-in rear-facing camera.

Looking Over the Home Screen

I won't kid you: You have a slight learning curve ahead of you if you're coming from a more basic cellphone (but if you own another smartphone, you've got a head start). For example, your previous phone might not have had a Multi-Touch screen and onscreen keyboard.

The good news is that getting anything done on the iPhone is simple, once you know the ropes. In fact, using your fingers to do things is a very intuitive way to communicate with your computing device, which is just what iPhone is.

In this chapter, you turn on your iPhone, register it, and then take your first look at the Home screen. You also practice using the onscreen keyboard, see how to interact with the touchscreen in various ways, get pointers on working with cameras, and get an overview of built-in applications (apps).

 Have a soft cloth handy, like the one you might use to clean your eyeglasses. Although the iPhone's screen has been treated to repel oils, you're about to deposit a ton of fingerprints on your iPhone — one downside of a touchscreen device.

See What You Need to Use iPhone

You need to be able, at a minimum, to connect to the Internet to take advantage of most iPhone features, which you can do using a Wi-Fi network (a network that you set up in your own home or access in a public place such as a library) or a 3G/4G connection from your cellular provider. You might want to have a computer so that you can connect your iPhone to it to download photos, videos, music, or applications and transfer them to or from your iPhone through a process called *syncing* (see Chapter 3 for more about syncing). An Apple service called iCloud syncs content from all your Apple iOS devices (such as the iPhone or iPad), so anything you buy on your iPad that can be run on an iPhone, for example, will automatically be pushed to your iPhone. In addition, you can sync without connecting a cable to a computer using a wireless Wi-Fi connection to your computer.

Your phone will probably arrive registered and activated, or if you buy it in a store, the person helping you can handle that procedure.

For an iPhone 6s or 6s Plus, Apple's *iPhone User Guide* recommends that you have

➡ A Mac or PC with a USB 2.0 or later port and one of these operating systems:

  • Mac OS X Lion version 10.6.8 or later

  • Windows 10, 8.1, 8, 7, Vista, or XP Home or Professional with Service Pack 3 or later

➡ iTunes 11.4 or later, available at www.itunes. com/download

➡ An Apple ID

➡ Internet access

Turn On iPhone for the First Time

1. The first time you turn on your iPhone, it will probably have been activated and registered by your phone carrier or Apple, depending on whom you've bought it from.

2. Press and hold the Sleep/Wake button a little bit below the top of the upper-right side of your iPhone until the Apple logo appears. In another moment, a series of screens appears, asking you to enter a password if you have an Apple ID. If you don't have one, you can follow the instructions to create one.

3. Next, follow the series of prompts to make choices about your language and location, using iCloud (Apple's online sharing service), whether to use a passcode, and connecting with a network, and so on.

 You can choose to have certain items transferred to your iPhone from your computer when you sync the two devices using iTunes, including music, videos, downloaded apps, audiobooks, e-books, podcasts, and browser bookmarks. Contacts and Calendars are downloaded via iCloud, or, if you're moving to iPhone from an Android phone, you can download an app called Move to iOS to copy your current settings to your iPhone. You can also transfer to your computer any content you download directly to your iPhone using iTunes, the App Store, or non-Apple stores. See Chapters 12 and 13 for more about these features.

Meet the Multi-Touch Screen

When the iPhone Home screen appears (see **Figure 2-1**), you see a pretty background and two sets of icons. One set appears in the Dock, along the bottom of the screen. The *Dock* contains the Mail, Phone,

Music, and Safari app icons by default, though you can swap out one app for another. You can add new apps to populate as many as 10 additional Home screens for a total of 11 Home screens. The Dock appears on every Home screen.

Other icons appear above the Dock and are closer to the top of the screen. (I cover all these icons in the "Take Inventory of Preinstalled Apps" task, later in this chapter.) Different icons appear in this area on each Home screen. You can also nest apps in folders, which theoretically gives you the possibility of storing limitless apps on your iPhone. You are, in fact, limited — but only by your phone's memory.

App icons

The Dock

Figure 2-1

 Treat the iPhone screen carefully. It's made of glass and will smudge when you touch it (and will shatter if you throw it at the wall or drop it on concrete).

If you have an iPhone 6s Plus model and you hold it horizontally, the Home screen will appear with some differences (see **Figure 2-2**).

Figure 2-2

The iPhone uses *touchscreen technology:* When you swipe your finger across the screen or tap it, you're providing input to the device just as you do to a computer using a mouse or keyboard. You hear more about the touchscreen in the next task, but for now, go ahead and play with it for a few minutes — really, you can't hurt anything. Use the pads of your fingertips (not your fingernails) and follow these steps:

1. Tap the Settings icon. The various settings (which you read more about throughout this book) appear, as shown in Figure 2-3.

2. To return to the Home screen, press the Home button.

3. Swipe a finger or two from right to left on the Home screen. This action moves you to the next Home screen. Note that the little dots at the bottom of the screen, above the Dock icons, indicate which Home screen is displayed.

4. To experience the screen rotation feature, hold the iPhone firmly while turning it sideways. The screen flips to the horizontal orientation. To flip the screen back, just turn the device so that it's oriented like a pad of paper again. (Note that some apps force iPhone to stay in one orientation or the other.)

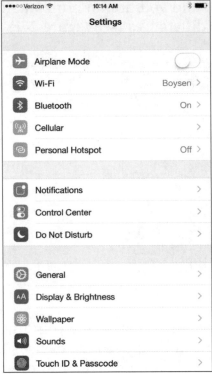

Figure 2-3

5. Drag your finger down from the very top edge of the screen to reveal the Notification Center items, such as reminders, calendar entries, and so on (covered in Chapter 22); drag up from the very bottom edge of the Home screen to hide Notification Center, and then drag up to display Control Center (containing commonly used controls and tools and discussed later in this chapter).

6. To close either Notification Center or Control Center, tap or drag the arrow at the bottom (Notification Center) or top (Control Center) of the display.

 You can customize the Home screen by changing its *wallpaper* (background picture) and brightness. You can read about making these changes in Chapter 7.

Discover 3D Touch and Quick Actions

New with iPhone 6s/6s Plus comes 3D Touch and Quick Actions. These are made possible by the multi-touch screen. 3D Touch allows you to get different results depending on the amount of pressure you apply to the screen, and get feedback on your actions with taps from the screen. For example, if you open the Photos app, you can tap lightly to select a photo, press a bit harder to see a preview of that photo, and press harder to open the photo full screen. The ability to preview items such as emails, websites, maps, and photos before opening them can save you time. The medium press is called a Peek and the hard press is called a Pop.

| Light Press | Peek | Pop |

Quick Actions involve pressing an icon on the screen to see items you're likely to want to select. For example, if you press on the Phone icon, you'll get a shortcut list of commonly called contacts. If you press on the Maps app, you see a list of places you often go, such as your home, to quickly display a map of that location. Quick Actions provide a shortcut menu to your most frequently used items, saving you time and effort.

(continued)

Say Hello to Tap and Swipe

You can use several methods for getting around and getting things done in iPhone using its Multi-Touch screen, including

⟹ **Tap once.** To open an application on the Home screen, choose a field, such as a search box, choose an item in a list, use an arrow to move back or forward one screen, or follow an online link, tap the item once with your finger.

⟹ **Tap twice.** Use this method to enlarge or reduce the display of a web page (see Chapter 10 for more about using the *Safari* web browser) or to zoom in or out in the Maps app.

➡ **Pinch.** As an alternative to the tap-twice method, you can pinch your fingers together or move them apart on the screen (see **Figure** 2-4) when you're looking at photos, maps, web pages, or email messages to quickly reduce or enlarge them, respectively. This method allows you to grow or contract the screen to a variety of sizes rather than a fixed size, as with the double-tap method.

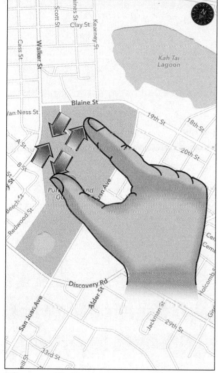

Figure 2-4

 You can use the three-finger tap to zoom your screen to be even larger or use multitasking gestures to swipe with four or five fingers (see the "Learn Multitasking Basics" task, later in this chapter). This method is handy if you have vision challenges. Go to Chapter 7 to discover how to turn on this feature using Accessibility settings.

➡ **Drag to scroll (known as *swiping*).** When you press your finger to the screen and drag to the right or left, the screen moves (see **Figure 2-5**). Swiping to the left on the Home screen, for example, moves you to the next Home screen. Swiping down while reading an online newspaper moves you down the page; swiping up moves you back up the page.

Figure 2-5

➡ **Flick.** To scroll more quickly on a page, quickly flick your finger on the screen in the direction you want to move.

➡ **Tap the Status bar.** To move quickly to the top of a list, web page, or email message, tap the Status bar at the top of the iPhone screen. Note that for some sites you have to tap twice to get this to work.

⟶ **Press and hold.** If you're using Notes or Mail or any other application that lets you select text, or if you're on a web page, pressing and holding text selects a word and displays editing tools that you can use to select, cut, or copy and paste the text.

 Notice that when you rock your phone backward or forward, the background moves as well, a feature called parallax. You can disable this feature if it makes you seasick. From the Home screen, tap Settings ⇨ General ⇨ Accessibility and then tap and turn off the Reduce Motion setting.

 Your iPhone offers the ability to perform bezel gestures, which involves sliding from the very outer edge of the phone left to right on the glass to go backward and sliding right to left to go forward in certain apps.

Try these methods now by following these steps:

1. Tap the Safari button in the Dock at the bottom of any iPhone Home screen to display the web browser.

2. Tap a link to move to another page.

3. Double-tap the page to enlarge it; then pinch your fingers together on the screen to reduce its size.

4. Drag one finger around the page to scroll.

5. Flick your finger quickly on the page to scroll more quickly.

6. Press and hold your finger on a word that isn't a link (links are usually blue and take you to another location on the web). The word is selected, and the Copy/Define/Share tool is displayed, as shown in **Figure 2-6**. (You can use this tool to get a definition of a word or copy it.)

7. Press and hold your finger on a link or an image. A menu appears with commands that you select to open the link or picture, open it in a new tab, add it to your Reading

List (see Chapter 10), or copy it. If you press and hold an image, the menu also offers the Save Image command. Tap Cancel to close the menu without making a selection.

8. Position your fingers slightly apart on the screen and then pinch your fingers together to reduce the page; next, with your fingers already pinched together on the screen, move them apart to enlarge the page.

9. Press the Home button to go back to the Home screen.

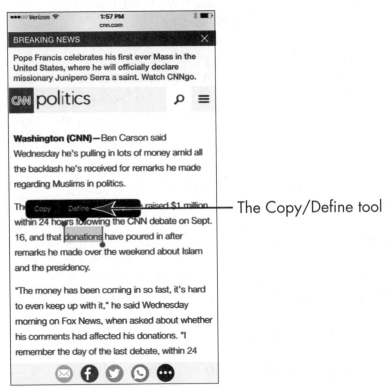

The Copy/Define tool

Figure 2-6

Display and Use the Onscreen Keyboard

1. The built-in iPhone keyboard appears whenever you're in a text-entry location, such as a search field or an email message form. Tap the Notes icon on the Home screen to open this easy-to-use notepad and try the onscreen keyboard.

2. Tap the note page or if you've already created some notes, tap one to display the page and then tap anywhere on the note; the onscreen keyboard appears.

3. Type a few words using the keyboard, as shown in **Figure 2-7**. To make the keyboard display as wide as possible, rotate your iPhone to landscape (horizontal) orientation (note that if you've locked the screen orientation in Control Center, you have to unlock it to do this).

Figure 2-7

4. If you make a mistake while using the keyboard — and you will, especially when you first use it — tap the Delete key (it's near the bottom corner, with the little *x* on it) to delete text to the left of the insertion point.

5. To create a new paragraph, tap the Return button, just as you would do on a computer keyboard.

6. To type numbers and symbols, tap the number key (labeled 123) on the left side of the spacebar (refer to Figure 2-7). The characters on the keyboard change (see **Figure 2-8**). If you type a number and then tap the spacebar, the keyboard returns to the letter keyboard automatically. To return to the letter keyboard at any time, simply tap the key labeled ABC on the left side of the spacebar.

Figure 2-8

7. Use the Shift button (it's a thick, upward-facing arrow in the lower-left corner of the keyboard) just as you would on a regular keyboard to type uppercase letters. Tapping one of these buttons once causes just the next letter you type to be capitalized.

8. Double-tap the Shift key to turn on the Caps Lock feature so that all letters you type are capitalized until you turn the feature off. Tap the Shift key once to turn off Caps Lock.

(You can control whether this feature is available in iPhone Settings under the General category by tapping Keyboard.)

9. To type a variation on a symbol or letter (for example, to see alternative presentations for the letter *A* when you press the A button on the keyboard), hold down the key; a set of alternative letters/symbols appears (see **Figure 2-9**). Note that this trick works with only certain letters and symbols.

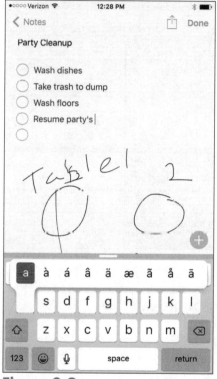

Figure 2-9

10. Tap the smiley-faced Emoji button to display the Emoji keyboard containing symbols that you can insert, including numerical, symbol, and arrow keys, as well as a row of symbol sets along the bottom of the screen. Tapping one of these displays a portfolio of icons from smiley faces and hearts to pumpkins, cats, and more. Tap the ABC button to close the Emoji keyboard and return to the letter keyboard.

11. Press the Home button to return to the Home screen.

12. If you own an iPhone 6s Plus, turn it into horizontal orientation. Tap Notes and then tap in a note to display the onscreen keyboard, which now takes advantage of the wider screen and includes some extra keys such as Cut, Copy, and Paste (see **Figure 2-10**).

Copy

Cut   Paste

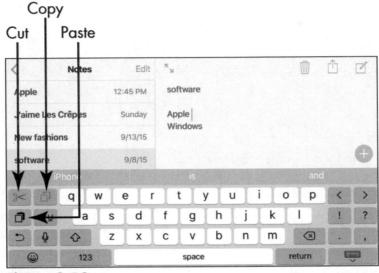

Figure 2-10

 To type a period and space, just double-tap the spacebar.

 Note that a small globe symbol will appear instead of the Emoji button on the keyboard if you've enabled multilanguage functionality in iPhone settings.

 With the latest version of the Notes app, you can display a shortcut keyboard that allows you to create a checklist, choose a font style, insert a photo, or create a drawing within your note. See Chapter 23 for more about using the Notes app.

 QuickType provides suggestions above the keyboard as you type. You can turn this feature off or on by tapping and holding the Emoji (the smiley face) or

International icon on the keyboard to display a menu. Tap the Predictive item on this menu to turn the feature off or on.

Flick to Search

1. The Spotlight Search feature in iPhone helps you find suggestions from the web, Music, iTunes, and the App Store as well as suggestions for nearby locations and more. Swipe down on any Home screen (but not from the very top or bottom of the screen) to reveal the Search feature (see **Figure 2-11**).

Figure 2-11

2. Begin entering a search term. In the example in **Figure 2-12**, after I typed the letters *dogs*, the Search feature displayed a map and search results. As you continue to type a search term or phrase, the results narrow to match it.

Figure 2-12

3. Scroll down and tap Show More in Bing, Search Web, or Search App Store to view more results.

4. Tap an item in the search results to open it in its appropriate app or player.

Update the Operating System to iOS 9

1. This book is based on the latest version of the iPhone operating system at the time: iOS 9. To be sure that you have the latest and greatest features, update your iPhone to the latest iOS now (and do so periodically to receive minor upgrades to iOS 9 or future versions of the iOS). If you have set up an iCloud account on your iPhone, you'll receive an alert and can choose to install the update or not, or you can update manually. Tap Settings. Be sure you have Wi-Fi enabled and that you're connected to a Wi-Fi network to perform these steps.

2. Tap General.

3. Tap Software Update (see **Figure** 2-13).

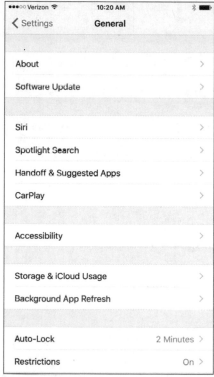

Figure 2-13

4. Read the note next to the Check for Update button to see whether your iOS is up-to-date. If it isn't, click the Check for Update button. Your iPhone checks to find the latest iOS version and walks you through the updating procedure.

Learn Multitasking Basics

1. *Multitasking* lets you easily switch from one app to another without closing the first one and returning to the Home screen. With iOS 9, this is accomplished by previewing all open apps and jumping from one to another; you quit an app by simply swiping upward. First, open an app.

2. Press the Home button twice.

3. On the Running Apps list that appears (see **Figure 2-14**), flick to scroll to the left or right to locate another app that you want to switch to.

Figure 2-14

4. Tap an app to open it.

 Press the Home button to remove the Running Apps list from the Home screen and return to the app that you were working in.

Examine the iPhone Cameras

iPhones have front- and back-facing cameras. You can use the cameras to take still photos (covered in more detail in Chapter 16) or shoot videos (covered in Chapter 17).

For now, take a quick look at your camera by tapping the Camera app icon on the Home screen. The app opens, as shown in **Figure 2-15**.

Timed Photo

Figure 2-15

You can use the controls on the screen to

⮕ Switch between the front and rear cameras

⮕ Change from still-camera to video-camera operation by using the slider at the bottom of the screen

⮕ Take a picture or start recording a video

 ⮕ Choose a 3- or 10-second delay with the new Timed Photos button

⟶ Turn HDR (high dynamic range for better contrast)
on or off

⟶ Tap the Flash button to set flash to On, Off, or Auto

⟶ Open previously captured images or videos

When you view a photo or video, you can use an iPhone sharing feature to send the image via AirDrop (iPhone 5 and later only), Message, Notes, Mail, and other options depending on which apps you've installed. You can also share through iCloud Photo Sharing, a tweet, Facebook, or Flickr. More things that you can do with images are to print them, use a still photo as wallpaper (that is, as your Home or lock screen background image) or assign it to represent a contact, and run a slideshow. See Chapters 16 and 17 for more detail about using the iPhone cameras.

Understand Lock Screen Rotation

Sometimes you don't want your screen orientation to flip when you move your phone around. Use these steps to lock the iPhone into portrait orientation:

1. Swipe up from the bottom of any screen to open Control Center.

2. Tap the Lock Screen button; it's the button in the top-right corner of Control Center.

3. Swipe down from the top of Control Center to hide it.

Explore the Status Bar

Across the top of the iPhone screen is the *Status bar* (see **Figure 2-16**). Tiny icons in this area can provide useful information, such as the time, battery level, and wireless-connection status. **Table 2-1** lists some of the most common items you find on the Status bar.

← Status bar

Figure 2-16

Table 2-1		Common Status Bar Icons
Icon	**Name**	**What It Indicates**
	Wi-Fi	You're connected to a Wi-Fi network.
	Activity	A task is in progress — a web page is loading, for example.
12:36 PM	Time	You guessed it: You see the time.
	Screen Rotation Lock	The screen is locked in portrait orientation and doesn't rotate when you turn the iPhone.
	Battery Life	This shows the charge percentage remaining in the battery. The indicator changes to a lightning bolt when the battery is charging.

If you have GPS, 3G, 4G cellular, or Bluetooth service or a connection to a virtual private network (VPN), a corresponding symbol appears on the Status bar whenever a feature is active. (If you can't conceive what a virtual private network is, my advice is not to worry about it.)

Take Inventory of Preinstalled Apps

The iPhone comes with certain functionality and applications — or *apps*, for short — built in. When you look at the Home screen, you see icons for each app. This task gives you an overview of what each app does. (You can find out more about every one of them as you read different chapters in this book.) The following icons appear in the Dock at the bottom of every Home screen (refer to Figure 2-1), from left to right:

➡ **Mail:** You use this application to access email accounts that you have set up in iPhone. Your email is then displayed without you having to browse to the site or sign in. You can use tools to move among a few preset mail folders, read and reply to email, and download attached photos to your iPhone. Read more about email accounts in Chapter 11.

➡ **Phone:** Use this app to make and receive phone calls, view a log of recent calls, create a list of favorite contacts, access your voice mail, and view contacts.

➡ **Music:** *Music* is the name of your media player. Though its main function is to play music, you can use it to play audio podcasts and audiobooks as well.

➡ **Safari:** You use the Safari web browser (see **Figure 2-17**) to navigate on the Internet, create and save bookmarks of favorite sites, and add web clips to your Home screen so that you can quickly visit favorite sites from there. You may have used this web browser (or another, such as Mozilla Firefox) on your desktop computer.

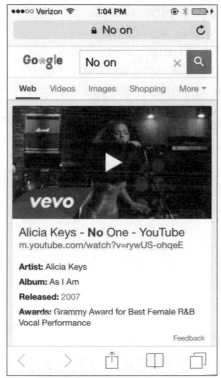

Figure 2-17

Apps with icons above the Dock on the Home screen include

↦ **Messages:** For those who love to instant message, the Messages app comes to the rescue. The Messages app has been in iPhone for quite some time. Now you can engage in live text- and image-based conversations with others via their phones or other devices that use email. You can also send video or audio messages.

↦ **Calendar:** Use this handy onscreen daybook to set up appointments and send alerts to remind you about them.

↦ **Photos:** The Photos app in iPhone (see Figure 2-18) helps you organize pictures in folders, send photos via email, use a photo as your iPhone wallpaper, and assign pictures to contact records. You can also run slideshows of your photos, open albums, pinch or unpinch to shrink or expand photos, and scroll photos with a simple swipe. Your iPhone can use the Photo Sharing feature to share photos among your friends. Since iOS 7, Photos displays images by collections, including Years and Moments.

Figure 2-18

⟶ **Camera:** As you may have read earlier in this chapter, the Camera app is Control Center for the still and video cameras built into the iPhone.

⟶ **Weather:** Get the latest weather for your location and others instantly with this handy app (see **Figure 2-19**). You can easily add other locations to check for weather where you're going or where you've been.

Figure 2-19

⟶ **Clock:** This app allows you to display clocks from around the world, set alarms, and use timer and stopwatch features.

⟶ **Maps:** With this iPhone mapping app, you can view classic maps or aerial views of addresses and find directions from one place to another whether traveling by car, foot, or public transportation (though this last requires that a third-party app be installed). You can even get your directions read aloud via a spoken narration feature.

⟶ **Videos:** This media player is similar to Music but specializes in playing videos and offers a few features specific to this type of media, such as chapter breakdowns and information about a movie's plot and cast.

➡ **Notes:** Enter text or cut and paste text from a website into this simple notepad app. You can't do much except save notes or email them — the app has no features for formatting text or inserting objects. You'll find Notes handy, though, for simple notes on the fly.

➡ **Reminders:** This useful app centralizes all your calendar entries and alerts to keep you on schedule and allows you to create to-do lists.

➡ **Stocks:** See in one place, anytime you like, the latest information about stock exchanges and individual stocks as well as trending information.

➡ **Game Center:** This app helps you browse games in the App Store and play them with other people online. You can add friends and track your scores. See Chapter 18 for more about Game Center.

➡ **News:** News is a customizable aggregator for stories from your favorite news sources.

➡ **iTunes Store:** Tapping this icon takes you to the iTunes store, where you can shop 'til you drop (or until your iPhone battery runs out of juice) for music, movies, TV shows, and audiobooks and then download them directly to your iPhone. (See Chapter 12 for more about how iTunes works.)

➡ **App Store:** Here you can buy and download applications that do everything from enabling you to play games to building business presentations. You can also subscribe to periodicals for use with the Newsstand app. Some of these are even free!

➡ **iBooks:** The iBooks app is now bundled with the iPhone out of the box. Because the iPhone has been touted as being a good small screen *e-reader* — a device that enables you to read books on an electronic device, similar to the Amazon Kindle Fire HD — you

should definitely check this one out. (To work with the
iBooks e-reader application itself, go to Chapter 14.)

➡ **Health:** This is exciting very useful app that you can
use to record various health and exercise statistics
and even send them to your doctor. See Chapter 20
for more about the Health app.

➡ **Wallet:** This Apple Pay feature lets you store a virtual
wallet of plane or concert tickets, coupons, and more
and use them with a swipe of your iPhone across a
point of purchase device.

➡ **Settings:** Settings is the central location on the
iPhone where you can specify settings for various
functions and do administrative tasks, such as set up
email accounts or create a password.

There are also some preinstalled apps located on the second Home
screen by default, including some in an Extras folder. Wrapped up in
the Extras folder are some other handy tools: Compass, Contacts, and
Voice Memos.

Additionally, on the second Home screen, you'll find:

➡ **FaceTime:** Use FaceTime to place phone calls using
video of the sender and receiver to have a more personal conversation.

➡ **Calculator:** Use this simple app to add, subtract, and
so on.

➡ **Podcasts:** Before iOS 8, you had to download the
free Podcast app, but now it's built into your iOS
iPhone. Use this app to listen to recorded informational programs.

➡ **News:** This app, new with iOS 9, is a news aggregator
that assembles news stories from a variety of sources.
See Chapter 24 for more about this useful app.

Several useful apps are free for you to download from the App Store. These include iMovie and iPhoto, as well as the Pages, Keynote, and Numbers apps of the iWork suite.

Discover Control Center

1. Control Center is a one-stop screen for common features and settings such as connecting to a network, increasing screen brightness or volume, and even turning a built-in flashlight on or off. To display Control Center, swipe up from the bottom of the screen.

2. In the screen that appears, tap a button or tap and drag a slider to access or adjust a setting (see **Figure** 2-20).

3. Swipe the top of Control Center down to hide it.

Figure 2-20

Lock iPhone, Turn It Off, or Unlock It

Earlier in this chapter, I mention how simple it is to turn on the power to your iPhone. Now it's time to put it to *sleep* (a state in which the screen goes black, though you can quickly wake up the iPhone) or turn off the power to give your new toy a rest. Here are the procedures you use to put the phone to sleep or turn it off:

➠ **Sleep:** Press the Sleep/Wake button just below the top of the right side of the phone. The iPhone goes to sleep. The screen goes black and is locked.

➠ **Power Off:** From any app or Home screen press and hold the Sleep/Wake button until the Slide to Power Off bar appears at the top of the screen, and then swipe the bar. You've just turned off your iPhone.

➠ **Force Off:** If the iPhone becomes unresponsive, hold the Power and Home buttons simultaneously until the phone shuts itself off.

To wake the phone up from Sleep mode, do the following:

➠ **Press the Home button and swipe the onscreen arrow on the Slide to Unlock bar (see Figure 2-21).** The iPhone unlocks.

 The iPhone automatically enters Sleep mode after a few minutes of inactivity. You can change the time interval at which it sleeps by adjusting the Auto-Lock feature in General Settings. See this book's companion Cheat Sheet at www.dummies.com/cheatsheet/iphoneforseniors to review tables of various settings.

Figure 2-21

 Note that you can swipe the Camera icon at the bottom right of the lock screen to use the camera without waking up the iPhone from Sleep mode. Also, if you were playing music before putting iPhone to sleep, you will see music controls on the lock screen and your music will play from there.

Getting Going

Y our first step in getting to work with the iPhone is to make sure that its battery is charged. Next, if you want to find free or paid content for your iPhone from Apple, from movies to music to e-books to audiobooks, you'll need to have an iTunes account.

You can also use the wireless sync feature to exchange content between your computer and iPhone over a wireless network.

You can also take advantage of the iCloud service from Apple to store and push all kinds of content and data to all your Apple devices — wirelessly. You can pick up where you left off from one device to another through iCloud Drive, an online storage service that enables sharing content among devices so that edits that you make to documents in iCloud are reflected in all iOS devices and Macs running OS X Yosemite or later.

Chapter

3

Get ready to . . .

Charge the Battery

1. My iPhone showed up in the box fully charged, and let's hope yours did, too. Because all batteries run down eventually, one of your first priorities is to know how to recharge your iPhone battery. Gather your iPhone and its Lightning to USB Cable (iPhone 5 and later; if you have an earlier model, you have the Dock cable) and the Apple USB power adapter.

2. Gently plug the Lightning connector end (the smaller of the two connectors) of the Lightning to USB Cable into the iPhone.

Note that if you have a hard case for your iPhone, you should remove the phone from it if you're charging it over several hours because these cases retain heat, which is bad for the phone and the case.

3. Plug the USB end of the Lightning to USB Cable into the Apple USB power adapter (see **Figure 3-1**).

4. Plug the adapter into an electric outlet.

Connector cables from earlier versions of iPhone or other Apple devices such as iPad or iPod don't work with your iPhone 5 or later. Adapters are available, however, from Apple.

If you are moving from an Android phone to an iPhone, consider downloading the Move to iOS app. This app allows you to wirelessly transfer key content, such as contacts, message history, videos, mail accounts, photos and more from your old phone to your new one. If you had free apps on your Android device, iPhone will suggest you download them from the App Store. Any paid apps will be added to your iTunes Wish List.

Attach this end...   to the power adapter.

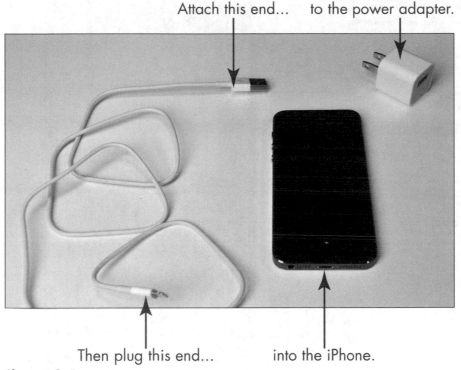

Then plug this end...   into the iPhone.

Figure 3-1

Sign into an iTunes Account for Music, Movies, and More

1. To be able to buy or download free items from the iTunes Store or the App Store on your iPhone, you must open an iTunes account. First, assuming you are not signed into an iTunes account, tap Settings on your iPhone.

2. Scroll down and tap App and iTunes Stores; the screen shown in **Figure 3-2** appears.

3. Tap Sign In (see **Figure 3-3**), and enter your Apple ID and password and tap the Sign In button.

Figure 3-2

Figure 3-3

4. In the Account Settings screen that follows (see **Figure** 3-4), fill in the information fields and then tap the Done button. A screen appears, confirming that your account information has been saved.

 If you prefer not to leave your credit card info with Apple, one option is to buy an iTunes gift card and provide that as your payment information. You can replenish the card periodically through the Apple Store.

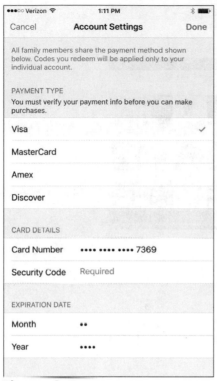

Figure 3-4

Sync Wirelessly

You can connect your iPhone to a computer and use the tools there to sync content on your computer to your iPhone. Also, with Wi-Fi turned on in Settings, use the iTunes Wi-Fi Sync setting to allow cordless syncing if you're within range of a Wi-Fi network that has a computer connected to it with iTunes installed and open. There are a few steps you have to take with your iPhone connected to your computer before you can perform a wireless sync with iTunes:

1. Open iTunes, remove the power adapter if necessary, and connect your iPhone to your computer using the Lightning to USB Cable.

2. Click the icon of an iPhone that appears in the tools in the left corner of the screen (refer to **Figure 3-5**).

Figure 3-5

3. Click the check box labeled Sync with This iPhone over Wi-Fi and then click Apply.

4. Disconnect your iPhone from your computer.

 Note that you can click any item on the left side of the screen shown in Figure 3-5 to handle settings for syncing items such as Movies, Music, and Apps. In the Apps category, you can also choose to remove certain apps from your Home screens. You can also tap the list of items On My Device on the left side to view and even play contents.

After you complete the preceding steps, you'll be able to wirelessly sync your iPhone with your computer. To do so, first back up your phone (see Chapter 25) and then follow these steps:

1. To initiate a wireless sync, on the iPhone, tap Settings ⇨ General ⇨ iTunes Wi-Fi Sync.

2. In the settings that appear, tap Sync Now to sync with a computer connected to the same Wi-Fi network. (If you need to connect your iPhone to a network, tap Settings ⇨ Wi-Fi and then tap a network to join.)

If you have your iPhone set up to sync wirelessly to your Mac or PC and both are within range of the same Wi-Fi network, iPhone will appear in your iTunes Devices list. This setup allows you to sync and manage syncing from within iTunes. Also, be aware that your iPhone will automatically sync with iTunes once a day if both are on the same Wi-Fi network, iTunes is running, and your iPhone is plugged in.

Understand iCloud

There's an alternative to syncing content by using iTunes. iCloud is a service offered by Apple that allows you to back up most of your content to online storage. (Some content, however, such as videos, isn't backed up, so consider doing an occasional backup of content to your computer, as well.) That content is then pushed automatically to all your Apple devices through a wireless connection. All you need to do is get an iCloud account, which is free, and make settings on your devices and in iTunes for which types of content you want pushed to each device. After you've done that, content that you create or purchase on one device — such as music, apps, and TV shows, as well as documents created in Apple's iWork apps, photos, and so on — is synced among your devices automatically.

 See Chapter 12 for more about using the new Family Sharing feature to share content that you buy online and more with family members through iCloud.

When you get an iCloud account, you get 5GB of free storage. Content that you purchase from Apple (such as apps, books, music, iTunes Match content, Photo Sharing contents, and TV shows) isn't counted against your storage. If you want additional storage, you can buy an upgrade from one of your devices. Having 20GB costs $0.99 a month; 200GB is $3.99 per month; and 500GB is $9.99 per month. If you are a storage sponge, you can get one terabyte for $19.99 a month. Most people will do just fine with the free 5GB of storage.

To upgrade your storage, go to iCloud in Settings, tap Storage, and then tap Buy More Storage. Tap the amount you need and then tap Buy.

 If you change your mind, you can get in touch with Apple within 15 days to cancel your upgrade.

 If you pay $24.99 a year for the iTunes Match service, you can sync up to 25,000 songs in your iTunes library to your devices, which may be a less expensive way to go than paying for added iCloud storage. Tap Match in iTunes or visit www.apple.com/itunes/itunes-match for more information.

Turn on iCloud Drive

Before you can use iCloud Drive, you need to be sure that iCloud Drive is turned on. By default, Apple assumes that you want to use the Apple ID you probably already have for an iTunes account. You can sign up for an iCloud account when first setting up your iPhone, and use Settings to turn on iCloud Drive for online storage and sharing.

1. When first setting up your phone after upgrading to iOS 9, in the sequence of screens that appear, you'll see the one in **Figure 3-6**. Tap Use iCloud.

2. In the next dialog, tap Backup to iCloud. Your account is now set up based on the Apple ID that you entered earlier in the setup sequence.

Here are the steps to turn on iCloud Drive on your iPhone if you didn't do so when first setting up iPhone:

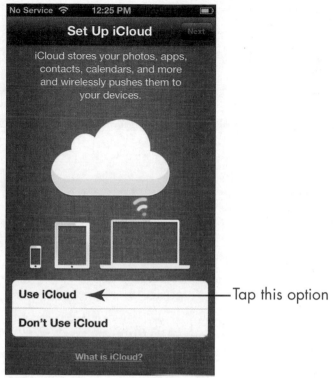

Tap this option

Figure 3-6

1. Tap Settings and then tap Mail, Contacts, Calendars. Next, under Accounts, tap iCloud and, on the next screen, tap iCloud Drive.

2. Tap the On/Off switch to turn on iCloud Drive (see **Figure 3-7**).

3. An alert may appear, asking whether you want to allow iCloud to use the location of your iPhone. Tap OK to use iCloud and features such as Find My iPhone. Your account is now set up.

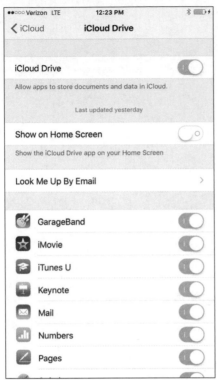

Figure 3-7

Make iCloud Sync Settings

1. When you have an iCloud account up and running (see the previous task), you have to specify which type of content should be synced with your iPhone via iCloud. To do so, tap Settings and then tap iCloud.

2. In the iCloud settings shown in **Figure 3-8,** tap the On/Off switch for any item that's turned off that you want to turn on (or vice versa). You can sync Photos, Mail, Contacts, Calendars, Reminders, News, Safari, Notes, Wallet, Keychain (an app that stores all your passwords and even credit card numbers across all Apple devices), and more.

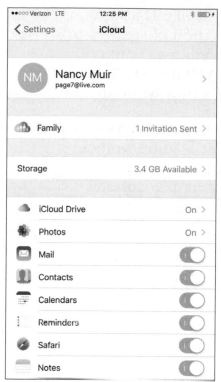

Figure 3-8

 If you want to allow iCloud to provide a service for locating a lost or stolen iPhone, tap the On/Off switch in the Find My iPhone field to activate it. This service helps you locate, send a message to, or delete content from your iPhone if it falls into other hands.

3. To enable automatic downloads of iTunes-purchased music, apps, and books, return to the main Settings screen by tapping the Settings button in the top-left corner of the screen (refer to Figure 3-8), and then tap App and iTunes Stores.

4. Tap the On/Off switch for Music, Apps, Books, or Updates to set up automatic downloads of any of this content to your iPhone via iCloud.

You might want to turn off the Cellular Data option, which you find in the Cellular section of Settings, to avoid having these downloads occur over your cellular connection, which can use up your data allowance. Wait until you're on a Wi-Fi connection to have iPhone perform the updates.

 If you need help with any of these features, you can always go to `http://manuals.info.apple.com/MANUALS/1000/MA1565/en_US/iphone_user_guide.pdf` to view the Apple manual.

Part II
Start Using Your iPhone

Visit www.dummies.com/extras/iphoneforseniors for information about working with Siri commands.

Making and Receiving Calls

If you're the type who wants a cellphone only to make and receive calls, you probably didn't buy an iPhone. Still, making and receiving calls is one of the primary functions of any phone, smart or not.

In this chapter, you discover all the basics of placing calls, receiving calls, and using available tools during a call to mute sound, turn on the speakerphone, and more. You also explore features that help you manage how to respond to a call that you can't take at the moment, how to receive calls when in your car, and how to change your ringtone.

Use the Keypad to Place a Call

1. Dialing a call with a keypad is an obvious first skill for you to acquire, and it's dead simple. On any Home screen, tap Phone in the Dock, and the app opens; tap the keypad button at the bottom of the screen, and the keypad appears (see **Figure 4-1**). (Note that if anything other than the keypad appears, you can just tap the Keypad button at the bottom of the screen to display the keypad.)

Keypad

Figure 4-1

2. Enter the number you want to call by tapping the number buttons; as you do, the number appears above the keypad.

3. If you enter a number incorrectly, use the Delete button that appears on the keypad after you've begun to enter a number (a backward-pointing arrow with an X in it) to clear numbers one at a time.

4. Tap the Call button shaped like a telephone headset. The call is placed and tools appear, as shown in **Figure 4-2**.

Figure 4-2

 When you enter a phone number, before you place the call, you can tap Add to Contacts (the + symbol to the left of the phone number) to add the person to your Contacts app. You can create a new contact or add the phone number to an existing contact using this feature.

 If you're on a call that requires you to punch in numbers or symbols such as a pound sign, tap the Keypad button on the tools that appear during a call to display the keypad. See more about using calling tools in the "Use Tools During a Call" task, later in this chapter.

Car Play is a feature new with iOS 9 that provides the ability to interact with your car and place calls using Siri voice commands and your iPhone. Apps designed for Car Play allow you to interact with controls while avoiding taking your attention from the road. At the time of this writing, car manufacturers are in the process of producing cars that can take advantage of Car Play.

End a Call

In the following tasks, I tell you several other ways to place calls; however, I don't want to leave you on your first call without a way out. When you're on a phone call, the Call button changes to an End button shaped like a phone receiver (see **Figure 4-3**). Tap End, and the call is disconnected.

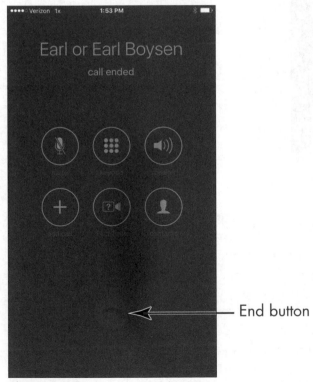

End button

Figure 4-3

Place a Call Using Contacts

1. If you've created a contact (see Chapter 5) and included a phone number in that contact record, you can use the Contacts app to place a call. Tap the Phone icon in any Home screen dock.

2. Tap the Contacts button at the bottom of the screen.

3. In the Contacts list that appears (see **Figure** 4-4), scroll up or down to locate the contact you need or tap a letter along the right side to jump to that section of the list.

Contacts button

Figure 4-4

4. Tap the contact to display his or her record. In the record that appears (see **Figure** 4-5), tap the phone number field. The call is placed.

Tap the phone number

Figure 4-5

 If you locate a contact and the record doesn't include a phone number, you can add it at this point by tapping the Edit button, entering the number, and then tapping Done. Place your call following Step 4 in the preceding steps.

Return a Recent Call

1. If you want to dial a number from a call you've recently made or received, you can use the Recents call list, which you get to by tapping Phone in the Dock on any Home screen.

2. Tap the Recents button at the bottom of the screen. A list of recent calls that you've both made and received appears (see **Figure** 4-6). Missed calls appear in red.

Recents button

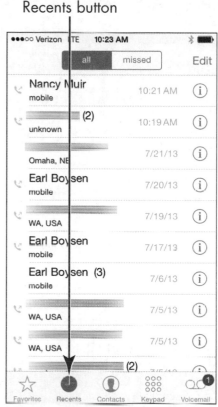

Figure 4-6

3. If you want to view only the calls you've missed, tap the Missed tab at the top of the screen.

4. Tap the Info icon (a small *i*) to the right of any item to view information about calls to or from this person or establishment (see **Figure** 4-7). The information displayed here might differ depending on the other phone and connection.

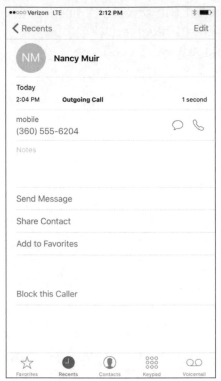

Figure 4-7

5. Tap the Back button to return to the Recents list, and then tap any call record to place a call to that number.

 Note that as of iOS 8, you can access folks you've recently contacted using the Multitasking feature. Double-tap your Home button and the Multitasking screen appears with a phone at the top of the screen indicating recent calls. Tap on one and you can then connect by tapping mobile, message, or FaceTime.

Use Favorites

1. You can save up to 50 contacts to Favorites in the Phone app so that you can quickly make calls to your A-list folks or businesses. Tap Phone on any Home screen.

2. Tap the Favorites button at the bottom of the screen.

3. In the Favorites screen that displays (see **Figure** 4-8), tap the Add button.

4. Your Contacts list appears and contact records that contain a phone number are bolded. Locate a contact that you want to make a Favorite and tap it. Next, in the menu that appears, select Home or Mobile for a voice call, FaceTime Audio, or FaceTime, depending on which type of call you prefer to make to this person most of the time (see **Figure** 4-9). The Favorites list reappears with your new favorite contact on it.

Favorites   Add button

Figure 4-8

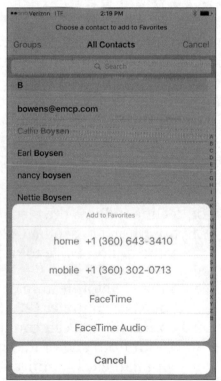

Figure 4-9

5. To place a call to a Favorite, display the Phone app, tap Favorites, and then tap a person on the list to place a call.

 If you decide to place a FaceTime call to a Favorite that you've created using the Voice Call setting, just tap the Information icon that appears to the right of the favorite's listing and tap the FaceTime call button in the contact record that appears. You can also create two contacts for the same person, one with a cellphone and one with a land phone, for instance, and place one or both in Favorites. See Chapter 9 for more about making FaceTime calls.

Receive a Call

There's one step to receiving a call. When a call comes in to you, the screen shown in **Figure 4-10** appears. Tap Accept to pick up the call, or Message to send a preset text message that you can select in Settings under Phone, Respond with Text without picking up. Tap Remind Me to have iPhone send you a reminder to return the call without answering it. If you don't tap either button, the call goes to your voice mail after a few rings.

 There's another quick way to send a call to voice mail or decline it: Press the Sleep/Wake button on the top of your phone to send a call to voice mail or press the same button twice to decline the call.

With the Handoff feature, if your iPhone is near an iPad or Mac computer (2012 model or later) and a call comes in, you can connect to the call via Bluetooth from any of the three devices by clicking or swiping the call notification. All devices have to be signed into the same iCloud account and have enabled Bluetooth and Handoff under Settings.

Figure 4-10

Use Tools During a Call

When you're on a call, whether you initiated it or received it, a set of tools, shown in **Figure 4-11**, is displayed.

Here's what these six buttons allow you to do, starting with the top-left corner:

⟶ **Mute:** Silences the phone call so that the caller can't hear you, though you can hear the caller. The Mute button background turns white, as shown in **Figure 4-12**, when a call is muted. Tap again to unmute the call.

⟶ **Keypad:** Displays the numeric keypad.

Figure 4-11

Figure 4-12

→ **Speaker:** Turns the speakerphone feature on and off. If you are near a Bluetooth device and have Bluetooth turned on in your iPhone Settings, you will see a list of sources (such as a car Bluetooth connection for hands-free calls) and you can choose the one you want to use.

→ **Add Call:** Displays Contacts so that you can add a caller to a conference call.

→ **FaceTime:** Begins a video call with somebody who has an iPhone 4 or more recent model, iPod touch (4th generation or later), iPad 2 or third-generation or later, an iPad mini, or a Mac running OS X 10.7 or later.

→ **Contacts:** Displays a list of contacts.

You can pair your iWatch with your iPhone and then tap Start Pairing to use your watch to make calls. Tap the Watch app on your second Home screen to pair your watch with your phone.

Turn On Do Not Disturb

1. Do Not Disturb is a feature that has iPhone silence incoming calls when iPhone is locked, displaying only a moon-shaped icon to let you know that a call is coming in. To turn the feature on, tap Settings.

2. Tap Do Not Disturb and then tap the On/Off switch labeled Manual to turn the feature on.

 When you turn on the Do Not Disturb feature, be aware that calls from Favorites are automatically allowed through by default, though you can change that setting by tapping the Allow Calls From option in Settings.

Set Up Exceptions for Do Not Disturb

1. If there are people whose calls you want to receive even when the Do Not Disturb feature is turned on, you can set up that capability. You can also set up a feature that allows a second call from the same number made within three minutes of the first to ring through. The theory with this feature is that two calls within a few minutes of each other might suggest an emergency situation that you'll want to respond to. With the Do Not Disturb feature turned on (see the previous task), tap Settings.

2. Tap Do Not Disturb, and on the Do Not Disturb screen, tap the Repeated Calls On/Off switch (see **Figure 4-13**).

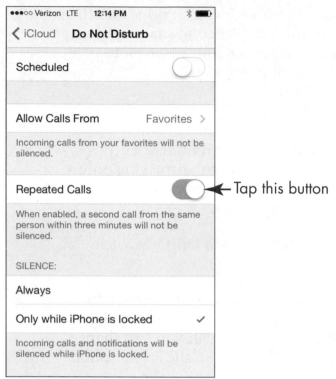

●●●○○ Verizon LTE   12:14 PM   ✳ ◾▸

❮ iCloud   **Do Not Disturb**

Scheduled   ⬭

Allow Calls From   Favorites ❯

Incoming calls from your favorites will not be silenced.

Repeated Calls   ⬭◖ ← Tap this button

When enabled, a second call from the same person within three minutes will not be silenced.

SILENCE:

Always

Only while iPhone is locked   ✓

Incoming calls and notifications will be silenced while iPhone is locked.

Figure 4-13

If you want to schedule Do Not Disturb to be active only during a certain time period, such as your lunch hour, tap the Scheduled feature, shown in Figure 4-13, and then set a time range.

Reply to a Call via Text or Set a Reminder to Call Back

1. You can reply with a text message to callers whose calls you can't answer. You can also set up a reminder to call the person back later. When a call comes in that you want to send a preset message to, tap Message.

2. Tap on a preset reply, or tap Custom and then enter your own message.

3. To set up a reminder, tap Remind Me when the call comes in and then tap In One Hour or When I Leave to be reminded when you leave your current location.

Change Your Ringtone

1. The music or sound that plays when a call is coming in is called a ringtone. Your phone is set up with a default ringtone, but you can choose among a large number of Apple-provided choices. Tap Settings.

2. Tap Sounds and then tap Ringtone.

3. Scroll down the list of ringtones and tap on one to preview it (see **Figure 4-14**).

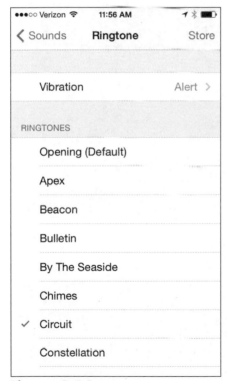

Figure 4-14

4. When you have selected the ringtone that you want in the list of ringtones, tap Sounds to return to the Sounds settings with your new ringtone in effect.

 You can also set custom ringtones for contacts using the Contacts app to give that person's calls a unique sound. Open a contact's record, tap Edit, and then tap the Ringtone setting to display a list of ringtones. Tap one and then tap Done to save it.

Managing Contacts

*C*ontacts is the iPhone equivalent of the
dog-eared address book that used to sit by
your phone. The Contacts app is simple to set
up and use, and it has some powerful features
beyond simply storing names, addresses, and
phone numbers.

For example, you can pinpoint a contact's
address in iPhone's Maps app. You can use
your contacts to address email and Facebook
messages and Twitter tweets quickly. If you
store a contact record that includes a website,
you can use a link in Contacts to view that
website instantly. In addition, of course, you
can easily search for a contact by a variety of
criteria, including how people are related to
you, such as family or mutual friends, or by
groups you create.

In this chapter, you discover the various features of Contacts, including how to save yourself time spent entering contact information by
syncing a contacts list from services such as
Google, Facebook, or Yahoo! to your iPhone.

Chapter 5

Get ready to . . .

Add a Contact

1. Tap Phone on the Home screen and then tap the Contacts icon at the bottom of the screen. An alphabetical list of contacts appears, like the one shown in **Figure 5-1**.

2. Tap the Add button, the button with the small plus sign (+) on it. A blank Info page opens (see **Figure 5-2**). Tap in any field and the onscreen keyboard displays.

Add button

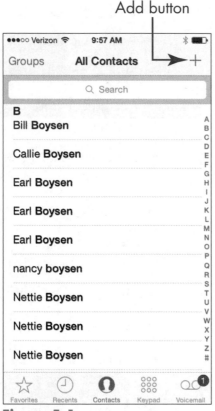

Figure 5-1

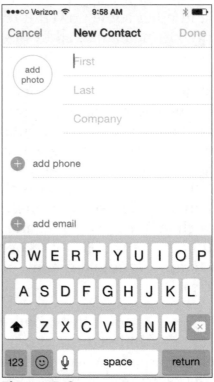

Figure 5-2

3. Enter any contact information you want. (Only one of the First, Last, or Company fields is required.)

4. To scroll down the contact's page and see more fields, flick up on the page with your finger.

5. If you want to add information such as a mailing or street address, you can tap the relevant Add field, which opens additional entry fields.

6. To add an information field such as Nickname or Job Title, tap Add Field toward the bottom of the page. In the Add Field dialog that appears (see **Figure 5-3**), choose a field to add. (You may have to flick the page up with your finger to view all the fields.)

7. Tap the Done button when you finish making entries. The new contact appears in your address book. Tap it to see details (see **Figure 5-4**).

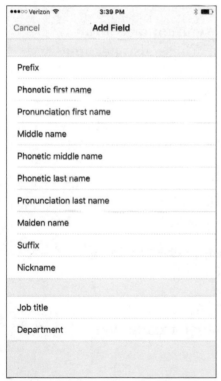

Figure 5-3

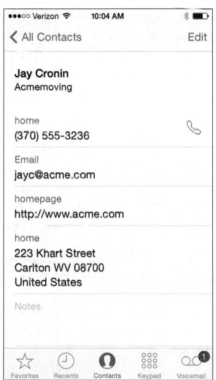

Figure 5-4

If your contact has a name that's difficult for you to pronounce, consider adding the Phonetic First Name or Phonetic Last Name field, or both, to that person's record (refer to Step 6).

 You can choose a distinct ringtone or text tone for a new contact. Just tap the Ringtone or Text Tone field in the New Contact form to see a list of options. When that person calls either on the phone or via FaceTime, or texts you via SMS, MMS, or iMessage, you will recognize him or her from the tone that plays.

Sync Contacts with iCloud

1. You can use your iCloud account to sync contacts from your iPad to iCloud to back them up. These also become available to your email account, if you set one up. On the Home screen, tap Settings and then tap iCloud.

2. In the iCloud settings shown in **Figure 5-5,** make sure that the On/Off switch for Contacts is set to On in order to sync contacts.

3. Tap the Back button in the top-left corner of the screen to return to Settings.

4. To choose which email account to sync with, tap Mail, Contacts, Calendars, and then tap iCloud.

5. In the following screen (see **Figure 5-6**), tap to turn Contacts on to merge contacts from that account via iCloud.

Set this to On   Set this to On

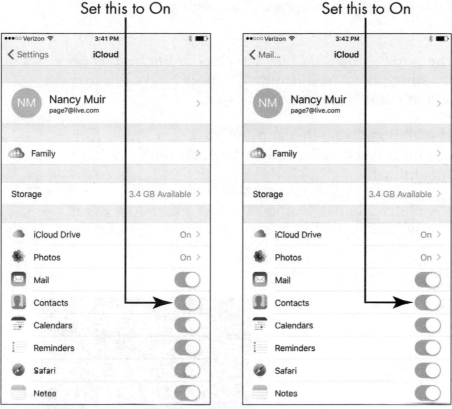

Figure 5-5   Figure 5-6

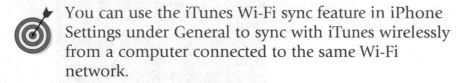

You can also use iTunes to sync contacts among all your Apple devices and even a Windows PC. See Chapter 3 for more about making iTunes settings.

You can use the iTunes Wi-Fi sync feature in iPhone Settings under General to sync with iTunes wirelessly from a computer connected to the same Wi-Fi network.

Assign a Photo to a Contact

1. With Contacts open, tap a contact to whose record you want to add a photo.

2. Tap the Edit button.

3. On the Info page that appears (see **Figure** 5-7), tap Add Photo.

4. In the popover that appears, tap Choose Photo to choose an existing photo. You could also choose Take Photo to take that contact's photo on the spot.

5. In the Photos dialog that appears, choose a source for your photo (such as Recently Added, Photo Sharing, or other album).

6. In the photo album that appears, tap a photo to select it. The Move and Scale dialog, shown in **Figure** 5-8, appears.

Tap here to add photo

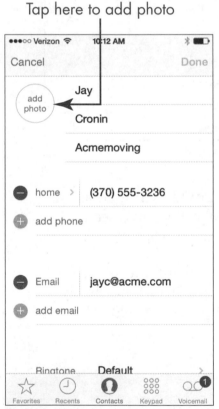

Figure 5-7

Figure 5-8

7. Tap the Choose button to use the photo for this contact.

8. Tap Done to save changes to the contact. The photo appears on the contact's Info page (see **Figure** 5-9).

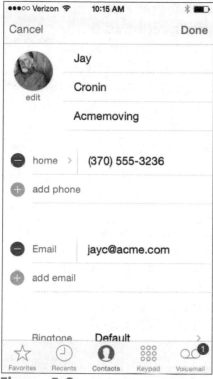

●●●○○ Verizon 🛜   10:15 AM   ✳ ▬)

Cancel   Done

Jay

Cronin

Acmemoving

⊖ home > (370) 555-3236

⊕ add phone

⊖ Email   jayc@acme.com

⊕ add email

Ringtone   Default   >

☆ Favorites   🕐 Recents   👤 Contacts   ⠿ Keypad   ⌬¹ Voicemail

Figure 5-9

 While in the Photos dialog, in Step 6, you can modify the photo before saving it to the contact information. You can unpinch your fingers on the iPhone screen to expand the photo and move it around the space to focus on a particular section and then tap the Choose button to use the modified version.

Add Twitter or Facebook Information

1. iPhone users can add Twitter information to their Contacts so that they can quickly tweet (send a short message to) others using Twitter. You can also add Facebook or LinkedIn information so that you can post a message to your contact's Facebook or LinkedIn account. Before you try this, go to Settings and click an app, such as Facebook, and then click Install. Next, with Contacts open, tap a contact.

2. Tap the Edit button.

3. Scroll down and tap Add Social Profile.

4. Tap in the Twitter Social Profile field and enter the contact's username information for an account.

 If you prefer to add Facebook information instead of Twitter, tap Facebook in Step 4 and enter the contact's Facebook information. (You can also click the Add Social Profile link again and choose Flickr, LinkedIn, Myspace, Sina Welbo, or Add Custom Service in the fields that appear.)

5. Tap Done and the information is saved. The account is now displayed when you select the contact, and you can send a tweet or Facebook message by simply tapping the username, tapping the service you want to use to contact the person, and then tapping the appropriate command (such as Facebook posting, as shown in **Figure 5-10**).

 To update contact information for people who use social media such as Twitter or Facebook, open Settings and scroll down to the service. Tap it and then tap Update All Contacts. iPhone updates your contacts with any new or changed information that the person has posted to the social media site.

Figure 5-10

Designate Related People

1. You can quickly designate relationships in a contact record if those people are saved to Contacts. One great use for this feature is using Siri to simply say, "Call Manager" to call someone who is designated in your contact information as your manager. Tap a contact and then tap Edit.

2. Scroll down the record and tap Add Related Name.

3. The field labeled Mother (see **Figure 5-11**) now appears.

4. Tap the Add Related Name, and the Father field appears. Tap again and the Assistant field appears.

5. Tap the blue Information arrow in a field, and your Contacts list appears. Tap the related person's name, and it appears in the field (see **Figure 5-12**). Tap Done to complete the edits.

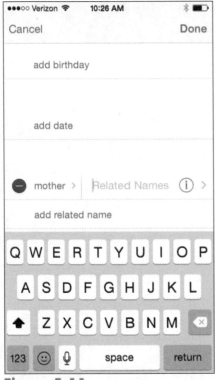

Figure 5-11

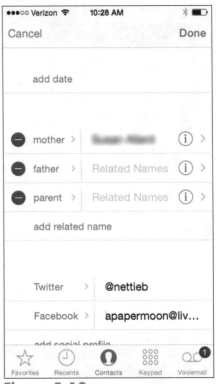

Figure 5-12

 After you add relations to a contact record, when you select the person in the Contacts main screen, all the related people for that contact are listed there.

 There's a setting for Linked Contacts in the Contacts app when you're editing a contact's record. Using this setting isn't like adding a relation; rather, if you have records for the same person that have been imported into Contacts from different sources such as Google or Twitter, you can link them to show only a single contact.

Set Ringtones and Text Tones

1. If you want to hear a unique tone when you receive a phone or FaceTime call from a particular contact, you can set up this feature in Contacts. For example, if you want to be sure that you know instantly whether your spouse, sick friend, or boss is calling, you can set a unique tone for that person. To do so, tap to add a new contact or select a contact in the list of contacts and tap Edit.

2. Tap the Ringtone field in a new contact or tap Edit and then the Ringtone field in an existing contact, and a list of tones appears (see **Figure 5-13**).

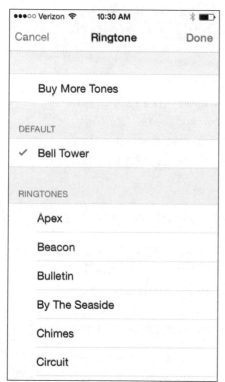

Figure 5-13

3. Tap a tone, and it previews. When you hear one you like, tap Done.

If you set a custom tone for someone, that tone will be used when that person calls or contacts you by FaceTime. You can also set a custom text tone to be used when the person sends you a text message — tap Text Tone instead of Ringtone in Step 2 in the preceding steps and follow the remaining steps.

If your Apple devices are synced via iCloud, setting a unique ringtone for an iPhone contact also sets it for use with FaceTime and Messages on your iPad and Mac. See Chapter 3 for more about iCloud.

Search for a Contact

1. With Contacts open, tap in the Search field at the very top of your Contacts list (see **Figure 5-14**). The onscreen keyboard opens.

2. Type the first letter of either the first or last name or company. All matching results appear, as shown in **Figure 5-15**. For example, typing *Me* might display *Megan and Melrose* and email addresses including *@metro* in the results, all of which have *Me* as the first two letters of the first or last part of the name or address.

3. Tap a contact in the results to display that person's Info page.

You can search by phone number simply by entering the phone number in the Search field until the list narrows to the person you're looking for. This might be a good way to search for all contacts in your town or company, for example.

You can use the alphabetical listing along the right side of All Contacts and tap a letter to locate a contact. Also, you can tap and drag to scroll down the list of contacts on the All Contacts page.

Search field

Search results

Figure 5-14

Figure 5-15

Go to a Contact's Website

1. If you entered website information in the Home Page field, it automatically becomes a link in the contact's record. Open a contact's record.

2. Tap a contact's name to display the organization or person's contact information, locate the Home Page field, and then tap the link (see **Figure 5-16**).

3. The Safari browser opens with the web page displayed (see **Figure 5-17**).

Tap this link

Figure 5-16

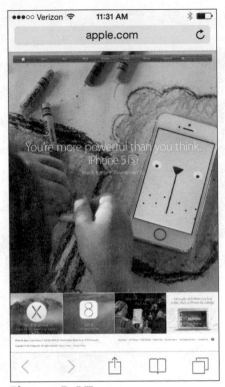

Figure 5-17

 You can't go directly back to Contacts after you follow a link to a website. You have to press the Home button and then tap the Contacts app again to reenter the application or use the multitasking feature by pressing the Home button twice and choosing Contacts from the icons that appear along the bottom of the screen.

Address Email Using Contacts

1. If you entered an email address for a contact, the address automatically becomes a link in the contact's record. Tap the Phone icon on the Home screen and then tap Contacts.

2. Tap a contact's name to display the person's contact information, and then tap the email address link in the field labeled Email (see **Figure 5-18**).

3. The New Message dialog appears, as shown in **Figure 5-19**. Initially, the title bar of this dialog reads *New Message*, but as you type a subject, *New Message* changes to the specific title.

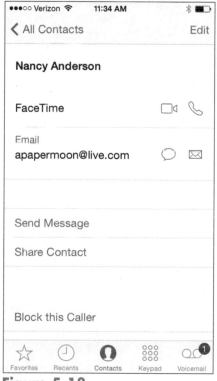

Figure 5-18

Figure 5-19

4. Tap in a field and use the onscreen keyboard to enter a subject and message.

5. Tap the Send button. The message goes on its way.

Share a Contact

1. After you've entered contact information, you can share it with others via an email or text message. With Contacts open, tap a contact name to display its information.

2. On the Information page, scroll down and tap Share Contact. In the dialog that appears, shown in **Figure 5-20,** tap Mail (at this point you could also tap Message). A New Message form appears.

Tap this option

Figure 5-20

 To share with an AirDrop-enabled device that is nearby, use the AirDrop button in the screen shown in Figure 5-20. Just select a nearby device, and your contact is transmitted to that person's device (such as a smartphone, Mac with OS X Yosemite with the AirDrop folder open in Finder, or tablet).

3. In the New Message form, use the onscreen keyboard to enter the recipient's email address. Note that if the person is saved in Contacts, you can just type his or her name here.

4. Modify the information in the Subject field, if you like.

5. Enter a message and then tap the Send button. The message goes to your recipient with the contact information attached as a .vcf file. (This *vCard* format is commonly used to transmit contact information.)

 When somebody receives a vCard containing contact information, he or she needs only to click the attached file to open it. At this point, depending on the email or contact management program, the recipient can perform various actions to save the content. Other iPhone, iPod touch, iPad, or iPhone users can easily import .vcf records as new contacts in their own Contacts apps.

View a Contact's Location in Maps

1. If you've entered a person's address in Contacts, you have a shortcut for viewing that person's location in the Maps application. Tap the Phone app on the Home screen and then tap Contacts.

2. Tap the contact you want to view to display that contact's information.

3. Tap Edit and then tap Add Address and enter the address information. Tap Done and then tap the address field. Maps opens and displays a map of the address (see **Figure 5-21**).

Figure 5-21

 This task works with more than your friends'
addresses. You can save information for your favorite
restaurant or movie theater or any other location and
use Contacts to jump to the associated website in the
Safari browser or to the address in Maps. For more
about using Safari, see Chapter 10. For more about
the Maps application, see Chapter 19.

Delete a Contact

1. When it's time to remove a name or two from your
Contacts, it's easy to do. With Contacts open, tap the
contact you want to delete.

2. On the Information page (refer to Figure 5-4), tap the
Edit button.

3. On the Info page that displays, drag your finger upward to scroll down and then tap the Delete Contact button at the bottom (see **Figure 5-22**).

4. The confirming dialog shown in **Figure 5-23** appears; tap the Delete Contact button to confirm the deletion.

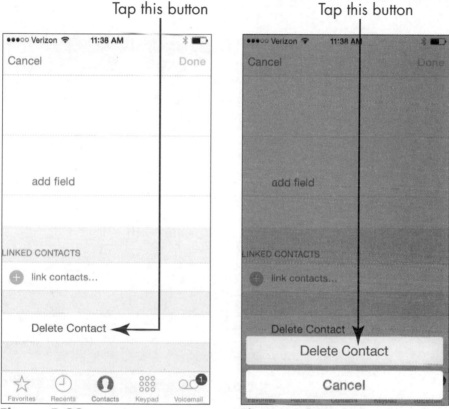

Figure 5-22   Figure 5-23

 During this process, if you change your mind before you tap Delete, tap the Cancel button in Step 4. Be careful: After you tap Delete, there's no going back! Your contact is deleted from not only your iPhone but also any other device that syncs to your iPhone via iCloud, Google, or other means.

Using Handy Utilities

*U*tilities are simple apps that can be very useful indeed to help with common tasks such as calculating your meal tip or finding your way on a hike in the woods.

In this chapter, I help you explore two apps: Compass to help you find your way, and Voice Memos so that you can record your best ideas for posterity. I also help you out with using the Calculator app to keep your numbers in line.

Use the Calculator

1. This one won't be rocket science. The Calculator app works like just about every calculator app you've ever used. Go to the second Home screen and tap Calculator to display the app (see **Figure 6-1**).

Figure 6-1

2. Tap a few numbers (see **Figure 6-2**) and then use any of these functions and additional numbers to perform calculations:

- **+, −, ×, and ÷:** These familiar buttons add, subtract, multiply, and divide the number you've entered.

- **+/−:** If the calculator is displaying a negative result, tap this to change it to a positive result, and vice versa.

- **AC/C:** This is the Clear button; its name will change depending on whether you've entered anything. (AC clears all; C clears just the last entry after you've made several entries.)

- **=:** This button produces the result of whatever calculation you've entered.

Figure 6-2

 If you have a scientific nature, you'll be delighted to see that if you turn your phone to a landscape orientation, you get additional features that turn the basic calculator into a scientific calculator so that you can play with calculations involving such functions as cosines and tangents. You can also use memory functions to work with stored calculations.

Find Your Way with Compass

1. Compass is a handy tool for figuring out where you are, assuming that you get 3G or 4G reception wherever you are. Tap the Extras folder on the second Home screen to open it and then tap Compass. The first time you do this, if you haven't enabled location access, a message appears, asking if iPhone can use your current location to provide information. Tap OK.

2. If you're using Compass for the first time, you'll be asked to tilt the screen to roll a little red ball around a circle; this helps iPhone to calibrate the Compass app. When you've completed this exercise, the Compass app appears (see **Figure 6-3**). Move around with your iPhone, and the compass indicates your current orientation in the world.

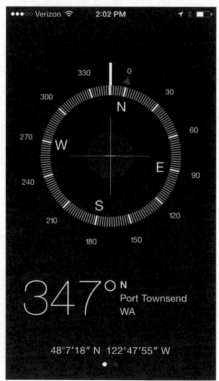

Figure 6-3

3. Tap the bold white line indicating your current location, as shown in **Figure 6-4,** and the display changes to True North and indicates with a red wedge how far off True North you are when you move the compass; tap it again to display Magnetic North.

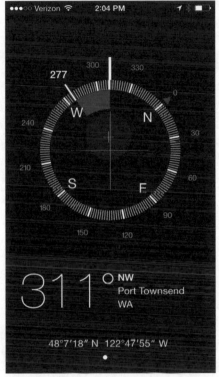

Figure 6-4

4. Swipe to the left to view a compass view with information about how many degrees off of zero a surface is (see **Figure 6-5**). If a surface beneath your phone is flat, the screen turns green. Use this to check to see whether a surface is level.

Figure 6-5

 True North refers to the direction you follow from where you are to get to the North Pole; Magnetic North is correlated relative to the Earth's magnetic field. True North is the more accurate measurement because of the tilt of the Earth.

 You will know that you have a 4G connection if you see LTE in the Status bar. Not every location has this capability yet, so this is a good way to check whether you're connected.

Record Voice Memos

1. Voice Memos is perhaps the most robust of the three apps covered in this chapter. The app allows you to record memos, edit memos by trimming them down, share them via email or instant message with Messages, and label recordings so that you find them again. On the second Home screen, tap the Extras folder to open it and then tap Voice Memos.

2. In the Voice Memos app (see **Figure 6-6**), tap the red Record button to record a memo. (This button changes to a red Pause button when you're recording.)

Record button

Figure 6-6

3. A blue line moving from left to right shows that you're in recording mode (see **Figure 6-7**). While recording, you can tap the red Pause button to pause the recording and then tap Done to stop recording.

Pause button

Figure 6-7

4. When you're done recording, a New Voice Memo dialog appears where you can enter a name for the recording and tap Save. A list of recorded memos appears (see **Figure 6-8**). Tap one to play it back; share it via AirDrop, Messages, Music, or Mail; edit it; save it as note in the Notes app; or delete it.

 AirDrop is a feature that, with a fifth-generation iPhone or later, allows you to share items such as photos, voice memos, music, and more with another person who has an AirDrop-enabled device and is nearby. You can also share via AirDrop with a Mac using OS X Yosemite or later. Learn more about AirDrop in Chapter 10.

Figure 6-8

Trim a Voice Memo

1. Perhaps you repeated yourself at the beginning of your memo. If you want to cut part of a recorded memo, you can trim it. With the list of recordings displayed (refer to Figure 6-8), tap any recording. The recording details display, as shown in **Figure 6-9**.

2. Tap Edit.

3. In the Edit screen shown in **Figure 6-10**, tap the Trim button (it's a little square with dots coming off of the left and right sides) and then drag the lines on the right or left of the memo bar and drag inward to trim a portion of the recording.

Trim button

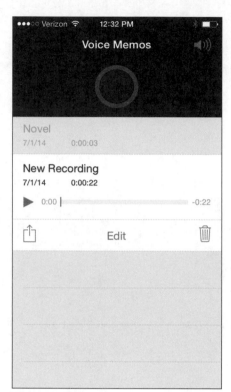

Figure 6-9   Figure 6-10

4. Tap Trim and a dialog appears. Tap Trim Original to apply the trim and save the recording, or Save As New Recording to apply the trim and save it as a new version of the recording.

5. Tap Done to go back to the list of voice memos.

 If you begin to trim a memo and change your mind, tap the Cancel button in the dialog mentioned in Step 4.

Rename a Voice Memo

1. You may occasionally have to rename a voice memo. With the list of memos displayed (refer to Figure 6-8), tap a memo to display its details.

2. Tap the name of the recording and the name becomes available for editing, as shown in **Figure 6-11**.

3. Tap Backspace on your iPhone keyboard to delete the current name; enter a new name and then tap the Done button at the lower-right corner of the screen to return to the list of memos, where you see the memo now named with the label you just gave it (see **Figure 6-12**).

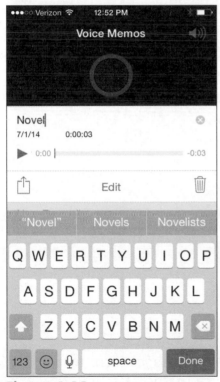

Figure 6-11

Figure 6-12

Share a Voice Memo

1. Tap a memo in the list of memos (refer to Figure 6-8) to select it.

2. Tap the Share button (the box with an arrow pointing out of the top), shown in **Figure 6-13**.

Share button

Figure 6-13

3. In the menu shown in **Figure 6-14**, tap Mail to display an email form or Message to display a Messages form to send an instant message with the voice memo attached (see **Figure 6-15**).

Tap this option

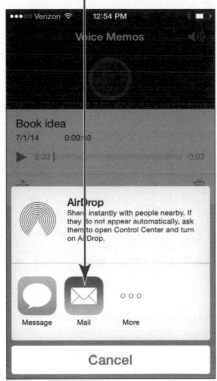

Figure 6-14

Figure 6-15

4. Fill in the recipient's information by typing it or beginning to type and selecting it from your Contacts list. Enter
a subject if you're sending an email, and a message, and
tap Send. The voice memo and your message go on
their way.

Making Your iPhone More Accessible

*i*Phone users are all different, and some face visual, motor, or hearing challenges. If you're one of these folks, you'll be glad to hear that iPhone offers some handy accessibility features.

To make your screen easier to read, you can adjust the brightness or change wallpaper. You can also set up the VoiceOver feature to read onscreen elements out loud. Then there are a slew of features you can turn on or off, including Zoom, Invert Colors, Speak Selection, Large Type, and more.

If hearing is your challenge, you can do the obvious and adjust the system volume. If you wear hearing aids, you can choose the correct settings for using Bluetooth or another hearing aid mode. The iPhone also has settings for Mono Audio (useful when you're wearing headphones), using an LED flash when an alert sounds, and a Phone Noise Cancellation feature.

Features that help you deal with physical and motor challenges include an AssistiveTouch feature for those who have difficulty using the iPhone touchscreen, Switch Control for working with adaptive accessories, and the Home Button and Call Audio Routing settings that allow you to adjust how quickly you have to tap the iPhone screen to work with features and whether you can use a headset or speaker to answer calls.

Finally, the Guided Access feature provides help for those who have difficulty focusing on one task. It also provides a handy mode for showing presentations of content in settings where you don't want users to flit off to other apps, as in school or a public kiosk.

Set Brightness

1. Especially when using iPhone as an e-reader, you may find that a slightly less-bright screen reduces strain on your eyes. To adjust screen brightness, tap the Settings icon on the Home screen.

2. In Settings, tap Display & Brightness.

3. To control brightness manually, tap the Auto-Brightness On/Off switch (see **Figure 7-1**) to turn off this feature.

4. Tap and drag the Brightness slider (refer to Figure 7-1) to the right to make the screen brighter or to the left to make it dimmer.

5. Press the Home button to close Settings.

If glare from the screen is a problem for you, consider getting a *screen protector*. This thin film not only protects your screen from damage but also can reduce glare.

In the iBooks e-reader app, you can set a sepia tone for the page, which might be easier on your eyes. See Chapter 14 for more about using iBooks.

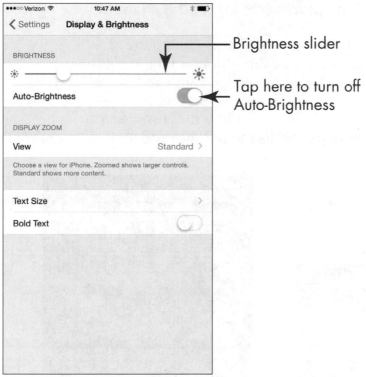

Brightness slider

Tap here to turn off Auto-Brightness

Figure 7-1

Change the Wallpaper

1. The default iPhone background image on your iPhone may be pretty, but it may not be the one that works best for you. Choosing different wallpaper may help you to see all the icons on your Home screen. Start by tapping the Settings icon on the Home screen.

2. In Settings, tap Wallpaper (tap the Back button to go back to the main Settings window if necessary).

3. In the Wallpaper settings that appear, tap Choose a New Wallpaper and then tap a wallpaper category such as Dynamic or Stills, as shown in **Figure 7-2,** to view choices. Tap a sample to select it; if you choose Photos on the Wallpaper screen, tap an album in Photos to locate a picture to use as your wallpaper and tap it.

4. In the preview that appears (see **Figure** 7-3), tap Set.

5. In the following menu, tap Set Lock Screen (the screen that appears when you lock the iPhone by tapping the power button), Set Home Screen, or Set Both.

6. Press the Home button to return to your Home screen with the new wallpaper set as the background.

Figure 7-2

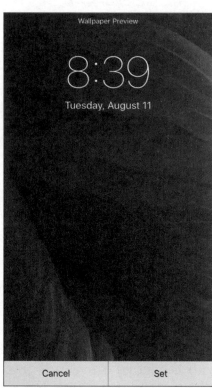

Figure 7-3

Set Up VoiceOver

1. VoiceOver reads the names of screen elements and settings to you, but it also changes the way you provide input to the iPhone. In Notes, for example, you can have VoiceOver read the name of the Notes buttons to you, and when you enter notes, it reads words or characters that you've entered. It can also tell you whether features such as Auto-Correction are on. To turn on this feature, tap the Settings icon on the Home screen. Tap General and then tap Accessibility.

2. In the Accessibility pane, shown in **Figure** 7-4, tap the VoiceOver button.

3. In the VoiceOver pane, shown in **Figure** 7-5, tap the VoiceOver On/Off switch to turn on this feature. With VoiceOver on, you must first single-tap to select an item such as a button, which causes VoiceOver to read the name of the button to you. Then you double-tap the button to activate its function. (VoiceOver reminds you about this if you turn on Speak Hints, which is helpful when you first use VoiceOver, but it soon becomes annoying.)

Tap this option

Tap to turn on VoiceOver

Figure 7-4

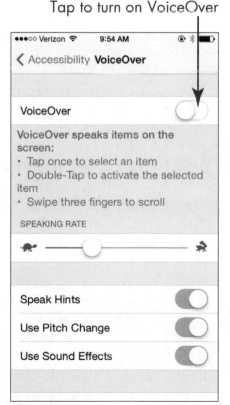

Figure 7-5

4. Tap the VoiceOver Practice button to select it, then double-tap the button to open VoiceOver Practice. (This is the new method of tapping that VoiceOver activates.) Practice using gestures such as pinching or flicking left, and VoiceOver tells you what action each gesture initiates.

5. Tap the Done button and then double-tap the same button to return to the VoiceOver dialog. Tap the Speak Hints On/Off switch and then double-tap the switch; VoiceOver speaks the name of each tapped item.

6. If you want VoiceOver to read words or characters to you (for example, in the Notes app), scroll down and then tap and double-tap Typing Feedback.

7. In the Typing Feedback dialog, tap and then double-tap to select the option you prefer. The Words option causes VoiceOver to read words to you, but not characters, such as the "dollar sign" ($). The Characters and Words option causes VoiceOver to read both, and so on.

8. Press the Home button to return to the Home screen. Read the next task to find out how to navigate your iPhone after you've turned on VoiceOver.

 You can change the language that VoiceOver speaks. In General settings, tap Language & Region, tap iPhone Language, and then select another language. This action, however, also changes the language used for labels on Home icons and various settings and fields in iPhone.

 You can use the Accessibility Shortcut setting to help you more quickly turn the VoiceOver, Zoom, Switch Control, AssistiveTouch, Grayscale, or Invert Colors features on and off. In the Accessibility dialog, tap Accessibility Shortcut. In the dialog that appears, choose what you want three presses of the

Home button to activate. Now three presses with a single finger on the Home button provide you with the option you selected wherever you go in iPhone.

Use VoiceOver

After VoiceOver is turned on, you need to figure out how to use it. I won't kid you — using it is awkward at first, but you'll get the hang of it! Here are the main onscreen gestures you should know how to use:

➡ **Tap an item to select it.** VoiceOver then speaks its name.

➡ **Double-tap the selected item.** This action activates the item.

➡ **Flick three fingers.** It takes three fingers to scroll around a page with VoiceOver turned on.

Table 7-1 provides additional gestures to help you use VoiceOver. If you want to use this feature often, I suggest that you read the VoiceOver section of the iPhone online *User Guide*, which goes into great detail about using VoiceOver. You'll find the *User Guide* at `http://manuals.info.apple.com/MANUALS/1000/ MA1565/en_US/iphone_user_guide.pdf`. You can also get an iBooks version of the manual through that app in the iBooks Store.

Table 7-1	VoiceOver Gestures
Gesture	*Effect*
Flick right or left.	Select the next or preceding item.
Tap with two fingers.	Stop speaking the current item.
Flick two fingers up.	Read everything from the top of the screen.
Flick two fingers down.	Read everything from the current position.

(continued)

Table 7-1 *(continued)*

Gesture	Effect
Flick three fingers up or down.	Scroll one page at a time.
Flick three fingers right or left.	Go to the next or preceding page.
Tap three fingers.	Speak the scroll status (for example, line 20 of 100).
Flick four fingers up or down.	Go to the first or last element on a page.
Flick four fingers right or left.	Go to the next or preceding section (as on a web page).

 If tapping with two or three fingers seems difficult for you, try tapping with one finger from one hand and one or two from the other. When double- or triple-tapping, you have to perform these gestures as quickly as you can for them to work.

 Check out some of the settings for VoiceOver, including a choice for Braille, Language Rotor for making language choices, the ability to navigate images, and a setting to have iPhone speak notifications.

Several Vision features are simple on/off settings, so rather than repeatedly give you the steps to get to those settings, I provide this useful bullet list of additional features that you can turn on or off after you tap Settings ➪ General ➪ Accessibility:

➡ **Zoom:** The Zoom feature enlarges the contents displayed on the iPhone screen when you double-tap the screen with three fingers. The Zoom feature works almost everywhere in iPhone: in Photos, on web pages, on your Home screens, in your Mail, in Music, and in Videos — give it a try!

➡ **Invert Colors:** The Invert Colors setting reverses colors on your screen so that white backgrounds are black and black text is white.

The Invert Colors feature works well in some places and not so well in others. For example, in the Photos application, pictures appear almost as photo negatives. Your Home screen image will likewise look a bit strange. And don't even think of playing a video with this feature turned on! However, if you need help reading text, White on Black can be useful in several apps.

➡ **Larger Text:** If having larger text in apps such as Contacts, Mail, and Notes would be helpful to you, you can turn on the Larger Text feature and choose the text size that works best for you.

➡ **Bold Text:** Turning on this setting restarts your iPhone (after asking you for permission to do so) and then causes text in various apps and in Settings to be bold.

➡ **Increase Contrast:** Use this setting to set up backgrounds in some areas of iPhone and apps with greater contrast, which should improve visibility.

➡ **Reduce Motion:** Tap this accessibility feature and then tap the On/Off setting to turn off the parallax effect, which causes the background of your Home screens to appear to float as you move the phone around.

➡ **On/Off Labels:** If you have trouble making out colors and therefore find it hard to tell when an On/Off setting is On (green) or Off (white), use this setting to add a circle to the right of a setting when it's off and a white vertical line to a setting when it's on (see **Figure 7-6**).

On/Off Labels option

Figure 7-6

Use iPhone with Hearing Aids

1. If you have Bluetooth enabled or use another style of hearing aid, your iPhone may be able to detect it and work with its settings to improve sound on your phone calls. Tap Settings on the Home screen and then tap General.

2. Tap Accessibility and then scroll down to the Hearing section and tap Hearing Aids.

3. On the following screen, shown in **Figure 7-7,** your iPhone searches for hearing aid devices. When yours appears, tap it.

4. Tap Hearing Aid Mode to turn on a feature that could improve audio quality when you're using your hearing aid.

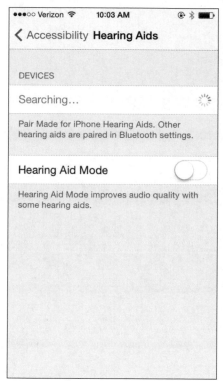

Figure 7-7

Adjust the Volume

1. Though individual apps such as Music and Video have their own volume settings, you can set your iPhone system volume for your ringer and alerts as well to help you better hear what's going on.

2. Tap Settings on the Home screen and then tap Sounds.

3. In the Sounds settings that appear (see **Figure 7-8**), tap and drag the Ringer and Alerts slider to the right to increase the volume of these audible attention grabbers, or to the left to lower it.

4. Press the Home button to return to the Home screen.

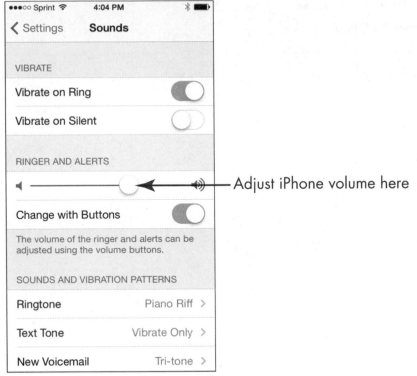

Adjust iPhone volume here

Figure 7-8

 In the Sounds settings, you can turn on or off the sounds that iPhone makes when certain events occur (such as receiving new Mail or Calendar alerts). These sounds are turned on by default.

 Even those of us with perfect hearing sometimes have trouble hearing a phone ring, especially in busy public places. Consider using the Vibrate settings in the Sounds settings to have your phone vibrate when a call is coming in.

Set Up Subtitles and Captioning

1. Closed captioning and subtitles help folks with hearing challenges enjoy entertainment and educational content. Tap Settings on the Home screen, tap General, and then tap Accessibility. Scroll down to the Media section and tap Subtitles & Captioning.

2. On the following screen, shown in **Figure 7-9,** tap the On/Off switch to turn on Closed Captions + SDH (Subtitles for the Deaf and Hard of Hearing). If you'd like, you can also tap Style and choose a text style for the captions.

3. Press the Home button to return to the Home screen.

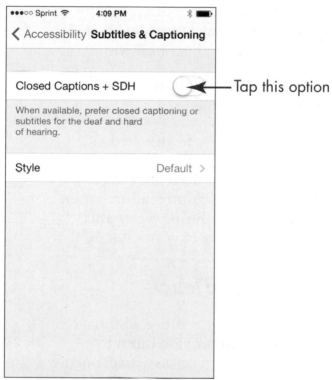

Figure 7-9

Manage Other Hearing Settings

Several hearing accessibility settings are simple On/Off settings, including:

⟶ **Mono Audio:** Using the stereo effect in headphones or a headset breaks up sounds so that you hear a portion in one ear and a portion in the other ear.

The purpose is to simulate the way your ears process sounds. If there is only one channel of sound, that sound is sent to both ears. However, if you're hard of hearing or deaf in one ear, you're hearing only a portion of the sound in your hearing ear, which can be frustrating. If you have such hearing challenges and want to use iPhone with a headset connected, you should turn on Mono Audio. When it's turned on, all sound is combined and distributed to both ears. You can use the slider below Mono Audio to direct more sound to the ear you hear best with.

⟶ **LED Flash for Alerts:** If you need a visual clue when an alert is spoken, turn this setting on.

⟶ **Phone Noise Cancellation:** If you're annoyed at ambient noise when you make a call in public (or noisy private) settings, with an iPhone 5 or later, turn on the Phone Noise Cancellation feature. When you hold the phone to your ear during a call, this feature reduces background noise to some extent.

Turn On and Work with AssistiveTouch

1. The AssistiveTouch Control panel helps those who have challenges working with buttons to provide input to iPhone using the touchscreen. To turn on AssistiveTouch, tap Settings on the Home screen and then tap General and Accessibility.

2. In the Accessibility pane, scroll down and tap AssistiveTouch. In the pane that appears, tap the On/Off switch for AssistiveTouch to turn it on (see **Figure 7-10**). A gray square (called the AssistiveTouch Control panel) then appears on the right side of the screen. This square now appears in the same location in whatever apps you display on your iPhone, though you can move it around with your finger.

3. Tap the AssistiveTouch Control panel to display options, as shown in **Figure 7-11**. The panel now includes Notification Center and Control Center options.

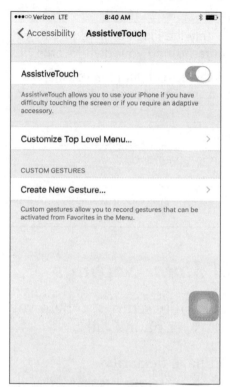

Figure 7-10

Figure 7-11

4. You can tap Custom or Device on the panel to see additional choices, tap Siri to activate the personal assistant feature, tap Notification Center or Control Center to display those panels, or press Home to go directly to the Home screen. After you've chosen an option, pressing the Home button takes you back to the Home screen.

Table 7-2 shows the major options available in the AssistiveTouch Control panel and their purpose.

Table 7-2	AssistiveTouch Controls
Control	*Purpose*
Siri	Activates the Siri feature, which allows you to speak questions and make requests of your iPhone.
Custom	Displays a set of gestures with only the Pinch gesture preset; you can tap any of the other blank squares to add your own favorite gestures.
Device	You can rotate the screen, lock the screen, turn the volume up or down, mute or unmute sound, or shake iPhone to undo an action using the presets in this option.
Home	Sends you to the Home screen.
Control Center	Open the Control Center common commands.
Notification Center	Open Notification Center with reminders, Calendar appointments, and so on.

Turn On Additional Physical and Motor Settings

Use these On/Off settings in the Accessibility settings to help you deal with how fast you tap and how you answer phone calls:

⟹ **Home Button:** Sometimes if you have dexterity challenges, it's hard to double-press or triple-press the Home button fast enough to make an effect. Choose the Slow or Slowest option when you tap this setting to allow you a bit more time to make that second or third tap.

⟹ **Call Audio Routing:** If you prefer to use your speaker phone to receive incoming calls, or you typically use a headset with your phone that allows you to tap a button to receive a call, tap this option and then choose Headset or Speaker. Speakers and headsets can both provide a better hearing experience for many.

If you have certain adaptive accessories that allow you to control devices with head gestures, you can use them to control your iPhone, highlighting features in sequence and then selecting one. Use the Switch Control feature in the Accessibility settings to turn this mode on and make settings.

Focus Learning with Guided Access

1. Guided Access is a feature that you can use to limit a user's access to iPhone to a single app, and even limit access in that app to certain features. This feature is useful in several settings, ranging from a classroom, for use by someone with attention deficit disorder, and even to a public setting such as a kiosk where you don't want users to be able to open other apps. Tap Settings and then tap General.

2. Tap Accessibility and then scroll down and tap Guided Access; then, on the screen that follows (see **Figure 7-12**), tap Guided Access to turn the feature on.

3. Tap Passcode Settings and then tap Set Guided Access Passcode to activate a passcode so that those using an app cannot return to the Home screen to access other apps. In the Set Passcode dialog that appears (see **Figure 7-13**), enter a passcode using the numeric pad. Enter the number again when prompted.

4. Press the Home button and tap an app to open it.

5. Press the Home button three times. You are presented with an Options button along the bottom of the screen; tap the button to display these options:

- **Sleep/Wake Button:** You can put your iPhone to sleep or wake it up with three presses of the Home button.

Tap to turn on Guided Access

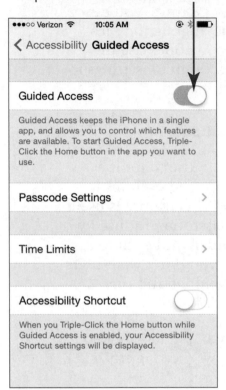

Figure 7-12

Figure 7-13

- **Volume Buttons:** You can tap Always On or Always Off. If you don't want users to be able to adjust volume using the volume toggle on the side of the iPhone, for example, use this setting.

- **Motion:** Turn this setting off if you don't want users to move the iPhone around — for example, to play a race car driving game.

- **Keyboards:** Use this setting to prohibit people using this app from entering text using the keyboard.

- **Touch:** If you don't want users to be able to use the touchscreen, turn this off.

- **Time Limit:** Tap this and use settings that are displayed to set a time limit for the use of the app.

6. Tap Done to hide the options. At this point, you can also use your finger to circle areas of the screen that you want to disable, such as a Store button in the Music app.

7. Press the Start button and then press the Home button three times. Enter your passcode, if you set one, and tap End. Tap the Home button again to return to the Home screen.

Talking to Your iPhone with Siri

One of the hottest features on iPhone is Siri, a personal assistant feature that responds to the commands you speak to your iPhone 4s or later. With Siri, you can ask for nearby restaurants, and a list appears. You can dictate your email messages rather than type them. You can open apps with a voice command or open the App Store. Calling your mother is as simple as saying, "Call Mom." Want to know the capital of Rhode Island? Just ask. Siri checks several online sources to answer questions ranging from the result of a mathematical calculation to the next scheduled flight to Dubai. With iOS 9, Siri searches more broadly, more quickly, and returns more results.

You can also have Siri perform tasks such as returning calls and controlling iTunes Radio. Finally, you can even play music or have Siri identify tagged songs (songs that contain embedded information that identifies them by categories such as artist or genre of music) for you.

With iOS 9, Siri has gained some other improvements. For example, you can have Siri search photos and videos and locate what you need by date, location, or album name. You can also ask Siri to remind you about an app you're working in, such as Safari, Mail, or Notes at a later time so you can pick up where you left off.

Activate Siri

When you first go through the process of registering your phone, making settings for your location, using iCloud, and so on, at one point you will see the screen in **Figure 8-1.** To activate Siri at this point, just tap Use Siri. As you begin to use your phone, iPhone reminds you about using Siri by displaying a message.

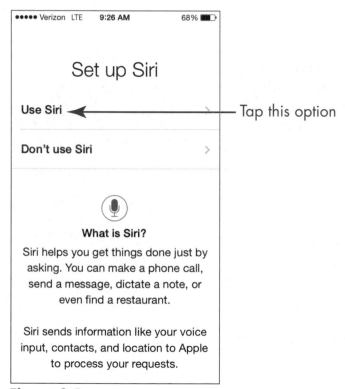

Figure 8-1

If you didn't activate Siri during the registration process, you can use Settings to turn Siri on by following these steps:

1. Tap the Settings icon on the Home screen.

2. Tap General and then tap Siri (see **Figure 8-2**).

Tap this option

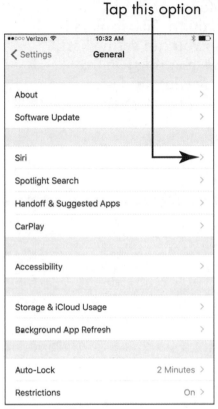

Figure 8-2

3. In the dialog in **Figure 8-3,** tap the On/Off switch to turn Siri on.

4. If you want to change the language Siri uses, tap Language and choose a different language in the list that appears.

5. To change the nationality or gender of Siri's voice from American to British or Australian, or from female to male, tap Siri Voice and make your selections.

6. If you want to be able to activate Siri Hands-Free (a feature that arrived with iOS 8), tap the Allow "Hey Siri" switch to turn on the feature. With your iPhone plugged into an outlet, car, or computer, just say

"Hey, Siri" and Siri opens up, ready for a command. In addition, with streaming voice recognition, Siri displays in text what it's hearing as you speak, so you can verify that it has understood you correctly. This streaming feature makes the whole process of interacting with Siri faster.

Tap to turn Siri on

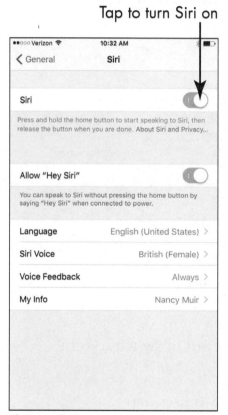

Figure 8-3

 If you want Siri to verbally respond to your requests only when the iPhone isn't in your hands, tap Voice Feedback and choose Hands-Free Only. Here's how this setting works and why you might want to use it: In general, if you're holding your iPhone, you can read responses on the screen, so you might choose not to have your phone talk to you out loud. But if you're puttering with an electronics project and want to speak requests for mathematical calculations and hear the answers rather than have to read them, Hands-Free is a useful setting.

 Siri is available only on iPhone 4s and later with Internet access, and cellular data charges could apply when Siri checks online sources. In addition, Apple warns that available features may vary by area.

Understand All That Siri Can Do

Siri allows you to interact by voice with many apps on your iPhone. Note that no matter what kind of action you want to perform, first press and hold the Home button until Siri opens.

You can pose questions or ask to do something like make a call or add an appointment to your calendar, for example. Siri can also search the Internet or use an informational service called Wolfram Alpha to provide information on just about any topic.

Siri also checks with Wikipedia, Bing, and Twitter to get you the information you ask for. In addition, you can use Siri to tell iPhone to return a call, play your voice mail, open and search the App Store, or control iTunes Radio playback.

Siri knows what app you're using, though you don't have to have that app open to make a request involving it. However, if you are in the Messages app, you can make a statement like "Tell Susan I'll be late," and Siri knows that you want to send a message. You can also ask Siri to remind you about what you're working on and Siri notes what you're working on, in which app, and reminds you about it at a later time you specify.

Siri requires no preset structure for your questions; you can phrase things in several ways. For example, you might say, "Where am I?" to see a map of your current location, or you could say, "What is my current location?" or "What address is this?" and get the same results.

If you ask a question about, say, the weather, Siri responds to you both verbally and with text information (see **Figure 8-4**) or by opening a form, as with email, or by providing a graphic display for some items such as maps. When a result appears, you can tap it to make a choice or open a related app.

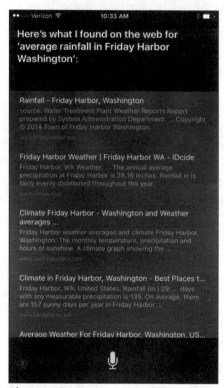

Figure 8-4

Siri works with Phone, the App Store, Music, Messages, Reminders, Calendar, Maps, Mail, Weather, Stocks, Clock, Contacts, Notes, social media apps such as Twitter, Safari, and iTunes Radio (see **Figure 8-5**). In the following tasks, I provide a quick guide to some of the most useful ways you can use Siri.

 If you want to dictate text in an app like Notes, use the Dictation key on the onscreen keyboard to do so. See the task "Use Dictation," later in this chapter, for more about this feature.

Figure 8-5

 Siri now supports 22 languages, so you can finally show off those language lessons you took in high school.

Get Suggestions

 With iOS 9 on recent iPhone models, Siri anticipates your needs by making suggestions when you swipe from left to right on the initial Home screen. Siri will list contacts you've communicated with recently, apps you've used, and nearby businesses, such as restaurants, gas stations, or coffee spots. If you tap on an app in the suggestions, it will open displaying the last viewed or listened to item.

Additionally, Siri lists news stories that may be of interest to you based on items you've viewed before.

Call Contacts

First, make sure that the person you want to call is entered in your Contacts app and include that person's phone number in his record. If you want to call somebody by stating your relationship to her, such as "Call sister," be sure to enter that relationship in the Related field in her contact record. Also make sure that the settings for Siri (refer to Figure 8-3) include your own contact name in the My Info field. (See Chapter 5 for more about creating contact records.) Follow these steps:

1. Press and hold the Home button until Siri appears.

2. Speak a command such as "Call Harold Smith," "Return Joe's call," or "Call Mom." If you want to make a FaceTime call, you can say "FaceTime Mom."

3. If you have two contacts who might match a spoken name, Siri responds with a list of possible matches (see **Figure 8-6**). Tap one in the list or state the correct contact's name to proceed.

4. The call is placed. To end the call before it completes, press the Home button and then tap End.

 To cancel any spoken request, you have three options: Say "Cancel," tap the Microphone button on the Siri screen, or press the Home button. If you're using a headset or Bluetooth device, tap the end button on the device.

You can also access your voice mail using Siri. Just press and hold the Home button until Siri activates and then say something like "Check voice mail." Siri responds by telling you whether you have a new voice mail message and displays a list of any new messages. Press one and then tap the Play button to play it back. If you want to get rid of it, tap Delete. It's that simple.

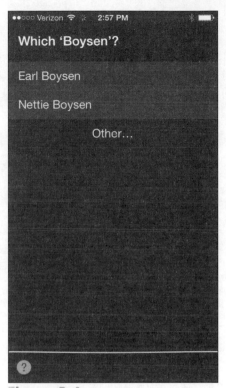

Figure 8-6

Create Reminders and Alerts

1. You can also use Siri with the Reminders app. To create a reminder or alert, press and hold the Home button and then speak a command, such as "Remind me to call Dad on Thursday at 10 a.m." or "Wake me up tomorrow at 7 a.m."

2. A preview of the reminder or alert is displayed (see **Figure 8-7**). Tap Remove if you change your mind.

3. If you want a reminder ahead of the event that you created, activate Siri and speak a command, such as "Remind me tonight about the play on Thursday at 8 p.m." A second reminder is created, which you can confirm or cancel if you change your mind.

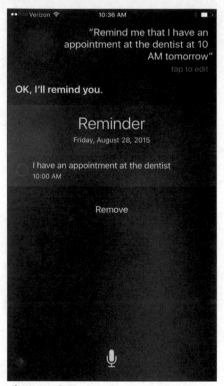

Figure 8-7

Add Tasks to Your Calendar

1. You can also set up events on your Calendar using Siri. Press and hold the Home button and then speak a phrase, such as "Set up meeting at 3 p.m. on September 2nd."

2. Siri sets up the appointment (see **Figure 8-8**) and asks whether you want to schedule the new appointment. You can say, "Yes" or "Cancel" at that point, or tap the Yes or Cancel button.

Figure 8-8

Play Music

1. You can use Siri to play music from the Music app and iTunes Radio. Press and hold the Home button until Siri appears.

2. To play music, speak a command, such as "Play music" or "Play Jazz radio station" to play a specific song, album, or radio station.

 3. You can use the integration of iPhone with Shazam, a music identifier app that arrived with iOS 8, to identify tagged music. First, when you're near an audio source playing music, press and hold the Home button to activate Siri.

4. Ask Siri a question such as "What music is playing?" or "What's this song?"

5. Siri listens for a bit and if Siri recognizes the song, it shows you the song name, artist, any other available information, and the ability to purchase the music in the iTunes Store.

 If you're listening to music or a podcast with earphones plugged in, and stop midstream, the next time you plug in earphones, Siri recognizes that you might want to continue with the same item.

Get Directions

You can use the Maps app and Siri to find your current location, get directions, find nearby businesses such as restaurants or a bank, or get a map of another location. Be sure to turn on Location Services to allow Siri to know your current location (go to Settings and tap Privacy⇨Location Services; make sure Location Services is on and that Siri & Dictation is turned on further down in these settings).

Here are some of the commands that you can try to get directions or a list of nearby businesses:

➡ **"Where am I?"**

Displays a map of your current location.

➡ **"Where is Apache Junction, Arizona?"**

Displays a map of that city.

➡ **"Find pizza restaurants."**

Displays a list of restaurants near your current location; tap one to display a map of its location, as shown in **Figure 8-9**.

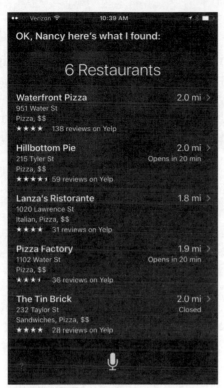

Figure 8-9

⇒ **"Find Bank of America."**

Displays a map with the location of the indicated business (or in some cases, several nearby locations, such as a bank branch and all ATMs).

⇒ **Get directions to the Empire State Building.**

Loads a map with a route drawn and provides a narration of directions to the site from your current location.

 After a location is displayed on a map, tap the Information button on the location's label to view its address, phone number, and website address, if available.

Ask for Facts

Wolfram Alpha is a self-professed online computational knowledge engine. That means that it's more than a search engine because it provides specific information about a search term rather than multiple search results. If you want facts without having to spend time browsing websites to find those facts, Wolfram Alpha is a very good resource.

Siri uses Wolfram Alpha and sources such as Wikipedia and Bing to look up facts in response to questions, such as "What is the capital of Kansas?" "What is the square root of 2,300?" or "How large is Mars?" Just press and hold the Home button and ask your question; Siri consults its resources and returns a set of relevant facts.

You can also get information about other things, such as the weather, stocks, or the time. Just say a phrase like one of these to get what you need:

➡ **"What is the weather?"**

This shows the weather report for your current location. If you want weather in another location, just specify the location in your question.

➡ **"What is the price of Apple stock?"**

Siri tells you the current price of the stock or the price of the stock when the stock market last closed.

➡ **"What time is it?"**

Siri tells you the time and displays a clock for your location (see **Figure 8-10**).

It's 3:12 PM.

Friday Harbor

Today

Figure 8-10

Search the Web

Although Siri can use its resources to respond to specific requests such as "Who is the Queen of England?" more general requests for information will cause Siri to search further on the web. Siri can also search Twitter for comments related to your search.

For example, if you speak a phrase such as "Find a website about birds" or "Find information about the World Series," Siri can respond in a couple of ways. The app can simply display a list of search results by using the default search engine specified in your settings for Safari or by suggesting, "If you like, I can search the web for such and such." In the first instance, just tap a result to go to that website. In the second instance, you can confirm that you want to search the web or cancel.

Send Email, Messages, or Tweets

You can create an email or an instant message using Siri and existing contacts. For example, if you say, "Email Jack Wilkes," a form opens that is already addressed to that stored contact. Siri asks for a subject and then a message. Speak your message contents and then say, "Send" to speed your message on its way.

Siri also works with messaging apps such as Messages. If you have the Messages app open and you say, "Tell Sarah I'll call soon," Siri creates a message for you to approve and send.

 Siri can also tweet, connect with Flickr and Vimeo, and post to Facebook. Go to Settings and turn on Flickr, Vimeo, Twitter, or Facebook support and provide your account information. Now you can say things to Siri such as "Post Tweet" or "Post to Facebook" and Siri asks what you want to say, lets you review it, and posts it.

Use Dictation

1. Text entry isn't Siri's strong point. Instead, you can use the Dictation key that appears with a microphone symbol on the onscreen keyboard (see **Figure 8-11**) to speak text rather than type it. This feature is called Dictation. Go to any app where you enter text, such as Notes or Mail, and tap in the document or form. The onscreen keyboard appears.

2. Tap the Dictation key on the keyboard and speak your text.

3. To end the dictation, tap Done.

 When you finish speaking text, you can use the keyboard to make edits to the text Siri entered, although as voice recognition programs go, Dictation is pretty darn accurate. If a word sports a blue underline, which means there may be an error, you can tap to select and make edits to it.

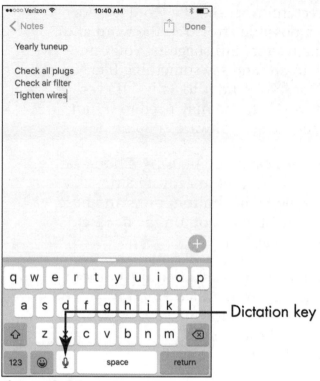

Dictation key

Figure 8-11

Get Helpful Tips

I know you're going to have a wonderful time learning the ins and outs of Siri, but before I close this chapter, here are some tips to get you going:

➡ **If Siri doesn't understand you:** With iOS 9, improvements have been made to how accurately Siri recognizes your voice. However, it's not perfect. When you speak a command and Siri displays what it thought you said, if it misses the mark, you have a few options. To correct a request you've made, you can tap Tap to Edit under the command Siri heard and edit the question by typing or tapping the Dictation key on the onscreen keyboard and dictating the correct information. If a word is underlined in blue, it's a possible error. Tap the word and then tap an alternative that Siri suggests. You can also simply speak to Siri and say something like "I meant Sri Lanka" or "No, send it to Sally." If even corrections aren't working, you may need to restart your phone to reset the Siri software.

➥ **Headsets and earphones:** If you're using iPhone earphones or a Bluetooth headset to activate Siri, instead of pressing the Home button, press and hold the center button (the little button on the headset that starts and stops a call).

➥ **Using Find My Friends:** There is a free app you can download from the App Store called Find My Friends that, in addition to allowing you to use it with keyboard input, allows you to ask Siri to locate your friends geographically.

➥ **Getting help:** To get help with Siri features, just press and hold the Home button and ask Siri, "What can you do?"

➥ **Joking around:** If you need a good laugh, ask Siri to tell you a joke. It has quite the sense of humor.

Getting Social with FaceTime, Twitter, and iMessage

FaceTime is an excellent video-calling app that's located on the second Home screen of iPhone out of the box. The app lets you call people who have FaceTime on their devices using either a phone number or an email address. You and your friend, colleague, or family member can see each other as you talk, which makes for a much more personal calling experience.

Twitter is a social networking service, referred to as a *microblog* because it involves posting short messages. You can set up Twitter credentials in Settings and use them to post tweets whenever you like.

Twitter is incorporated into the iOS in a way that allows you to "tweet" people from within Safari, Photos, Camera, Maps, and many other apps.

Finally, iMessage is a feature available through the preinstalled Messages app for instant messaging (IM). IM involves sending a text message to somebody's iPhone, iPod touch,

Mac running OS X 10.8 or later, or iPad (using the person's phone number or email address to carry on an instant conversation). You can even send audio and video via Messages.

In this chapter, I introduce you to FaceTime, Twitter, and the Messages app and review their simple controls. In no time, you'll be socializing with all and sundry.

Understand Who Can Use FaceTime

Here's a quick rundown of the device and information you need for using FaceTime's various features:

⟶ You can use FaceTime to call people over a Wi-Fi connection who have an iPhone 4 or later, an iPad 2 or a third-generation iPad or later, a fourth-generation iPod touch or later, or a Mac (running Mac OS X 10.6.6 or later). If you want to connect over a 3G/4G cellular connection, you're limited to iPhone 4s or later and iPad third generation or later.

⟶ You can use a phone number to connect with any-body with either an iOS device or a Mac and an iCloud account.

⟶ The person you're contacting has to have allowed FaceTime to be used in Settings.

Get an Overview of FaceTime

FaceTime works with the iPhone's built-in cameras so that you can call other folks who have a device that supports FaceTime. You can use FaceTime to chat while sharing video images with another person. This preinstalled app is useful for seniors who want to keep up with distant family members and friends and see (as well as hear) the latest-and-greatest news.

You can make and receive calls with FaceTime using a phone number or an email account and make calls to those with an iCloud account. Once connected, you can show the person on the other end what's going on around you. Just remember that you can't adjust audio volume from within the app or record a video call. Nevertheless, on the positive side, even though its features are limited, this app is straightforward to use.

You can use your Apple ID and iCloud account to access FaceTime, so it works pretty much right away. See Chapter 3 for more about getting an Apple ID.

 If you're having trouble using FaceTime, make sure that the FaceTime feature is turned on. That's quick to do: Tap Settings on the Home screen, tap FaceTime, and then tap the On/Off switch to turn it on, if it isn't already on. On this Settings screen, you can also select the phone number and/or email addresses that others can use to make FaceTime calls to you, as well as which one of those is displayed as your caller ID.

Make a FaceTime Call with Wi-Fi or 3G/4G

1. If you know that the person you're calling has FaceTime available on his device, adding that person to your iPhone Contacts is a good idea so you can initiate FaceTime calls from within Contacts if you like or from the Contacts list you can access through the FaceTime app.

2. Tap the FaceTime button on the second Home page. Tap to choose a Video or Audio call at the top of the screen. Video includes your voice and image; Audio includes only your voice.

3. If your contact doesn't appear in the Recents list, tap the Enter Name, Email, or Number field and begin to enter a contact's name; a list of matching contacts appears, or you can tap the plus sign (+) to open your complete Contacts list, scroll to locate a contact who has associated a device with FaceTime, tap that contact and then tap the appropriate method to initiate a call (see **Figure 9-1**).

Tap this for video

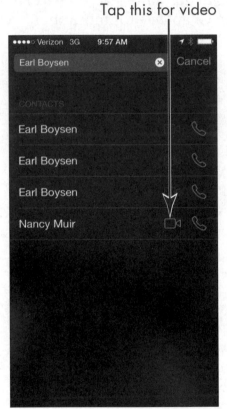

Figure 9-1

 You'll see a Camera button if that contact's device supports FaceTime video and a Phone button if the contact's device supports FaceTime audio.

(Note that if you haven't saved this person in your contacts and you know the phone number to call or email, you can just enter that information in the Enter Name, Email, or Number field.)

 When you call somebody using an email address, the person must be signed in to his Apple iCloud account and have verified that the address can be used for FaceTime calls. You can make this setting by tapping Settings and then FaceTime⟿Use Your Apple ID for FaceTime; FaceTime for Mac users make this setting by selecting FaceTime⟿Preferences.

4. When the person accepts the call, you see a large screen that displays the recipient's image and a small screen referred to as a Picture in Picture (PiP) containing your image superimposed (see **Figure 9-2**).

Figure 9-2

> To view recent calls, tap the FaceTime app on the second Home screen and then tap the Information button on a recent call, and iPhone displays that person's information. You can tap the contact to call the person back.

> If you have iOS 6 or later, you can use FaceTime over both a Wi-Fi network and your iPhone 3G or 4G connection. However, remember that if you use FaceTime over a phone connection, you may incur costly data usage fees. To avoid this, in Settings under Cellular, set the iPhone Cellular Calls switch for FaceTime to Off.

Accept and End a FaceTime Call

1. If you're on the receiving end of a FaceTime call, accepting the call is about as easy as it gets. When the call comes in, tap the Accept button to take the call or tap the Decline button to reject it (see **Figure 9-3**).

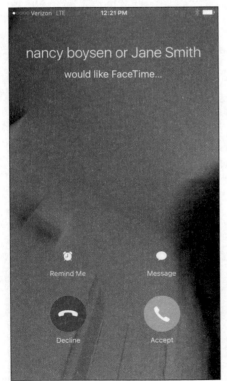

Figure 9-3

2. Chat away with your friend, swapping video images. To end the call, tap the End button (see **Figure 9-4**).

Switch Camera

End   Mute

Figure 9-4

 To mute sound during a call, tap the Mute button, which looks like a microphone with a line through it (refer to Figure 9-4). Tap the button again to unmute your iPhone.

 If you'd rather not be available for calls, you can go to Settings and turn on the Do Not Disturb feature. This stops any incoming calls or notifications other than for the people you've designated as exceptions to Do Not Disturb. After you turn on Do Not

Disturb, you can use the feature's settings to schedule when it's active, allow calls from certain people, or allow a second call from the same person in a three-minute interval to go through.

Switch Views

1. When you're on a FaceTime call, you might want to use iPhone's built-in, rear-facing camera to show the person you're talking to what's going on around you. Tap the Switch Camera button (refer to Figure 9-4) to switch from the front-facing camera that's displaying your image to the back-facing camera that captures whatever you're looking at.

2. Tap the Switch Camera button again to switch back to the front camera displaying your image.

Experience Twitter on iPhone

Twitter is a social networking service for *microblogging,* which involves posting very short messages (limited to 140 characters) online so that your friends can see what you're up to. You can go to your Settings from the Home screen and install the app from the Twitter item in the left panel. After you have an account, you can post tweets for all to see, have people follow your tweets, and follow the tweets that other people post.

The ability to tweet is integrated into several apps. You can post tweets using the Share button within Safari, Voice Memos, Photos, Camera, Maps, and many third-party apps. First, using your computer or the Safari browser on your iPhone, sign up for a Twitter account at `https://twitter.com`. Go to Settings and tap Twitter. Then click Install and sign in to the iTunes Store. iPhone installs the Twitter app automatically.

Now when you're using Safari, Photos, Voice Memos, Camera, or Maps, you can choose Twitter in the screen that appears when you tap the Share button (see **Figure 9-5**). You'll see a tweet form. Just type your brief message in the form and then tap Send.

Figure 9-5

 See Chapters 10 and 16 for more about tweeting in the Safari and Photos apps.

Set Up an iMessage Account

1. iMessage is a feature available through the preinstalled Messages app that allows you to send and receive instant messages (IMs) to others using an Apple iOS device or suitably configured Macs. iMessage is a way of sending instant messages through a Wi-Fi network, but you can send messages through your cellular connection without having iMessage activated. Instant messaging differs from email or tweeting in an important way. Whereas you might email somebody and wait for days or weeks before that person responds, or you might post a tweet that could sit there awhile before anybody views it, with instant messaging, communication happens almost immediately. You send an IM, and it appears on some-body's Apple device right away. Assuming that the person wants to participate in a live conversation, the chat begins immediately, allowing a back-and-forth dialogue in real time. To set up Messages, tap Settings on the Home screen.

2. Tap Messages, and the settings shown in **Figure** 9-6 appear.

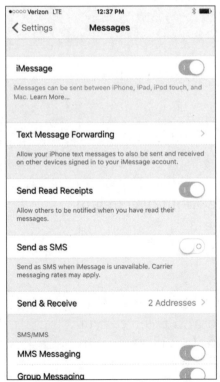

Figure 9-6

3. If iMessage isn't set to On (refer to Figure 9-6), tap the On/Off switch to turn it on.

4. You should be sure that the phone number and/or email account associated with your iPhone under the Send & Receive setting is correct. (This should be set up automatically based on your iCloud settings.) If it's not, tap the Send & Receive field, add an email or phone, and then tap Messages to return to the previous screen.

5. To allow a notice to be sent to the sender when you've read a message, tap the On/Off switch for Send Read Receipts. You can also choose to show a subject field in your messages.

6. Press the Home button to leave Settings.

 To change the email account used by Messages, tap Send & Receive, tap the Information button to the right of an email address, and then tap Remove This Email and then confirm the deletion; next, follow the preceding steps to add another account.

Use Messages to Address, Create, and Send Messages

1. Now you're ready to use Messages. From the Home screen, tap the Messages button. Tap the New Message button in the top-right corner to begin a conversation.

2. In the form that appears (see **Figure 9-7**), you can address a message in a couple of ways:

- Begin to type a name in the To field, and a list of matching contacts appears.

- Tap the Dictation key on the onscreen keyboard and speak the address.

- Tap the plus (+) button on the right side of the address field, and the All Contacts list is displayed.

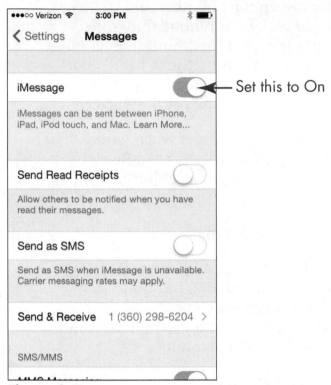

Figure 9-7

3. Tap a contact on the list you chose from in Step 2. If the contact has both an email address and a phone number stored, the Info dialog appears, allowing you to tap one or the other, which addresses the message.

4. To create a message, simply tap in the message field near the bottom of the screen (see **Figure 9-8**) and type your message.

Figure 9-8

5. To send the message, tap the Send button (refer to Figure 9-8). When your recipient (or recipients) responds, you'll see the conversation displayed on the screen. Tap in the message field again to respond to the last comment.

 You can address a message to more than one person by simply choosing more recipients in Step 2 of the preceding list.

Read Messages

1. Tap Messages on the Home screen.

2. When the app opens, you see a list of all text messages and all attachments that have appeared in your Messages app.

3. Tap a message to see the message string, including all attachments, as shown in **Figure 9-9**.

Message field

Send button

Figure 9-9

4. To view all attachments of a message, tap Details and scroll down.

Clear a Conversation

1. When you're done chatting, you might want to delete a conversation to remove the clutter before you start a new chat. With Messages open and your conversations displayed, swipe to the left on the message you want to delete.

2. Tap the Delete button next to the conversation you want to get rid of (see **Figure 9-10**).

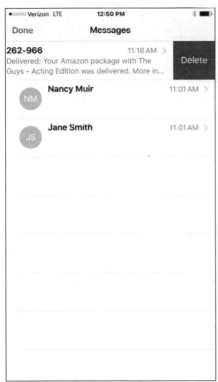

Figure 9-10

Send and Receive Audio

1. When you're creating a message, you can also create an audio message. With Messages open, tap the New Message button in the top-right corner.

2. Enter an addressee's name in the To field.

3. Tap and hold the Audio button (the microphone symbol to the right of the screen).

4. Speak your message or record a sound or music near you.

5. Tap the Send button (an upward-pointing arrow at the top of the recording circle). The message appears as an audio track in the recipient's Messages inbox (see **Figure 9-11**). To play the track, she just holds the phone up to her ear or taps the Play button.

Figure 9-11

Send a Photo or Video

1. When you're creating a message, you can also create a short video message. With Messages open, tap the New Message button in the top-right corner.

2. Press and hold the Camera button. In the tool palette that appears (see **Figure 9-12**), tap the Photo button to take a picture and then return to the message.

Figure 9-12

3. If you prefer to capture a video, with the palette in Figure 9-12 displayed, tap the Video button and move the phone around to take a video; tap the red Stop button when you've recorded what you want to record. Tap the Send button. Your video is attached to your message.

4. To send multiple photos or videos, repeat these steps and then tap Send to send your message and attachments.

Send a Map of Your Location

When responding to a message, you can also send a map showing your current location. Tap a message and then tap Details. Tap Send My Current Location (see **Figure 9-13**), and a map will be inserted as a message attachment.

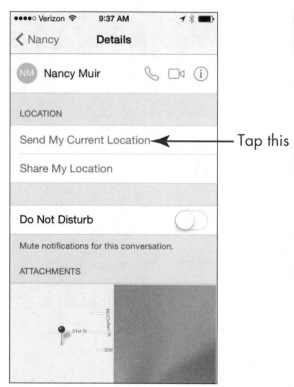

Tap this

Figure 9-13

 You can also share your location in the middle of a conversation rather than send a map attachment with your message. In the screen shown in Figure 9-13, tap Share My Location and then tap Share for One Hour, Share Until End of Day, or Share Indefinitely. A map showing your location appears above your conversation until you stop sharing.

You can share a map from within the Maps app by tapping the Share button and then tapping Message or Mail.

Understand Group Messaging

If you want to start a conversation with a group of people, you can use group messaging. Group messaging is great for keeping several people in the conversational loop.

With iOS 8 came a lot of group messaging functionality, including the following features:

➡ When you participate in a group message, you see all participants in the Details for the message (see **Figure 9-14**). You can drop people whom you don't want to include any longer and leave the conversation yourself when you want to by simply tapping Details and then tapping Leave This Conversation.

➡ When you turn on Do Not Disturb by tapping Details in a message (see Figure 9-14), you won't get notifications of messages from this group, but you can still read the group's messages at a later time (this also works for individuals).

Taking you further into the workings of group messages is beyond the scope of this book, but if you're intrigued, go to www.apple.com/ios/ios/whats-new/messages/ for more information.

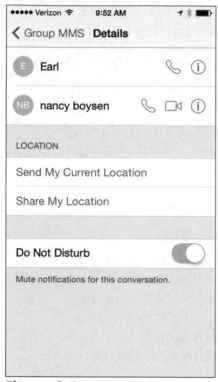

Figure 9-14

Activate the Do Not Disturb Feature

1. If you don't want to get notifications of new messages from an individual or group for a while, you can use the Do Not Disturb feature. With a message open, tap Details.

2. Tap the Do Not Disturb switch to turn the feature on (refer to Figure 9-14).

3. Later, return to Details and tap the Do Not Disturb switch again to turn the feature off.

You can turn on the Do Not Disturb feature for everyone in the Control Center (drag up from the bottom edge of the screen to display it) and tapping the half-moon shaped button. You can also allow selected callers to get through in the Do Not Disturb settings by choosing everyone, no one, people you've tagged as favorites, or people in one or more groups.

Part III
Taking the Leap Online

 Visit www.dummies.com/extras/iphoneforseniors for recommendations of great News and Weather apps for iPhone.

Browsing the Internet with Safari

Getting on the Internet with your iPhone is easily done using its Wi-Fi or 3G/4G capabilities. After you're online, the built-in browser (software that helps you navigate the Internet's contents), *Safari,* is your ticket to a wide world of information, entertainment, education, and more. Safari will look familiar to you if you've used it on a PC or Mac device before, though the way you move around by using the iPhone touchscreen might be new to you. In case you've never used Safari, this chapter takes you by the hand and shows you all the basics of making it work for you.

In this chapter, you discover how to go online with your iPhone. You see how to navigate among web pages and use iCloud tabs to share your browsing experience among devices. Along the way, you see how to place a bookmark for a favorite site or place a web clip on your Home screen. You can also view your browsing history, save online images to your Photo Library, post photos to sites from within Safari, or email or tweet a link to a friend. You also explore Safari's Reader and Reading List features and learn how to keep yourself safer while online by using private browsing. Finally, you review the simple steps involved in printing what you find online.

Chapter 10

Get ready to . . .

Connect to the Internet

How you connect to the Internet depends on what connections are available:

➠ You can connect to the Internet via a Wi-Fi network. You can set up this type of network in your own home using your computer and some equipment from your Internet provider. You can also connect over public Wi-Fi networks, referred to as *hotspots*. You'll probably be surprised to discover how many hotspots your town or city has. Look for Internet cafés, coffee shops, hotels, libraries, and transportation centers such as airports or bus stations, for example. Many of these businesses display signs alerting you to their free Wi-Fi.

➠ You can also use the paid data network provided by AT&T, Sprint, T-Mobile, or Verizon to connect using 3G or 4G from just about anywhere you can get cell-phone coverage via a cellular network.

To enable 3G/4G data, tap Settings and then Cellular. Tap to turn on the Cellular Data setting. Do note that browsing the Internet using a 3G/4G connection can eat up your data plan allotment quickly if your plan doesn't include unlimited data access.

To connect to a Wi-Fi network, you have to complete a few steps.

1. Tap Settings on the Home screen and then tap Wi-Fi. Be sure that Wi-Fi is set to On and choose a network to connect to. Network names should appear automatically when you're in range of them. When you're in range of a public hotspot, if access to several nearby networks is available, you may see a message asking you to tap a network name to select it. After you select one (or if only one network is available), you may see a message asking for your password. Ask the owner of the hotspot (for example, a hotel desk clerk or business owner) for this password, or if you're connecting to your home network, enter your network password.

2. Tap the Join button, and you're connected. Your iPhone will now recognize the network and be able to connect without entering the password.

 Free public Wi-Fi networks typically don't require passwords, or the password is posted prominently for all to see. However, remember that after you connect, someone else can track your online activities because these are *unsecured* networks. Avoid accessing financial accounts or sending emails with sensitive information in them when connected to a public hotspot.

Explore Safari

1. After you're connected to a network, tap Safari on the Dock at the bottom of the Home screen. Safari opens, probably displaying the Apple iPhone Home page the first time you go online (see **Figure 10-1**).

2. Put two fingers together on the screen and unpinch them to expand the view. Double-tap the screen with a single finger to restore the default view size.

3. Put your finger on the screen and flick upward to scroll down on the page.

4. To return to the top of the web page, put your finger on the screen and drag downward or tap the Status bar at the very top of the screen twice.

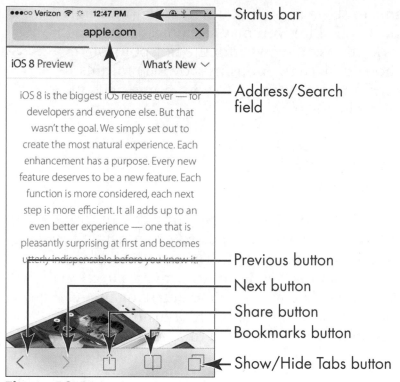

Status bar

Address/Search field

Previous button

Next button

Share button

Bookmarks button

Show/Hide Tabs button

Figure 10-1

 Using your fingers on the screen to enlarge or reduce the size of a web page allows you to view what's displayed at various sizes, giving you more flexibility than the double-tap method.

 When you enlarge the display, you gain more control using two fingers to drag from left to right or from top to bottom on the screen. On a reduced display, one finger works fine for making these gestures.

Navigate among Web Pages

1. Tap in the Address field just under the Status bar. The onscreen keyboard appears (see **Figure 10-2**).

2. Enter a web address; for example, you can go to www.wiley.com.

Go key   Delete key

Figure 10-2

3. Tap the Go key on the keyboard (refer to Figure 10-2). The website appears.

• If, for some reason, a page doesn't display, tap the Reload button at the right end of the Address field.

Cancel • If Safari is loading a web page and you change your mind about viewing the page, you can tap Cancel, which appears at the right end of the Address field during this process, to stop loading the page.

4. Tap the Previous button to go to the last page you displayed.

5. Tap the Next button to go forward to the page you just backed up from.

6. To follow a link to another web page (links are typically indicated by colored text or graphics), tap the link with your finger. To view the destination web address of the link before you tap it, just touch and hold the link; a menu appears that displays the address at the top, as shown in **Figure 10-3.**

The link's web address

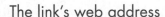

Figure 10-3

By default, AutoFill is turned on in iPhone, causing entries you make in fields such as the Address field and password fields to automatically display possible matching entries. You can turn off AutoFill by using iPhone Settings for Safari.

 Apple QuickType supports predictive text in the onscreen keyboard. This feature adds the capability for iPhone to spot what you probably intend to type from text you've already entered and suggests it to save you time typing.

Use Tabbed Browsing

1. *Tabbed browsing* is a feature that allows you to have several websites open at one time so that you can move easily among those sites. With Safari open and a web page already displaying, tap the Show/Hide Tabs button in the bottom-right corner (refer to Figure 10-1). The new Tab view appears.

2. To add a new page (meaning that you're opening a new website), tap the New Page button (shaped like a plus [+] symbol) in the lower middle of the screen (see **Figure 10-4**). A page with your favorite sites and an address bar appears. (Note that you can get to the same new page by simply tapping in the address bar from any site.)

3. Tap in the Address field and use the onscreen keyboard to enter the web address for the website you want to open. Tap the Go key. The website opens on the page.

 Repeat Steps 1 to 3 to open as many new web pages as you'd like.

New Page button

Figure 10-4

4. You can now switch among open sites by tapping outside the keyboard to close it and tapping the Show/Hide Tabs button and scrolling among recent sites. Find the one you want and then tap it.

5. To delete a tab, tap the Show/Hide Tabs button, scroll to locate the tab, and then tap the Close button in the upper-left corner of the tab.

 Using multipage browsing, you can make available not only a site but also a search results screen. If you recently searched for something, those search results will be on your Recent Searches list.

View Browsing History

1. As you move around the web, your browser keeps a record of your browsing history. This record can be handy when you want to visit a site that you viewed previously but whose address you've now forgotten. With Safari open, tap the Bookmarks button.

2. On the menu shown in **Figure 10-5**, tap the History item.

Tap this item

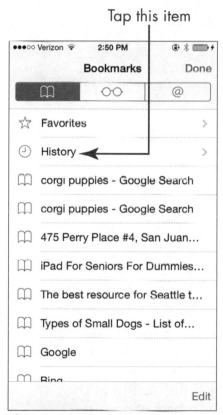

Figure 10-5

3. In the History list that appears (see **Figure 10-6**), tap a
site to navigate to it. Tap Bookmarks and then Done to
leave the History and then the Bookmarks features.

History list   Clear button

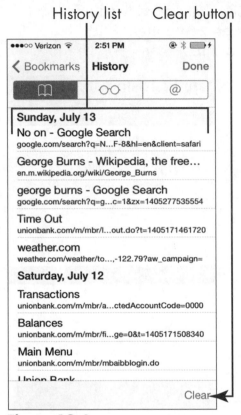

Figure 10-6

 After you master the use of the Bookmarks button
options, you might prefer a shortcut to view your
History list. Tap and hold the Previous button at the
bottom left on any screen, and your browsing history for the current session appears. You can also tap
and hold the Next button to look at sites you back-
tracked from.

To clear the history, tap the Clear button (refer to Figure 10-6) and on the screen that appears, tap an option: The Last Hour, Today, Today and Yesterday, or All Time. This button is useful when you don't want your spouse or grandchildren to see where you've been browsing for anniversary, birthday, or holiday presents!

Search the Web

1. If you don't know the address of the site that you want to visit (or you want to research a topic or find other information online), get acquainted with Safari's Search feature on iPhone. By default, Safari uses the Google search engine. With Safari open, tap in the Address field (refer to Figure 10-1). The onscreen keyboard appears.

2. Enter a search term. With recent versions of Safari, the search term can be a topic or a web address because of what's called the Unified smart search field. You can tap one of the suggested sites or complete your entry and tap the Go key (see **Figure 10-7**) on your keyboard.

3. In the search results that are displayed, tap a link to visit that site.

 To change your default search engine from Google to Yahoo!, Bing, or DuckDuckGo, from the Home screen, tap Settings, tap Safari, and then tap Search Engine. Tap Yahoo!, Bing, or DuckDuckGo, and your default search engine changes.

Enter the search term here

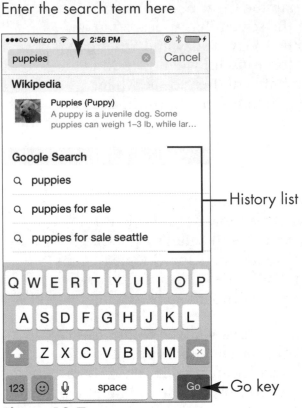

History list

Go key

Figure 10-7

 You can browse for specific items, such as web, images, or videos, by tapping the corresponding link at the top of the search results screen. Also, tap the More button in this list to see additional options to narrow your results, such as searching for books, news, or shopping resources on the subject.

Add and Use Bookmarks

 1. Bookmarks are a way to save favorite sites so that you can easily visit them again. With a site open that you want to bookmark, tap the Share button.

2. On the menu that appears (see **Figure 10-8**), tap Add Bookmark.

Tap this option

Figure 10-8

3. In the Add Bookmark dialog, shown in **Figure 10-9,** edit the name of the bookmark if you want. To do so, tap the name of the site and use the onscreen keyboard to edit its name.

4. Tap the Save button. The item is saved to your Favorites by default.

5. To go to the bookmark, tap the Bookmarks button.

Edit the name here

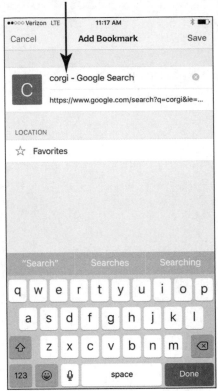

Figure 10-9

6. On the Bookmarks menu that appears (see **Figure 10-10**), if you saved a site to a folder tap to open the folder and then tap the bookmarked site that you want to visit.

> If you want to sync your bookmarks on your iPhone browser, go to Settings on iPhone and make sure that iCloud is set to sync with Safari.

> When you tap the Bookmarks button, you can tap Edit and then use the New Folder option to create folders to organize your bookmarks or folders. When you next add a bookmark, you can then choose, from the dialog that appears, any folder to which you want to add the new bookmark.

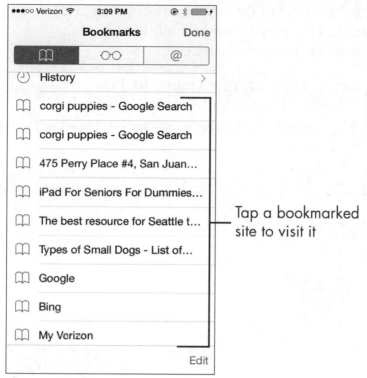

Tap a bookmarked site to visit it

Figure 10-10

Save Links and Web Pages to Safari Reading List

1. The Safari Reading List provides a way to save content that you want to read at a later time so that you can easily call up that content again. You essentially save the content rather than a web page address, which allows you to read the content even when you're offline. You can scroll from one item to the next easily. With a site that you want to add to your Reading List displaying, tap the Share button.

2. On the menu that appears (refer to Figure 10-8), tap the Add to Reading List link. The site is added to your Reading List.

3. To view your Reading List, tap the Bookmarks button and then tap the Reading List tab (the middle tab with the eyeglasses icon near the top of the page).

4. On the Reading List that appears (see **Figure 10-11**), tap the content that you want to revisit and resume reading.

Tap an item to resume reading

Figure 10-11

If you want to see both the Reading List material you've read and the material you haven't read, tap the Show Unread button in at the bottom-right corner of the Reading List. To see all reading material, tap the Show All button.

To save an image to your Reading List, tap and hold the image until a menu appears, and then tap Add to Reading List (this is available for only some images).

To delete an item, with the Reading List displaying, swipe right to left on an item; a Delete button appears. Tap this button to delete the item from the Reading List.

Enjoy Reading More with Safari Reader

1. The Safari Reader feature gives you an e-reader type of experience right within your browser, removing other stories and links as well as those distracting advertisements. When you're on a site where you're reading content such as an article, Safari displays a Reader button on the left side of the Address field for sites that support this feature (see **Figure 10-12**). Tap the Reader button. The content appears in a reader format (see **Figure 10-13**).

Reader button

Figure 10-12

Welsh Corgi

Welsh corgi

Brindle and white Cardigan Welsh corgi

Nicknames	Corgi	
Country of origin	Wales Cardigan: Believed to have its origins in Roman Britain Pembroke: Believed to have been introduced to Wales by Flemish weavers in the Middle Ages	
Traits		
Weight	Male	27 lbs (12¼ kg)
	Female	25 lbs (11⅓ kg)
Height	Male	10–12.5" (25.5–30.5 cm)
	Female	10–12.5" (25.5—30.5 cm)

Figure 10-13

2. Scroll down the page. The entire content is contained in this one long page.

3. When you finish reading the material, just tap the Reader button again to leave that view.

 Tap the small or large letter *A* at the top right of the Address field to adjust the font size for the article.

Add Web Clips to the Home Screen

 1. The Web Clips feature allows you to save a website as an icon on your Home screen so that you can go to the site at any time with one tap. With Safari open and displaying the site you want to add, tap the Share button.

2. On the menu that appears (refer to Figure 10-8), tap Add to Home Screen.

3. In the Add to Home dialog that appears (see **Figure 10-14**), you can edit the name of the site to be more descriptive, if you like. To do so, tap the name of the site and use the onscreen keyboard to edit its name.

Edit the name here

Figure 10-14

4. Tap the Add button. The site is added to your Home screen.

Remember that you can have as many as 11 Home screens on your iPhone to accommodate all the web clips you create and apps you download. (There is a limit to how many items will fit on these screens; however, you can place an unlimited number of apps in folders on Home screens.)

 If you want to delete an item from a Home screen for any reason, press and hold the icon on the Home screen until all items on the screen start to jiggle and Delete badges appear on all items except preinstalled apps. Tap the Delete badge (the X) on each item that you want to delete, tap to verify the deletion, and it's gone. (To get rid of the jiggle, press the Home button.)

Save an Image to Your Photo Library

1. Display a web page that contains an image you want to copy.

2. Tap and hold the image. The menu shown in **Figure 10-15** appears.

3. Tap the Save Image option (refer to Figure 10-15). The image is saved to your Camera Roll.

 Be careful about copying images from the Internet and using them for business or promotional activities. Most images are copyrighted, and you may violate the copyright even if you simply use an image in (say) a brochure for your association or a flyer for your community group. Note that some search engines' advanced search settings offer the option of browsing only for images that aren't copyrighted.

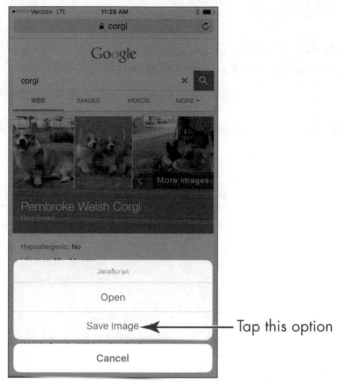

Tap this option

Figure 10-15

 Some websites are set up to prevent you from copying images on them, or they display a pop-up stating that the contents on the site are copyrighted and should not be copied.

Send a Link

 1. If you find a great site that you want to share, you can do so easily by sending a link in an email (this also works for sending a site via Messages, Twitter, or Facebook, or even saving a link to Reminders or Notes). With Safari open and the site that you want to share displaying, tap the Share button.

2. On the menu that appears (refer to Figure 10-8), tap Mail.

3. On the message form that appears (see **Figure 10-16**), enter a recipient's email address, a subject, and your message.

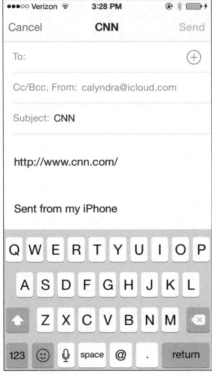

Figure 10-16

4. Tap Send, and the email is sent.

 The email is sent from the default email account that you have set up on iPhone. For more about setting up an email account, see Chapter 11.

To tweet the link using your Twitter account, in Step 2 of this task, choose Twitter, enter your tweet in the form that appears, and then tap Send. For more about using Twitter with iPhone, see Chapter 9. You can also choose AirDrop in the same menu with any fifth-generation iPhone or later to share with someone in your immediate vicinity who has an AirDrop-enabled device.

Make Private Browsing and Cookie Settings

Apple has provided some privacy settings for Safari that you should consider using. Private Browsing automatically stops Safari from using AutoFill to save information used to complete certain entries as you type, and erases some browsing history information. These features can keep your online activities more private.

Cookies are small files that document your browsing history so that you can be recognized by a site the next time you go to or move within that site. Go to Settings from the Home screen and in Safari settings turn on the Block Cookies setting, which allows you to stop the downloading of cookies to your phone. Tap the arrow on Block Cookies and choose to always block cookies, never block cookies, or block cookies only from third parties and advertisers.

Tap to turn on the Do Not Track feature (see **Figure 10-17**). This setting stops sites from tracking your online activities.

You can also tap the Clear History and Website Data option (refer to Figure 10-17) to manually clear your browsing history, saved cookies, and other data.

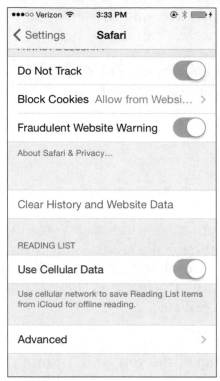

●●●○○ Verizon 🤏 3:33 PM ⓔ ✳ ▭◀

‹ Settings **Safari**

PRIVACY & SECURITY

Do Not Track ⬤

Block Cookies Allow from Websi... ›

Fraudulent Website Warning ⬤

About Safari & Privacy...

Clear History and Website Data

READING LIST

Use Cellular Data ⬤

Use cellular network to save Reading List items
from iCloud for offline reading.

Advanced ›

Figure 10-17

Print a Web Page

1. If you have a wireless printer that supports Apple's AirPrint technology, you can print web content using a wireless connection. With Safari open and the site that you want to print displaying, tap the Share button.

2. On the menu that appears (refer to Figure 10-8), scroll to the right in the bottom row of buttons and then tap Print.

3. In the Printer Options dialog that appears (see **Figure 10-18**), tap Select Printer. In the list of printers that appears, tap the name of your wireless printer.

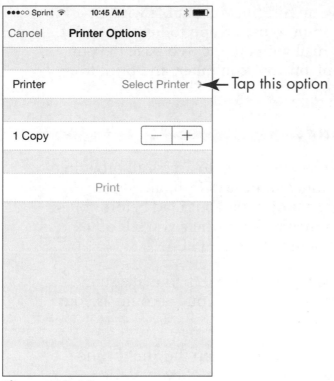

Figure 10-18

4. Tap either the plus or minus button in the Copy field to adjust the number of copies to print. If your printer supports two-sided printing, you'll also see a Double-Sided On/Off switch.

5. Tap Print to print the displayed page.

 The Mac applications Printopia and HandyPrint make any shared or network printer on your home network visible to your iPhone. Printopia has more features, but will cost you, whereas HandyPrint is free.

If you don't have an AirPrint-compatible wireless printer or don't want to use an app to help you print wirelessly, just email a link to the web page to yourself, open the link on your computer, and print from there.

Understand iCloud Tabs

1. The iCloud Tabs feature allows you to access all browsing history among your different devices from any device. If you begin to research a project on your iPad before you leave home, you can then pick up where you left off as you sit in a waiting room with your iPhone.

2. Tap Settings and then tap iCloud; check to make sure that the iPhone is using the same iCloud account as your other devices.

3. Open Safari on another device and tap the Show/Hide Tabs button. Scroll down to see a list of every device using your iCloud account. All items in your iPhone's browsing history are displayed on the other devices.

Working with Email in Mail

Chapter 11

Staying in touch with others by using email is a great way to use your iPhone. You can access an existing account using the handy Mail app supplied with your iPhone or sign in to your email account using the Safari browser. In this chapter, you take a look at using Mail, which involves adding an existing email account by way of Settings. Then you can use Mail to write, format, retrieve, and forward messages from that account.

Mail offers the capability to mark the messages you've read, delete messages, and organize your messages in a small set of folders, as well as use a handy search feature. You can create a VIP list so that you're notified when that special person sends you an email.

iOS 9 includes a feature that makes jumping between a draft email and your inbox possible; the ability to quickly swipe to mark an email as read or flag it for future action; and the ability to create an event from information about a reservation, flight number, or phone number within an email.

In this chapter, you read all about Mail and its various features.

Get ready to . . .

Add an Email Account

1. You can add one or more email accounts, including the email account associated with your iCloud account, using iPhone Settings. If you have an iCloud, Microsoft Exchange (often used for business accounts), Gmail, Yahoo!, AOL, or Outlook.com (this includes Microsoft accounts from Live, Hotmail, and so on) account, iPhone pretty much automates the setup. To set up iPhone to retrieve messages from your email account at one of these popular providers, first tap the Settings icon on the Home screen.

2. In Settings, tap Mail, Contacts, Calendars. The settings shown in **Figure 11-1** appear.

3. Tap Add Account. The options shown in **Figure 11-2** appear.

Tap this option   Select your email provider

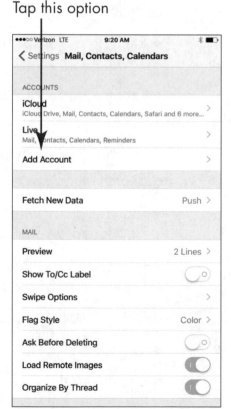

Figure 11-1   **Figure 11-2**

4. Tap iCloud, Google, Yahoo!, AOL, Exchange, or Outlook. com. Enter your account information in the form that appears and tap Sign In, or, for AOL and Outlook accounts, tap Next.

5. After iPhone takes a moment to verify your account information, on the next screen (shown in **Figure 11-3**) you can tap any On/Off switch to have Mail, Contacts, Calendars, or Reminders from that account synced with iPhone.

6. When you're done, tap Save. The account is saved, and you can now open it using Mail.

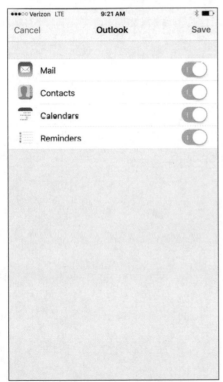

Figure 11-3

Set Up a POP3 Email Account

1. You can also set up most popular email accounts, such as those available through Earthlink or a cable provider's service, by obtaining the host name from the provider. To set up an existing account with a provider other than iCloud, Gmail, Yahoo!, AOL, Exchange, or Outlook.com, you enter the account settings yourself. First, tap the Settings icon on the Home screen.

2. In Settings, tap Mail, Contacts, Calendars, and then tap the Add Account button (refer to Figure 11-1).

3. On the screen that appears (refer to Figure 11-2), tap Other.

4. On the screen shown in **Figure 11-4,** tap Add Mail Account.

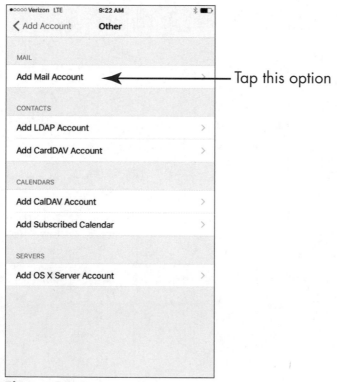

— Tap this option

Figure 11-4

5. In the form that appears (refer to Figure 11-3), enter your name and an account email address, password, and description, and then tap Next. iPhone takes a moment to verify your account and then returns you to the Mail, Contacts, Calendars page, with your new account displayed.

 iPhone will probably add the outgoing mail server (SMTP) information for you, but if it doesn't, you may have to enter it yourself. If you have a less mainstream email service, you may have to enter the mail server protocol (POP3 or IMAP — ask your provider for this information) and your password.

6. To make sure that the Account field is set to On for receiving email, tap the account name. In the dialog that appears, tap the On/Off switch for the Mail field and then tap the Mail button to return to Mail settings. You can now access the account through iPhone's Mail app.

 If you turn on Calendars in the Mail account settings, any information that you've put into your calendar in that email account is brought over into the Calendar app on your iPhone and reflected in the Notification Center (discussed in more detail in Chapter 22).

Open Mail and Read Messages

1. Tap the Mail app icon, located in the Dock on the Home screen (see **Figure 11-5**). A red circle on the icon, called a badge, indicates the number of unread emails in your Inbox.

2. In the Mail app (see **Figure 11-6**), tap the Inbox whose contents you want to display.

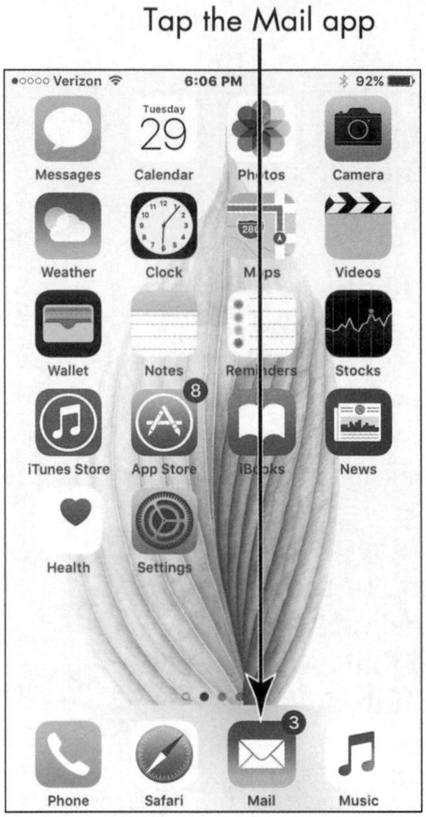

Tap the Mail app

Figure 11-5

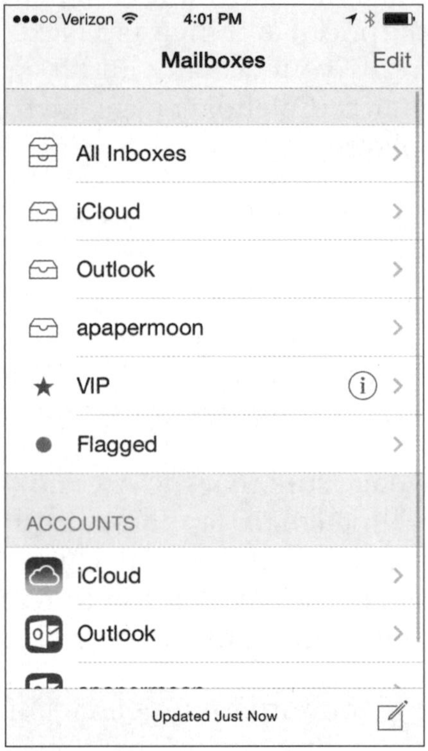

Figure 11-6

3. Tap a message to read it. It opens (see **Figure 11-7**).

4. If you need to scroll to see the entire message, just place your finger on the screen and flick upward to scroll down. You can swipe right while reading a message to open the Inbox's list of messages, and then swipe right again to return to your list of mailboxes.

 The new 3D Touch feature allows you to preview an email before you open it. Simply press lightly to select the message, press with medium pressure to preview it, and press a bit harder to open the message.

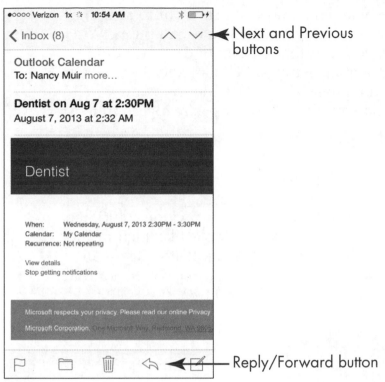

Figure 11-7

 You can tap the Next or Previous buttons (top-right corner of the message) to move to the next or previous message in the Inbox or tap All Inboxes in the top-left corner to return to your Inbox.

 Email messages that you haven't read are marked with a blue circle in your Inbox. After you read a message, the blue circle disappears. You can mark a read message as unread to help remind you to read it again later. With the inbox displayed, swipe to the right (starting your swipe just a little in from the edge of the screen) and a message and then tap Mark as Unread.

 If you have an iPhone 6s or 6s Plus and you hold it horizontally, you will view both the Inbox and currently selected message. This is because the larger 5.5" screen can accommodate more content, and apps such as Mail and Weather take advantage of this.

To escape your email now and then (or to avoid having messages retrieved while you're at a public Wi-Fi hotspot), you can stop retrieval of data including email by tapping Settings, Cellular, and then the On/Off switch on the Cellular Data option. Now you'll get data on your device only if you're logged in to a Wi-Fi network.

Reply To or Forward Email

1. With an email message open (see the previous task), tap the Reply/Forward button, which looks like a left-facing arrow (refer to Figure 11-7). Then tap Reply, Reply All (available if there are multiple recipients), or Forward in the menu that appears (see **Figure 11-8**).

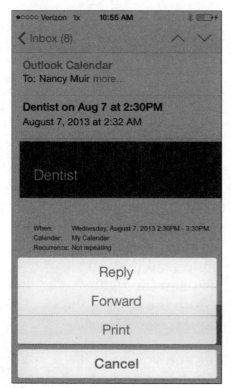

Figure 11-8

2. In the form that appears (see **Figure 11-9**), tap in the To field and enter another addressee if you like (you have to do this if you're forwarding); next, tap in the message body and enter a message (see **Figure 11-10**).

3. Tap the Send button. The message goes on its way.

If you want to move an address from the To field to the Cc or Bcc field, tap and hold the address and drag it to the other field.

If you tap Forward to send the message to somebody else and the original message had an attachment, you're offered the option of including or not including the attachment.

Tap here to enter a recipient

Send button

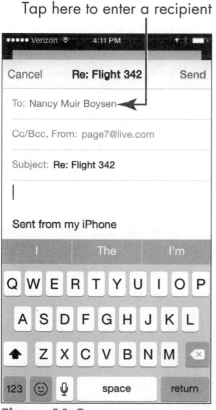

Figure 11-9

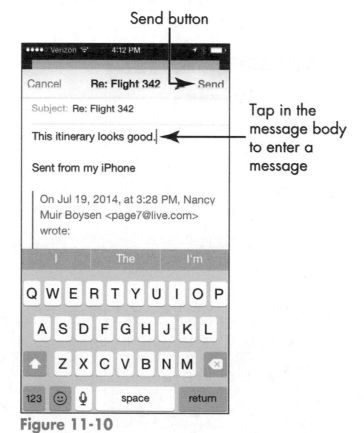

Tap in the message body to enter a message

Figure 11-10

Create and Send a New Message

1. With Mail open, tap the New Message button in the bottom-right corner (this looks like a page with a pen on it). A blank message form appears (see **Figure 11-11**).

2. Enter a recipient's address in the To field. If you have saved addresses in Contacts, tap the plus sign (+) in the Address field to choose an addressee from the Contacts list that appears.

3. If you want to send a copy of the message to other people, tap the Cc/Bcc field. When the Cc and Bcc fields open, enter addresses in either or both. Use the Bcc field to specify recipients of blind carbon copies, which means that no other recipients are aware that that person received this reply.

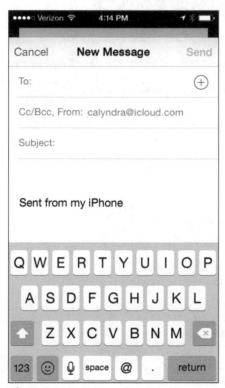

Figure 11-11

4. Enter the subject of the message in the Subject field.

5. Tap in the message body and type your message.

6. If you want to check a fact or copy and paste some part of another message into your draft message, swipe down near the top of the email to display your Inbox and other folders. Locate the message, and when you're ready to return to your draft, tap the Subject of the email, which is displayed near the bottom of the screen.

7. When you've finished creating your message, tap Send.

Format Email

1. You can apply some basic formatting to email text. You can use bold, underline, and italic formats, and indent text using the Quote Level feature.

2. Press and hold the text in a message you're creating and choose Select or Select All to select a single word or all the words in the email (see **Figure 11-12**). Note that when you make a selection, handles appear that you can drag to add adjacent words to your selection. If the menu disappears after you select the text, just tap one of the selection handles and it will reappear.

3. To see more tools, tap the arrow on the toolbar that appears; to apply bold, italic, or underline formatting, tap the B*I*U button.

4. In the toolbar that appears (see **Figure 11-13**), tap Bold, Italic, or Underline to apply formatting.

5. To change the indent level, tap and hold at the beginning of a line and then tap Quote Level.

6. Tap Increase to indent the text or Decrease to move indented text farther toward the left margin.

Tap this option

Make your selection here

Figure 11-12

Figure 11-13

 To use the Quote Level feature, make sure that it's on. From the Home screen tap Settings, tap Mail, Contacts, Calendars, and then tap the Increase Quote Level On/Off switch to turn it on.

Search Email

1. What do you do if you want to find all messages from a certain person or containing a certain word in the Subject field? You can use Mail's handy Search feature to find these emails (though you can't search message contents). With Mail open, tap an account to display its Inbox.

2. In the Inbox, tap and drag down near the top email to display the Search field. Tap in the Search field, and the onscreen keyboard appears.

3. Enter a search term or name, as shown in **Figure 11-14**. Matching emails are listed in the results (refer to Figure 11-14).

4. Tap the All Mailboxes tab to view messages that contain the search term in one of those fields in any mailbox, or tap the Current Mailbox tab to see only matches within the current mailbox (refer to Figure 11-14). Note that these options may vary slightly depending on what email service you use.

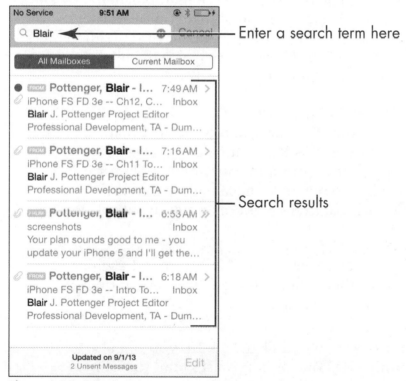

— Enter a search term here

— Search results

Figure 11-14

You can also use the Spotlight Search feature covered in Chapter 2 to search for terms in the To, From, or Subject lines of mail messages.

 To start a new search or go back to the full Inbox, tap the Delete icon (the circled X) on the far-right end of the Search field to delete the term or just tap the Cancel button.

Mark Email as Unread or Flag for Follow-Up

1. You can use a simple swipe to access tools that either mark an email as unread after you've read it (placing a blue dot before the message) or flag an email (which places an orange circle before it). These methods help you to remember to reread an email that you've already read or to follow up on a message at a later time. With Mail open and an Inbox displayed, swipe to the left to display three options: More, Flag, and Trash.

2. Tap More. On the menu shown in **Figure 11-15,** you're given several options, including Mark. Tapping Mark accesses both the Mark As Read/Unread and Flag commands. Tapping either command applies it and returns you to your Inbox. Note that you can also get to this command by swiping to the right on a message displayed in your Inbox.

3. There's another way to get to the Flag command. Swipe to the left on another email and then tap Flag. An orange circle appears before the email.

 On the menu shown in Figure 11-15, you can also select Notify Me. This option causes Mail to notify you whenever somebody replies to this email thread.

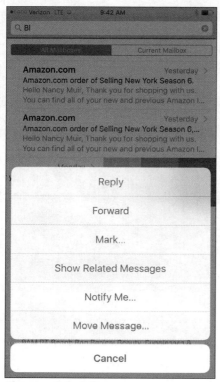

Figure 11-15

Create an Event from Email Contents

1. A neat feature in Mail is the ability to create a Calendar event from within an email. To check this out, create an email to yourself mentioning a reservation on a specific airline on a specific date and time; you can also mention another type of reservation, such as for dinner, or mention a phone number.

2. Send the message to yourself and then open Mail.

3. In your Inbox, open the email. Note that the pertinent information is displayed in blue, underlined text.

4. Tap the underlined text, and in the menu shown in **Figure 11-16,** tap Create Event. A New Event form from Calendar appears. Enter additional information about the event and then tap Done.

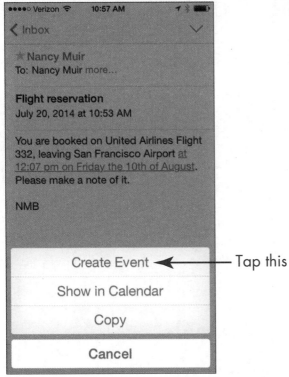

Figure 11-16

Delete Email

1. When you no longer want an email cluttering your Inbox, you can delete it. With the Inbox displayed, tap the Edit button. Circular check boxes are displayed to the left of each message (see **Figure 11-17**).

2. Tap the circle next to the message that you want to delete. (You can tap multiple items if you have several emails to delete.) A message marked for deletion shows a check mark in the circular check button (refer to Figure 11-17).

No Service 9:15 AM

2 Selected   Cancel

Q Search

Pottenger, Blair - In...   9:08 AM
iPhone FS FD 3e -- Figure 11-14
Don't get mad, but I need you to
reshoot Figure 11-15 again. It ne...   ————— Tap to select the message

DoNotReply@wsdot....   7:16 AM
Your WSF Reservation Order Co...
Dear Nancy Muir, Thank you for
your vehicle reservation(s). Your...

Apple   7:04 AM
How to reset your Apple ID pass...
Dear Nancy Muir, To reset your
Apple ID password, simply click...   ————— Selected messages

Outlook Calendar   3:08 AM
Casey, tree on Sep 18 at 3:00PM
Calendar

Dennis Cohen   Yesterday

Mark   Move   Trash

Figure 11-17

3. Tap the Trash button at the bottom of the Inbox dialog.
The message is moved to the Trash folder. Note that
some email services use different terms for Trash; for
example, Google calls this feature Archive, and its button
and menu options vary accordingly.

 You can also delete an open email by tapping the
Trash icon on the toolbar that runs across the bottom
of the screen, or swiping left on a message displayed
in an Inbox and tapping the Trash button that
appears.

Organize Email

1. You can move messages into any of several predefined folders in Mail (these will vary depending on your email provider and the folders you've created on your provider's server). After displaying the folder containing the message that you want to move (for example, Inbox), tap the Edit button. Circular check boxes are displayed to the left of each message (refer to Figure 11-17).

2. Tap the circle next to the message you want to move.

3. Tap the Move button.

4. In the Mailboxes list that appears (see **Figure 11-18**), tap the folder where you want to store the message. The message is moved.

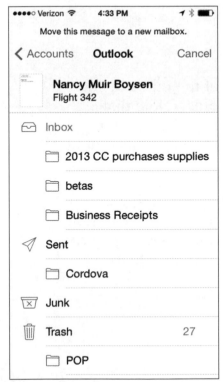

Figure 11-18

Create a VIP List

1. A VIP list is a way to create a list of senders. When any of these senders sends you an email, you'll be notified of it through the Notifications feature of iPhone. In the list of all Mailboxes, tap the Info button to the right of VIP (see **Figure 11-19**).

2. Tap Add VIP (see **Figure 11-20**), and your Contacts list appears. Tap a contact to add that person to the VIP list.

Tap this button   Tap this option

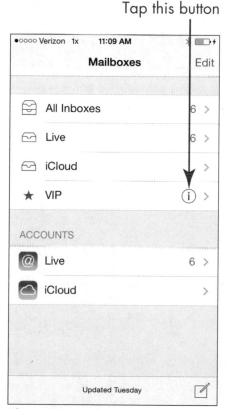

Figure 11-19

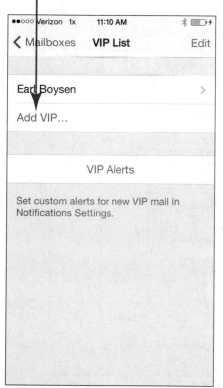

Figure 11-20

3. Tap a contact to make that person a VIP.

4. To make settings for whether VIP mail is flagged in the Notification Center, press the Home button and then tap Settings.

5. Tap Notifications and then tap Mail. In the settings that appear, shown in **Figure 11-21,** tap VIP.

6. Tap the Show in Notification Center On/Off switch to turn on notifications for VIP mail.

Tap this

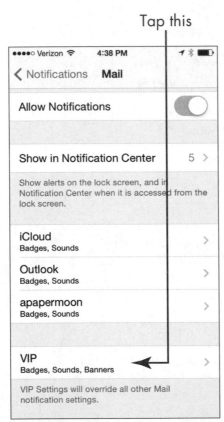

Figure 11-21

7. Tap an alert style and choose what Notification Sound should play or what badge icon should appear. You can also choose to have the notification displayed on your Lock screen (see **Figure 11-22**).

8. Press the Home button to close Settings. New mail from your VIPs should now appear in Notification Center when you swipe down from the top of the screen, and, depending on the settings you chose, may cause a sound to play or a badge icon to appear on your lock screen, and a blue star icon to appear to the left of these messages in the Inbox in Mail.

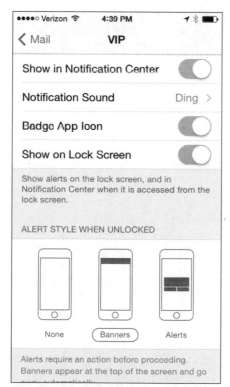

Figure 11-22

Shopping the iTunes Store

The iTunes Store app that comes preinstalled in iPhone lets you easily shop for music, movies, and TV shows. As Chapter 14 explains, you can also get electronic and audio books via the iBooks app.

In this chapter, you discover how to find content in the iTunes Store. You can download the content directly to your iPhone or to another device and then sync it to your iPhone. With the new Family Sharing feature, which I cover in this chapter, as many as six people in a family can share purchases using the same credit card. Finally, I cover a few options for buying content from other online stores and using Apple Pay to make real-world purchases using a stored payment method.

Note that I cover opening an iTunes account and downloading iTunes software to your computer in Chapter 3. If you need to, read Chapter 3 to see how to handle these two tasks before digging into this chapter.

Get ready to . . .

Explore the iTunes Store

1. Visiting the iTunes Store from your iPhone is easy with the built-in iTunes Store app. Tap the iTunes Store icon on the Home screen.

2. If you're not already signed in to iTunes, the dialog shown in **Figure** 12-1 appears, asking for your iTunes password. Enter your password and tap OK. If you see a prompt to set up Family Sharing, you can click Not Now to proceed and set it up at a later time. See the last task in this chapter for more about this feature.

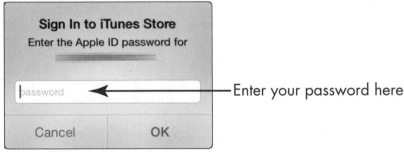

Enter your password here

Figure 12-1

3. Tap the Music button (if it isn't already selected) in the row of buttons at the bottom of the screen. You see several rows of categories of selections such as New Music, New Artists, and Hot Albums (these category names change from time to time).

4. Flick your finger up to scroll through the featured selections or tap the See All button to see more selections in any category, as shown in **Figure** 12-2.

5. Tap the Charts tab at the top of the screen. This displays lists of bestselling songs, albums, and music videos in the iTunes Store.

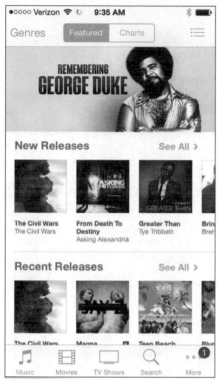

Figure 12-2

6. Tap any listed item to see more detail about it, as shown in **Figure 12-3,** and hear a brief preview when you tap the number to the left of a song.

> The navigation techniques in these steps work essentially the same in any of the content categories (the buttons at the bottom of the screen), which include Music, Movies, and TV Shows.

> If you want to use the Genius playlist feature, which recommends additional purchases based on the contents of your library in the iTunes app on your iPhone, tap the More button at the bottom of the screen and then tap Genius. If you've made enough purchases in iTunes, song and album recommendations appear based on those purchases as well as the content in your iTunes Match library (a fee-based service), if you have one.

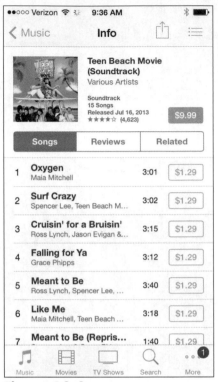

Figure 12-3

 If you're in search of other kinds of content, the Podcasts app and iTunes U app allow you to find and then download podcasts and online courses to your phone.

Find a Selection

You can look for a selection in the iTunes Store in several ways. You can use the Search feature, search by genre or category, or view artists' pages. Here's how these work:

➠ Tap the Search button at the bottom of the screen and the Search field shown in **Figure 12-4** appears. Tap in the field and enter a search term using the onscreen keyboard. Tap the Search button on the keyboard or, if a suggestion in the list of search results appeals to you, just tap that suggestion.

Enter a search term here

Figure 12-4

⟶ Tap an item such as Music at the bottom of the
screen; then tap the Genres button at the top of the
screen. A list of genres like the one shown in
Figure 12-5 appears.

⟶ On a description page that appears when you tap a
selection, you can find more offerings by the people
involved with that particular work. For example, for
a music selection, tap to display details about it and
then tap the Reviews tab at the middle of the page to
see all reviews of the album (see **Figure 12-6**). For a
movie (tap Movies at the bottom of the iTunes Store
Home page), tap to open details and then tap
Reviews, or tap the Related tab to see more movies
starring any of the lead actors.

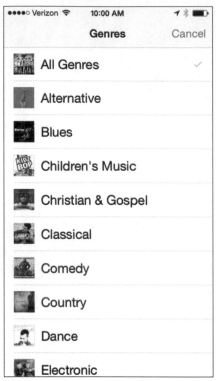

Figure 12-5

Reviews tab

Figure 12-6

 If you find a selection that you like, tap the Share button at the top of its description page to share your discovery with a friend via AirDrop, Mail, Message, Twitter, or Facebook. A message form appears with a link that your friend can tap to view information about the selection. Note that you must have set up an associated account (such as Twitter) before you can use this feature. Tap Settings from the Home screen to set up an account.

Preview Music, a Video, or an Audiobook

1. Because you've already set up an iTunes account (or if you haven't done so yet, refer to Chapter 3), when you choose to buy an item, it's automatically charged to the credit or debit card you have on file, to your PayPal

account, or against any allowance you have outstanding from an iTunes gift card. You might want to preview an item before you buy it. If you like it, buying and downloading are then easy and quick. Open iTunes and use any method outlined in earlier tasks to locate a selection that you might want to buy.

2. Tap the item to see detailed information about it, as shown in **Figure 12-7**.

3. For a TV show, tap an episode to get further information (refer to Figure 12-7). If you're looking at a music selection, tap the track number or name of a selection to play a preview. For a movie or audiobook selection, tap the Trailers Play button (movies) shown in **Figure 12-8**.

Tap an episode to get
additional info

Play button

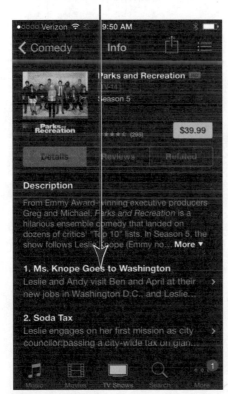

Figure 12-7

Figure 12-8

Buy a Selection

1. When you find an item that you want to buy, tap the button that shows either the price (if it's a selection available for purchase; see **Figure 12-9**) or the button with the word *Get* on it (if it's a selection available for free).

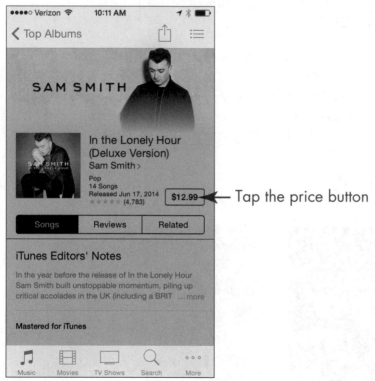

Figure 12-9

The button label changes to Buy *X*, where *X* is the type of content, such as a song or album, that you're buying. If the item is free, the label changes to Get Song (or whatever item you're purchasing).

2. Tap the Buy *X* button. The iTunes Password dialog appears (refer to Figure 12-1).

3. Enter your password and tap OK. The item begins down-loading, and the cost, if any, is automatically charged against your account. When the download finishes, tap OK in the Purchase Complete message and you can then view the content using the Music or Video app, depending on the type of content.

If you want to buy music, you can open the description page for an album and tap the album price, or buy individual songs rather than the entire album. Tap the price for a song and then proceed to purchase it.

Note the Redeem button on some iTunes screens. Tap this button to redeem any iTunes gift certificates that you might get from your generous friends, or from yourself.

If you don't want to allow purchases from within apps (for example, Music or Videos) but rather want to allow purchases only through the iTunes Store, you can go to the Settings app, tap General, tap Restrictions, and then tap Enable Restrictions and enter a passcode. After you've set a passcode, you can tap individual apps to turn on restrictions for them, as well as for actions such as installing apps, deleting apps, or using Siri.

You can allow content to be downloaded over your 3G/4G cellular network if you're not near a Wi-Fi hotspot. Be aware, however, that you could incur hefty data charges with your provider if you run over your allotted data. However, if you aren't near a Wi-Fi hotspot, downloading over your cellular network might be your only option. Tap Settings, tap App and iTunes Store, scroll down, and set the Use Cellular Data setting switch to On.

Rent Movies

1. In the case of movies, you can either rent or buy content. If you rent, which is less expensive but a one-time deal, you have 30 days from the time you rent the item to begin to watch it. After you have begun to watch it, you have 24 hours from that time left to watch it on the same device, as many times as you like. With the iTunes Store open, tap the Movies button.

2. Locate the movie you want to rent and tap it, as shown in **Figure 12-10.**

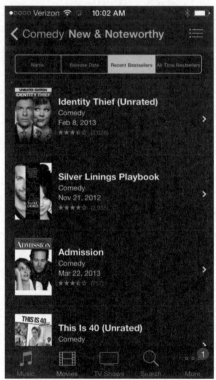

Figure 12-10

3. In the detailed description of the movie that appears, tap the Rent button (if it's available for rental); see **Figure 12-11.**

Rent button

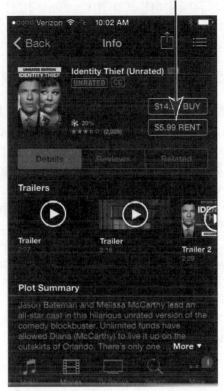

Figure 12-11

4. The gray Rent button changes to a green Rent Movie button; tap it to confirm the rental. The movie begins to download to your iPhone immediately, and your account is charged the rental fee.

5. After the download is complete, you can use the Videos app to watch it. (See Chapter 17 to read about how this app works.)

 Some movies are offered in high-definition versions. These HD movies look pretty good on that crisp, colorful iPhone screen. If your selection is available in SD it won't have quite as high quality, but it will take up less bandwidth to download or stream it to your phone. SD is also a bit cheaper than an HD movie to rent or purchase.

You can also download content to your computer and sync it to your iPhone. Refer to Chapter 3 for more about this process.

Shop Anywhere Else

One feature that's missing from the iPhone is support for Adobe Flash, a format of video playback that many online video-on-demand services and interactive games use. However, most online stores that sell content such as movies and music have added iPhone-friendly videos to their collections, so you do have alternatives to iTunes for your choice of movies and TV shows. You can also shop for music from sources other than iTunes, such as Amazon.com.

You can open accounts at one of these stores by using your computer or your iPhone's Safari browser and then following the store's instructions for purchasing and downloading content.

 For non–iPhone friendly formats, you can download the content on your computer and stream it to your iPhone using Air Video (for $2.99) on the iPhone and Air Video Server (for free) using your Mac or Windows computer. For more information, go to www.inmethod.com/air-video/index.html.

Use Apple Pay and Wallet

With iPhone 6 and 6 Plus, Apple announced a new electronic payment service, Apple Pay. Called a mobile wallet, this service uses the Touch ID feature in your iPhone's Home button to identify you and any credit cards you've stored at the iTunes Store to make payments via a feature called Wallet.

Your credit card information isn't stored on your phone, and Apple doesn't know a thing about your purchases. In addition, Apple considers Apple Pay safer because the store cashier doesn't even have to know your name.

There are 220,000 merchant locations that are set up to use Apple Pay, which launched in late fall 2014. Originally supported by Amex, Visa, MasterCard, and six of the largest banks in the United States, with iPhone 6s and 6s Plus, you'll find that even more credit cards (such as Discover) and store cards (such as Kohls or JCPenney) work with Apple Pay.

To set up Apple Pay, go to Settings and tap Wallet & Apple Pay. Add information about a credit card, and then double-tap the Home button when the lock screen is displayed to initiate a purchase. You can also make settings from within the Wallet app itself.

Enable Auto-Downloads of Purchases from Other Devices

1. With iCloud, you can make a purchase or download free content on any of your Apple devices, and iCloud automatically shares those purchases with all your Apple devices. To enable this auto-download feature on iPhone, start by tapping Settings on the Home screen.

> To use iCloud, first set up an iCloud account. See Chapter 3 for detailed coverage of iCloud, including setting up your account.

2. Tap App and iTunes Store.

3. In the options that appear, scroll down and then set the switch to On for any category of purchases you want to auto-download to your iPhone from other Apple devices: Music, Apps, or Books (see **Figure 12-12**).

> At this point, Apple doesn't offer an option of auto-downloading video content using these settings, probably because video is such a memory and bandwidth hog.

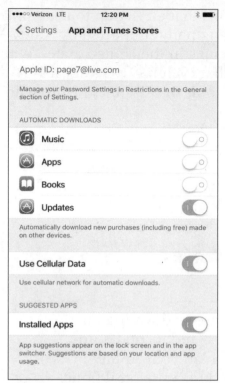

Figure 12-12

Set Up Family Sharing

Family Sharing is a feature that allows as many as six people in your family to share whatever anybody in the group has purchased from the iTunes, iBooks, and App Stores even though you don't share Apple IDs. Your family must all use the same credit card to purchase items (tied to whichever Apple ID is managing the family), but you can approve purchases by children 13 years old and younger. You can also share calendars, photos, and a family calendar (see Chapter 21 for information about Family Sharing and Calendar and Chapter 16 for information on sharing photos in a family album). Start by turning on Family Sharing.

1. Tap Settings.

2. Tap iCloud and then tap Set Up Family Sharing.

3. Tap Get Started. On the next screen, you can add a photo for your family. Tap Continue.

4. On the Share Purchases screen, tap Share Purchases from a different account to use another Apple account.

5. Tap Continue and check the payment method that you want to use. Tap Continue.

6. On the next screen, tap Add Family Member. Enter the person's name (assuming that this person is listed in your contacts) or email address. An invitation is sent to the person's email. When the invitation is accepted, the person is added to your family (see **Figure 12-13**).

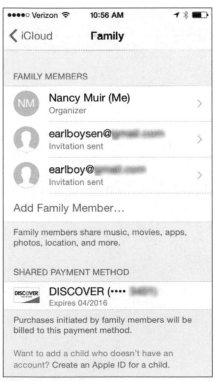

Figure 12-13

Note that the payment method for this family is displayed under Shared Payment Method in this screen. All those involved in a family have to use a single payment method for family purchases.

 There's also a link called Create an Apple ID for a Child. When you click this link and enter information to create the ID, the child's account is automatically added to your Family and retains the child status until he or she turns 13. If a child accesses iTunes to buy something, he or she gets a prompt to ask permission. You get an Ask to Buy notification on your phone as well as via email. You can then accept or decline the purchase, giving you control over family spending in the iTunes Store.

Expanding Your iPhone Horizons with Apps

*S*ome *apps* (short for *applications*) come pre-installed on your iPhone, such as Contacts and Videos. But you can choose from a world of other apps out there for your iPhone, some for free (such as iBooks) and some for a price (typically, ranging from 99 cents to about $10, though some can top out at $90 or more).

Apps range from games to financial tools such as loan calculators to apps that help you when you're planning or taking a trip.

In this chapter, I suggest some apps that you might want to check out and explain how to use the App Store feature of iPhone to find, purchase, and download apps.

Get ready to . . .

Explore Senior-Recommended Apps

As I write this book, new iPhone apps are in development, so even more apps that could fit your needs will be available. Still, to get you exploring what's possible, I provide a quick list of apps that might whet your appetite.

Access the App Store by tapping the App Store icon on the Home screen. You can start by exploring the Featured or Top Choices categories (see the buttons along the bottom of the screen). Or you can tap Explore and find apps divided into categories. Tap an app to see more information about it.

Here are some interesting apps to explore:

➡ **Sudoku2 (free):** If you like this mental logic puzzle in print, try it out on your iPhone (see **Figure 13-1**). It has three lessons and several levels ranging from easiest to nightmare, making it a great way to make time fly by in a doctor's or dentist's waiting room.

➡ **StockWatch Portfolio Tracking and Stock Market Quotes ($1.99):** Even though there's a Stocks app on the iPhone Home screen, this app will help you keep track of your investments in a portfolio format. You can use the app to create a watch list and record your stock performance.

➡ **SpaceEffect (free):** If you need a photo-sharing service with some cool features, try SpaceEffect. You can not only upload and share photos but also apply awesome effects to them.

➡ **Paint Studio ($3.99):** Get creative! You can use this powerful app to draw, add color, and even create special effects.

➡ **Virtuoso Piano Free 3 (free):** If you love to make music, you'll love this app, which gives you a virtual piano keyboard to play and compose on the fly.

Figure 13-1

→ **Travelzoo (free):** Get great deals on hotels, airfare, rental cars, entertainment, and more. This app also offers tips from travel experts.

→ **Nike+ Training Club (free):** Use this handy utility to help design personalized workouts, see step-by-step instructions to help you learn new exercises, and watch video demonstrations. The reward system in this app may just keep you going toward your workout goals.

 Note that you can work on documents using apps in the cloud. Use Keynote, Numbers, Pages, and more apps to get your work done from any device. See Chapter 3 for more about using iCloud Drive.

Search the App Store

1. Tap the App Store icon on the Home screen. The site shown in **Figure 13-2** appears.

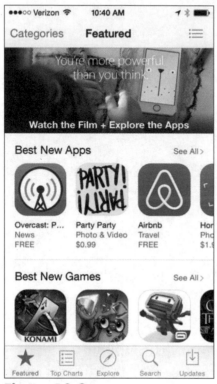

Figure 13-2

2. At this point, you have several options for finding apps:

- Scroll downward to view various categories of Featured apps such as Best New Apps and Best New Games.

- Tap the Top Charts tab at the bottom of the screen to see bestselling apps. Tap the Explore option to display apps in categories such as Books, Education, and Finance. Tap a category to display apps that fit within it.

- Tap the Categories button in the top-left corner of the screen on the Featured and Top Charts views as an alternative way to browse by type of app such as Education or Entertainment, as shown in **Figure 13-3**.

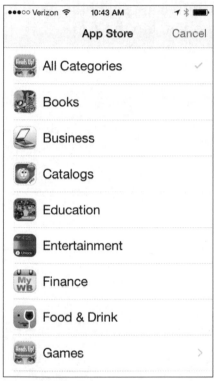

Figure 13-3

- Tap the Search button at the bottom of the screen and then tap in the Search field, enter a search term, and tap the result you want to view.

- Tap the See All button in any category shown in the Featured view to view all the items in that category.

- In the Top Charts view, use the Paid, Free, and Top Grossing tabs to narrow your search.

Get Applications from the App Store

1. Buying or getting free apps requires that you have an iTunes account, which I cover in Chapter 3. After you have an account, you can use the saved payment information there to buy apps or download free apps with a few simple steps. With the App Store open, tap the Top Charts button, and then tap the Free tab, as shown in **Figure 13-4**.

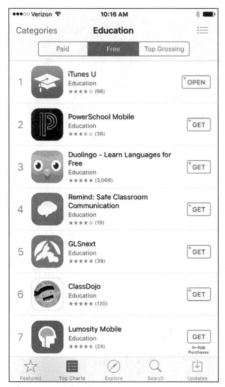

Figure 13-4

2. Tap the Get button for an app that appeals to you. (To get a *paid* app, you tap the same button, which is then labeled with a price.)

3. The Get button changes to read *Install* (or, in the case of a paid app, the button changes to read *Buy*. Tap the button and the button changes to read *Installing*. You may be asked to enter your iTunes password. Do so and then tap the OK button to proceed.

4. The app downloads, and if you purchase an app that isn't free, your credit card or gift card balance is charged at this point for the purchase price.

 Out of the box, only preinstalled apps are located on the first iPhone Home screen, with a few such as Voice Memos and Podcasts located on the second Home screen. Apps that you download are placed on available Home screens, and you have to scroll to view and use them; this procedure is covered later in this chapter. See the next task for help in finding your newly downloaded apps using multiple Home screens.

 If you've opened an iCloud account, you can set it up so that anything you purchase on your iPhone is automatically pushed to other Apple iOS devices and your iTunes library, and vice versa. See Chapter 3 for more about iCloud.

Organize Your Applications on Home Screens

1. iPhone can display up to 11 Home screens. By default, the first Home screen contains preinstalled apps, and the second contains a few more preinstalled apps, including Contacts and Calculator in the Extras folder. Other screens are created to contain any apps you download or sync to your iPhone. At the bottom of any iPhone Home screen (just above the Dock), dots indicate the number of Home screens you've filled with apps; a solid dot specifies which Home screen you're on now, as shown in **Figure 13-5.** Press the Home button to open the last displayed Home screen.

Screen you're on

Dots indicating the number
of Home screens

Figure 13-5

2. Flick your finger from right to left to move to the next Home screen. To move back, flick from left to right.

3. To reorganize apps on a Home screen, press and hold any app on that page. The app icons begin to jiggle (see **Figure 13-6**), and any apps you installed will sport a Delete button (a black circle with a white X on it).

4. Press, hold, and drag an app icon to another location on the screen to move it.

5. Press the Home button to stop all those icons from jiggling!

A Delete button

Figure 13-6

 To move an app from one page to another, while the apps are jiggling, you can press, hold, and drag an app to the left or right to move it to the next Home screen. You can also manage what app resides on what Home screen and change the order of the Home screens from iTunes when you've connected iPhone to iTunes via a cable or wireless sync.

 You can use the multitasking feature for switching between apps easily. Press the Home button twice and you get a preview of open apps. Scroll among the apps and tap the one you want to go to. You can also swipe an app upward from this preview list to close it.

Organize Apps in Folders

iPhone lets you organize apps in folders so that you can find them more easily. The process is simple:

1. Tap and hold an app until all apps do their jiggle dance.

2. Drag one app on top of another app. The two apps appear in a box with a placeholder name in a strip above them (see **Figure** 13-7).

Placeholder name

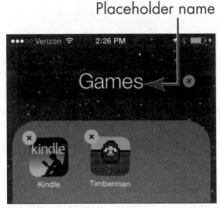

Figure 13-7

3. To change the name, tap in the field at the end of the placeholder name, and the keyboard appears.

4. Tap the Delete key to delete the placeholder name and type one of your own.

5. Tap Done, and then tap anywhere outside the box to close it.

6. Press the Home button to stop the icons from dancing around, and you'll see your folder appear on the Home screen where you began this process.

Delete Apps You No Longer Need

1. When you no longer need an app you have installed, it's time to get rid of it. (You can't delete apps that are preinstalled on the iPhone, however.) If you use iCloud to push content across all Apple iOS devices, note that deleting an app on your iPhone won't affect that app on other devices. Display the Home screen that contains the app you want to delete.

2. Press and hold the app until all apps begin to jiggle.

3. Tap the Delete button for the app you want to delete (refer to Figure 13-6).

4. A confirmation like the one shown in **Figure** 13-8 appears. Tap Delete to proceed with the deletion.

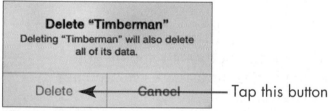

Delete "Timberman"
Deleting "Timberman" will also delete all of its data.

Delete ◄————— Cancel ————— Tap this button

Figure 13-8

 Don't worry about wiping out several apps at one time by deleting a folder. When you delete a folder, the apps that were contained within the folder are placed back on a Home screen if space is available, and you can still find the apps using the Spotlight Search feature.

Update Apps

1. App developers update their apps all the time, so you might want to check for those updates. The App Store icon on the Home screen displays the number of available updates in a red circle. Tap the App Store icon on the Home screen.

2. Tap the Updates button to access the Updates screen and then tap any item you want to update. Note that if you have Family Sharing turned on, there will be a folder titled Family Purchases that you can tap to display apps that are shared across your family's devices. To update all, tap the Update All button.

3. On the app screen that appears, tap Update. You may be asked to confirm that you want to update, or to enter your Apple ID; after you do, tap OK to proceed. You may also be asked to confirm that you are over a certain age or agree to terms and conditions; if so, scroll down the terms dialog and, at the bottom, tap Agree. The download progress is displayed.

 You can download multiple apps at one time. If you choose more than one app to update instead of downloading apps sequentially, several items will download simultaneously.

 If you have an iCloud account that you have activated on several devices and update an app on your iPhone, any other Apple iOS devices are also updated automatically and vice versa.

iOS 9 performs what Apple calls "intelligently scheduled updates," meaning that updates to apps and the iOS happen at times when your iPhone isn't using much power; for example, when you're connecting to the Internet via Wi-Fi. And speaking of updating, iOS 9 studies your habits and can update apps that require updated content, such as Facebook or Stocks, around the time you usually check them so that you have instant access to current information.

Part IV
Having Fun and Consuming Media

Visit www.dummies.com/extras/iphoneforseniors for information about the Apple Music service.

Using Your iPhone as an E-Reader

A traditional *e-reader* is a device that's used primarily to read the electronic version of books, magazines, and newspapers. If you're happy reading on your smaller iPhone screen, your phone can be a great e-reader, although it isn't a traditional e-reader device like the Kindle because it gets its functionality from an e-reader app.

Apple's free app that turns your iPhone into an e-reader is *iBooks*, which also enables you to buy and download books from Apple's iBooks Store. You can also use one of several other free e-reader apps — for example Kindle or Nook. Then you can download books to your iPhone from a variety of online sources, such as Amazon and Google, so that you can read to your heart's content.

In this chapter, you discover the options available for reading material and how to buy books. You also learn how to navigate a book or periodical and adjust the brightness and type, as well as how to search books and organize your iBooks libraries.

Discover E-Reading

An *e-reader* is any electronic device that enables you to download and read books, magazines, PDF files, or newspapers. Many e-readers use E Ink technology to create a paperlike reading experience. These devices are typically portable and dedicated only to reading the electronic version of published materials.

The iPhone is a bit different from an e-reader. It isn't only for reading books, and you have to use iBooks or download another e-reader app to enable it as an e-reader (though the apps are usually free). Also, the iPhone doesn't offer the paperlike reading experience — you read from a phone screen (though you can adjust the brightness and background color of the screen).

When you buy a book online (or get one of many free publications), it downloads to your iPhone in a few seconds using a Wi-Fi or 3G/4G connection. The iPhone offers several navigation tools to move around an electronic book, which you explore in this chapter.

Find Books with iBooks

1. To shop using iBooks, tap the iBooks application icon to open it. (It's on your first Home screen).

2. In the iBooks library that opens (see **Figure 14-1**), you see a bookshelf; yours probably has only one free book already downloaded to it. (If you don't see the bookshelf, tap the My Books button to go there.) Tap the Featured button, and you're taken to the iBooks Store with featured titles displayed.

3. In the iBooks Store, shown in **Figure 14-2**, featured titles are shown. You can do any of the following to find a book:

• Tap the Search button at the bottom of the screen and then tap in the Search field that appears and type a search word or phrase, using the onscreen keyboard.

Search button

Figure 14-1

Figure 14-2

- Tap the Featured button and then tap the Categories button along the top of the screen and scroll down to Browse Categories to see links to popular categories of books, as shown in **Figure 14-3**. Tap a category to view those selections.

- Press your finger on the screen and flick up to scroll to more suggested titles on a page.

- Tap the Top Charts button at the bottom of the screen to view both Paid and Free books listed on top best-seller lists.

- Tap Purchased to see only titles that you've already purchased on any Apple device connected via iCloud.

Figure 14-3

- Tap a suggested selection or featured book to read more information about it.

Many books let you download free samples before you buy. You get to read several pages of the book to see whether it appeals to you, and it doesn't cost you a dime! Look for the Sample button when you view book details.

Explore Other E-Book Sources

Beyond using iBooks, the iPhone is capable of using other e-reader apps to read book content from other bookstores. You first have to download another e-reader application such as Kindle from Amazon or the Barnes & Noble Nook reader from the App Store (see Chapter 13 for how to download apps). You can also download a nonvendor-specific app such as Bluefire Reader, which handles ePub and PDF formats, as well as the format that most public libraries use (protected PDF). Then use the app's features to search for, purchase, and download content.

The Kindle e-reader application is shown in **Figure 14-4.** After downloading the free app from the App Store, you just open the app and enter the email address and password associated with your Amazon account. Any content you've already bought from the Amazon.com Kindle Store from your computer or Kindle Fire tablet is archived online and can be placed on your Kindle Home page on the iPhone for you to read anytime you like. Tap the Device tab to see titles stored on iPhone rather than in Amazon's Cloud library. To enhance your reading experience, use features such as changing the background to a sepia tone or changing font. To delete a book from this reader, press the title with your finger, and the Remove from Device button appears.

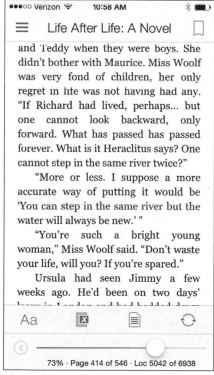

Figure 14-4

E-books are everywhere! You can get content from a variety of other sources: Project Gutenberg, Google Play, some publishers like Baen, and so on. Download the content using your computer, if you like, and then just add the items to Books in iTunes and sync them to your iPhone. You can also open items from a web link or email, and they're copied to iBooks for you. Just be aware that e-books come in different formats, and iBooks won't work with formats other than ePub or PDF (for example, it can't use formats such as the Kindle's Mobi and AZW). You can also make settings to iCloud so that books are pushed across your Apple devices or you can place them in an online storage service such as Dropbox and access them from there.

Buy Books

1. If you've set up an account with iTunes, you can buy books at the iBooks Store using the iBooks app. (See Chapter 3 for more about iTunes.) Open iBooks and tap Featured. When you find a book in the iBooks Store, either in Featured titles or by searching, you can buy it by tapping it and then tapping the Price button. The button changes to the Buy Book button, as shown in **Figure 14-5.** (If the book is free, these buttons are labeled Get.)

2. Tap the Buy Book or Get Book button. If you haven't already signed in, the iTunes Password dialog, shown in **Figure 14-6,** appears.

 If you have signed in, your purchase is accepted immediately. No returns are allowed as they are with Amazon Kindle devices, so tap carefully!

3. Enter your password and tap OK.

Buy Book button

Figure 14-5

Figure 14-6

4. The book appears on your bookshelf, and the cost is charged to whichever credit card you specified when you opened your iTunes account. Tap the Read button that appears to read your tome.

 Books that you've downloaded to your computer can be accessed from any Apple device through iCloud. Content can also be synced with your iPhone by using the Lightning to USB Cable and your iTunes account, or by using the wireless iTunes Wi-Fi Sync setting on the General Settings menu. See Chapter 3 for more about syncing.

Navigate a Book

1. Tap iBooks and, if your Library (the bookshelf) isn't already displayed, tap the My Books button.

2. Tap a book to open it. The book opens to its title page or the last spot you read on any compatible device, as shown in **Figure 14-7**.

Table of Contents button

Slider to move to another page
Figure 14-7

3. Take any of these actions to navigate the book:

- **To go to the book's Table of Contents:** Tap the Table of Contents button at the top of the page (refer to **Figure 14-7**) and then tap the name of a chapter to go to it (see **Figure 14-8**).

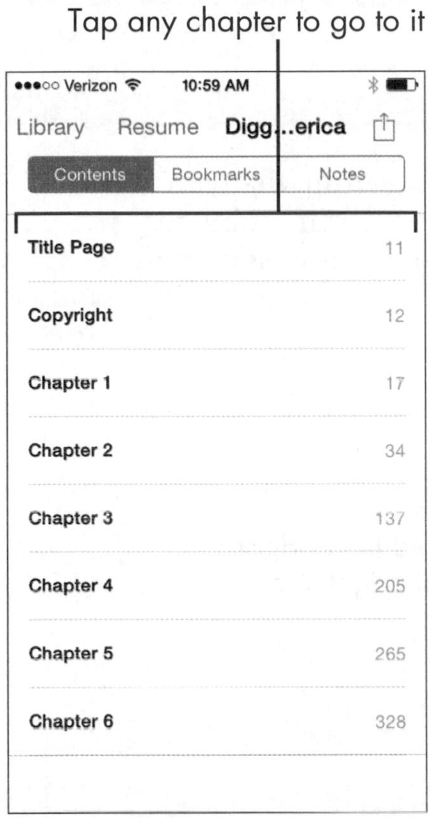
Tap any chapter to go to it
Verizon
10:59 AM
Library
Resume
Digg...erica
Contents
Bookmarks
Notes
Title Page 11
Copyright 12
Chapter 1 17
Chapter 2 34
Chapter 3 137
Chapter 4 205
Chapter 5 265
Chapter 6 328

Figure 14-8

- **To turn to the next page:** Place your finger anywhere along the right edge of the page and tap or flick to the left.

- **To turn to the preceding page:** Place your finger anywhere on the left edge of a page and tap or flick to the right.

- **To move to another page in the book:** Tap and drag the slider at the bottom of the page (refer to Figure 14-7) to the right or left.

 To return to the Library to view another book at any time, tap the Library button. If the button isn't visible, tap anywhere on the page, and the button and other tools appear.

Adjust Brightness in iBooks

1. iBooks offers an adjustable brightness setting that you can use to make your book pages more comfortable to read. With a book open, tap the Fonts button, shown in **Figure 14-9.**

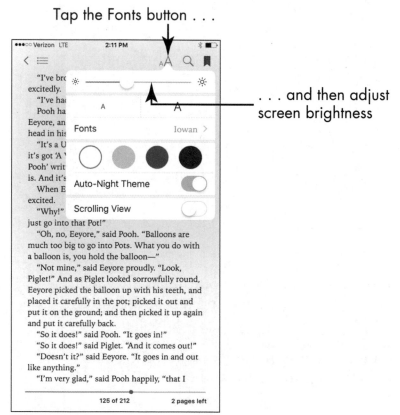

Tap the Fonts button . . .

. . . and then adjust screen brightness

Figure 14-9

2. On the Brightness setting that appears at the top (refer to Figure 14-9), tap and drag the slider to the right to make the screen brighter, or to the left to dim it.

3. Tap anywhere on the page to close the Fonts dialog.

 Experiment with the brightness level that works for you, or try out the Sepia setting, which you find by tapping Sepia in the Fonts dialog. Bright-white screens are commonly thought to be hard on the eyes, so setting the brightness halfway relative to its default setting or less is probably a good idea (and saves on battery life).

Change the Font Size and Type

1. If the type on your screen is a bit small for you to make out, you can change to a larger font size or choose a different font for readability. With a book open, tap the Fonts button (it sports a smaller capital *A* and a larger capital *A*, as shown in **Figure 14-10**).

2. In the Fonts dialog that appears (refer to Figure 14-10), tap the button with a smaller *A*, on the left, to use smaller text, or the button with the larger *A*, on the right, to use larger text.

3. Tap the Fonts button. The list of fonts shown in **Figure 14-11** appears.

4. Tap a font name to select it. The font changes on the book page.

5. If you want a sepia tint on the pages, which can be easier on the eye, tap the Back button to redisplay the Fonts dialog, and then tap the Normal, Sepia, or Night setting to activate it.

6. Tap outside the Fonts dialog to return to your book.

Tap the Fonts button

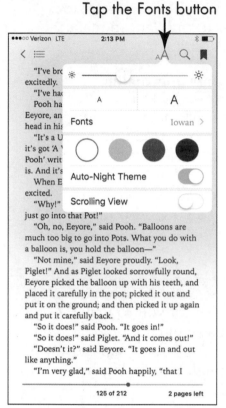

Figure 14-10

Figure 14-11

 Some fonts appear a bit larger on your screen than others because of their design. If you want the largest font, use Iowan.

Search in Your Book

1. You may want to find certain sentences or references in your book. To do so, with a book displayed, tap the Search button shown in **Figure 14-12**. The onscreen keyboard appears.

2. Enter a search term and then tap the Search key on the keyboard. iBooks searches for any matching entries.

3. Use your finger to scroll down the entries (see **Figure 14-13**).

Search button   Scroll through the entries

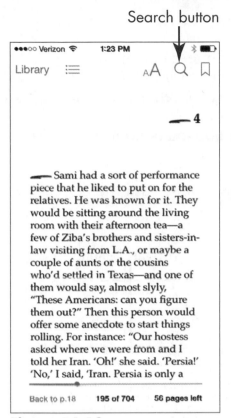

Figure 14-12

Figure 14-13

4. Flick your finger to scroll down the search results and then use either the Search Web or Search Wikipedia button at the bottom of the Search dialog if you want to search for information about the search term online. Tap a result and you're taken to the page containing that result with a highlight applied to it.

 You can also search for other instances of a particular word while in the book pages by pressing your finger on the word and tapping the right-facing arrow and then Search on the toolbar that appears.

Use Bookmarks and Highlights

1. Bookmarks and highlights in your e-books operate like favorite sites that you save in your web browser: They enable you to revisit a favorite passage or refresh your memory about a character or plot point. To bookmark a page, display that page and tap the Bookmark button in the top-right corner (see **Figure 14-14**).

2. To highlight a word or phrase, press a word until the toolbar shown in **Figure 14-15** appears.

Bookmark button   Tap this button

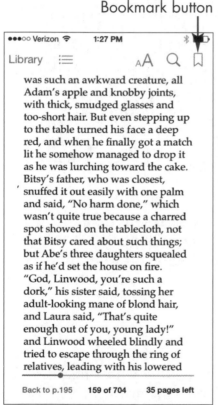

Figure 14-14

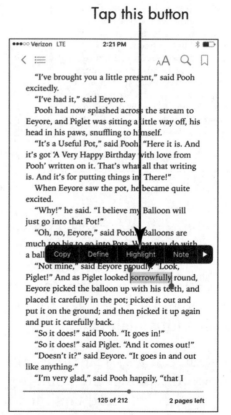

Figure 14-15

3. Tap the Highlight button. A colored highlight is placed on the word, and the toolbar shown in **Figure 14-16** appears.

Figure 14-16

4. Tap one of these four buttons (from left to right):

- **Colors:** Displays a menu of colors that you can tap to change the highlight color as well as an underline option.

- **Remove Highlight:** Removes the highlight.

- **Note:** Lets you add a note to the item.

- **Share:** Allows you to share the highlighted text with others via AirDrop, Messages, Mail, Notes, Twitter, or Facebook, or to copy the text.

5. You can also tap the arrow button at the right side of the toolbar to access Copy, Define, Highlight, and Note tools. Tap outside the highlighted text to close the toolbar.

6. To go to a list of bookmarks and notes (including high-lighted text), tap the Table of Contents button shown in **Figure 14-17.**

Bookmarks tab

Figure 14-17

7. In the Table of Contents, tap the Bookmarks tab; all bookmarks are displayed. If you want to see highlighted text and associated notes, you display the Notes tab.

8. Tap a bookmark in the bookmark list to go to that location in the book.

iPhone automatically bookmarks where you left off reading in a book so that you don't have to mark your place manually. If you use any other device registered to your iTunes or iCloud account, you also pick up where you left off reading.

Check Words in the Dictionary

1. As you read a book, you may come across unfamiliar words. Don't skip over them — take the opportunity to learn a new word! With a book open, press your finger on a word and hold it until the toolbar shown in **Figure 14-18** appears.

2. Tap the Define button. A definition dialog appears, as shown in **Figure 14-19**.

Tap this option

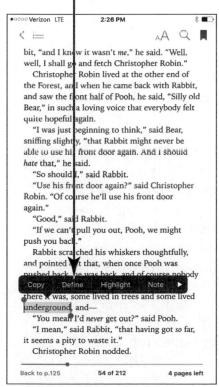

Figure 14-18

Figure 14-19

3. Tap the definition and scroll down to view more.

4. When you finish reviewing the definition, tap Done, and the definition disappears.

 If a definition doesn't appear, you can tap the Manage button to choose the dictionary from which your definitions should come from.

Organize Books in Collections

1. iBooks lets you create and name collections of books to help you organize them by your own logic, such as Tear Jerkers, Work-Related, and Great Recipes. You can place a book in only one collection, however. To create a collection from the Library bookshelf, tap Select.

2. On the screen that appears, tap a book and then tap Move. In the Collections screen shown in **Figure 14-20,** tap New Collection. On the blank line that appears, type a name.

3. Tap Done, which closes the dialog and returns you to the Collection. To add a book to a collection from the Library, repeat these steps.

4. Tap a book and then tap the Move button that appears in the top of the screen (see **Figure 14-21**). In the dialog that appears, tap the collection to which you'd like to move the book, and the book now appears on the bookshelf in that collection. To change which collection you're viewing, tap the button with the current collection's name to display other collections and then tap the one you want.

5. To delete a book from a collection with the collection displayed, tap Select, tap the book, and then tap Delete.

Tap this

Tap this button

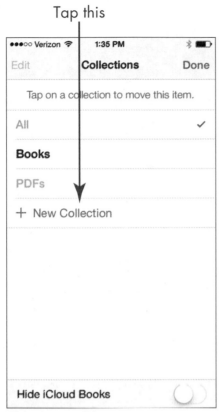

Figure 14-20

Figure 14-21

To delete a collection with the Collections dialog displayed, select the collection that you want to delete and then tap Edit. Tap the minus sign (–) to the left of the collection and then tap Delete to get rid of it. A message appears, asking you to tap Remove (to remove the contents of the collection from your iPhone) or Don't Remove. Note that if you choose Don't Remove, all titles within a deleted collection are returned to their original collections in your library, the default collection being Books.

Playing with Music on iPhone

*i*Phone includes an iPod-like app called Music that allows you to take advantage of its amazing little sound system to play your favorite music.

In this chapter, you get acquainted with the Music app and its features that allow you to sort and find music and control playback. You also get an overview of AirPlay for accessing and playing your music over a home network or over any connected device (this also works with videos and photos). Finally, I introduce you to iTunes Radio for your listening pleasure.

Chapter 15

Get ready to . . .

View the Library Contents

1. Tap the Music app, located in the Dock on the Home screen. The Music library appears (the Artists view is shown **Figure 15-1**).

Tap the Categories drop-down list

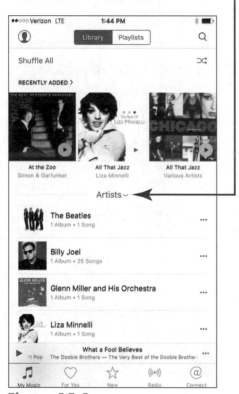

Figure 15-1

2. Tap the Categories drop-down list at the top of the library to view your music according to a criterion such as Songs or Genres (see **Figure 15-2**).

3. Tap a category (refer to Figure 15-2) to view music by album, genre, or composer, or to view any audiobooks you've acquired in iTunes.

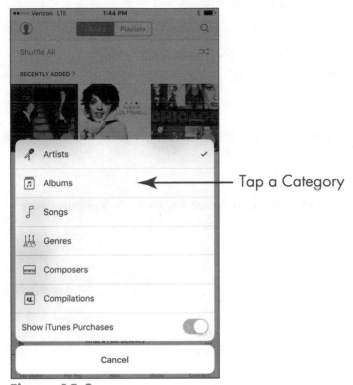

Figure 15-2

 iTunes has several free items that you can download and use to play around with the features in Music. You can also sync content, such as iTunes Smart Playlists stored on your computer or other Apple devices to your iPhone, and play it using the Music app. (See Chapter 3 for more about syncing and Chapter 12 for more about getting content from iTunes.)

 Apple offers a service called iTunes Match (visit www.apple.com/itunes/itunes-match for more information). You pay $24.99 per year for the capability to match the music you've bought from other providers (and stored in the iTunes Library on your computer) to what's in the iTunes Library. If there's a match (and there usually is), that content is added to your iTunes Library on iCloud. Then, using iCloud, you can sync the content among all your Apple devices.

Create Playlists

1. You can create your own playlists to put tracks from various sources into collections of your choosing. Tap the Playlists tab at the top of the Music screen.

2. Tap New. In the dialog that appears, enter a title for the playlist. Tap Add Songs and then tap a category, such as Songs or Artists, to display songs.

3. In the list of selections that appears (see **Figure 15-3**), tap the plus sign next to each item you want to include.

Tap the plus sign to include a
song in the playlist

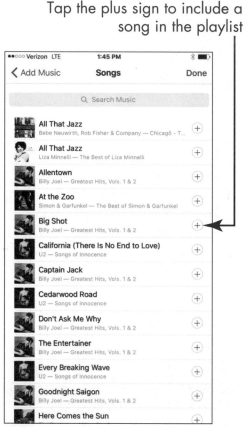

Figure 15-3

4. Tap the Done button and then tap Done on the next screen to return to the Playlists screen.

5. Your playlist appears in the list, and you can now play it by tapping the list name and then tapping a track to play it.

 To search for a song in your music libraries, use the Spotlight Search feature. From your first Home screen, you can swipe down from the screen outside the Dock and enter the name of the song. A list of search results appears.

Search for Music

1. You can search for an item in your Music library by using the Search feature. With Music open, tap the Search button (see **Figure 15-4**). The onscreen keyboard appears.

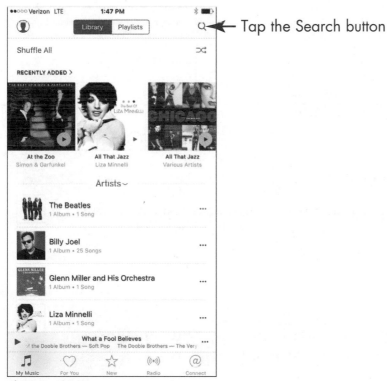

Figure 15-4

2. Enter a search term in the Search field. Results are displayed, narrowing as you type, as shown in **Figure 15-5.**

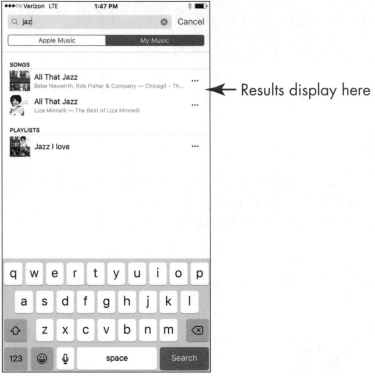

← Results display here

Figure 15-5

3. Tap an item to play it.

 You can enter an artist's name, a lyricist's or a composer's name, or a word from the item's title in the Search field to find what you're looking for.

Play Music

1. Locate the music that you want by using the methods described in previous tasks in this chapter.

2. Tap the item you want to play. Note that if you're displaying the Songs tab, you don't have to tap an album to open a song; you need only tap a song to play it. If you're using any other categories, you have to tap items such as albums (or multiple songs from one artist) to find the song you want to hear.

3. Tap the item you want to play from the list that appears; it begins to play (see **Figure 15-6**).

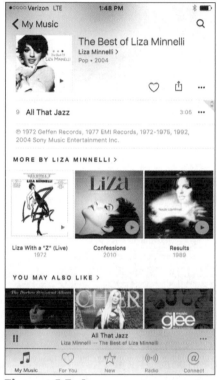

Figure 15-6

4. Tap the currently playing song title near the bottom of the screen to open it displaying playback controls. Use the Previous and Next buttons at the bottom of the screen shown in **Figure 15-7** to navigate the audio file that's playing. The Previous button takes you back to the beginning of the item that's playing; the Next button takes you to the next item. Use the Volume slider on the bottom of the screen (or the Volume buttons on the side of your iPhone) to increase or decrease the volume.

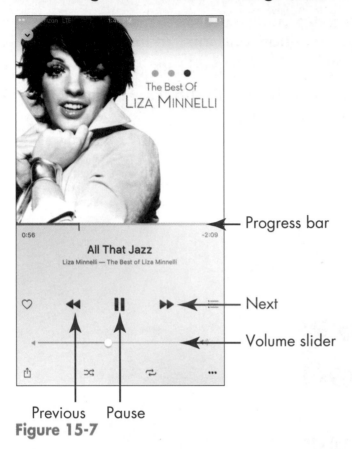

Progress bar

Next

Volume slider

Previous   Pause

Figure 15-7

5. Tap the Pause button to pause playback. Tap the button again to resume playing. Note that you can also use music controls for music that's playing from the lock screen.

6. Tap and drag the red line near the middle of the screen that indicates the current playback location. Drag the line to the left or right to "scrub" to another location in the song.

7. If you don't like what's playing, here's how to make another selection: Tap the Back arrow to the right of the playback controls to view other selections in the album that's playing. Tap My Music to go back to your music selections from this screen if you prefer.

You can use Siri to play music hands free. Just press and hold the Home button, and when Siri appears, say something like "Play 'Take the A Train'" or "Play *The White Album*."

 Home Sharing is a feature of iTunes that you can use to share music among up to five devices that have Home Sharing turned on. After Home Sharing is set up via iTunes, any of your devices can stream music and videos to other devices, and you can even click and drag content between devices using iTunes. For more about Home Sharing, visit this site: www. apple.com/support/homesharing.

 Family Sharing allows up to six members of your family to share purchased content even if they don't share the same iTunes account. You can set up Family Sharing under iCloud in Settings. See Chapter 12 for more about Family Sharing.

Shuffle Music

1. If you want to play a random selection of the music in an album on your iPhone, you can use the Shuffle feature. Tap the Categories button on the Home screen, tap Albums, and then tap an album.

2. Tap a currently playing song in at the bottom of the screen to open it and tap the Shuffle button, which looks like two lines crossing to form an X (see **Figure 15-8**). Your content plays in random order.

 If you're playing music and have set the Volume slider as high as it goes and you're still having trouble hearing, consider getting ear buds. These cut out extraneous noises and may improve the sound quality of what you're listening to, as well as add stereo to iPhone's mono speaker. Preferably, use 3.5 mm stereo ear buds; insert them in the headphone jack at the bottom of your iPhone.

Shuffle button

Figure 15-8

Use AirPlay

The AirPlay streaming technology is built into the iPhone, iPod touch, Macs and PCs running iTunes, and iPad. *Streaming* technology allows you to send media files from one device to be played on another. You can send (for example) a movie that you've purchased on your iPhone or a slideshow of your photos to be played on your Apple TV and then control the TV playback from your iPhone. You can also send music to be played over compatible speakers. Check out the Apple Remote app, which you can use to control your Apple TV.

You can use the AirPlay button in the Control Center, which you display by swiping up from the bottom edge of your iPhone screen, to take advantage of AirPlay in a few ways:

⟹ Purchase Apple TV and stream video, photos, and music to the TV.

⟹ Purchase AirPort Express and attach it to your speakers to play music.

⟹ If you buy AirPort Express, you can stream audio directly to your speakers. Because this combination of equipment varies, my advice — if you're interested in using AirPlay — is to visit your nearest Apple Store and find out which hardware combination will work best for you.

⟹ Get AirPlay-compatible speakers. With these, you don't need AirPort Express at all because you can AirPlay to the speakers directly.

To use AirPlay with another AirPlay-enabled device on your network or in close proximity, swipe up from the bottom of your screen and tap the AirPlay button in the Control Center; then select the AirPlay device to stream the content to, or choose your iPhone to move the playback back to it.

 If you get a bit antsy watching a long movie, one of the beauties of AirPlay is that you can still use your iPhone to check email, browse photos or the Internet, or check your calendar while the media file is playing on the other device.

Play Music with iTunes Radio

1. You can access iTunes Radio with any Apple device that has iOS 7 or later. Begin by tapping the Music icon in the Dock on any Home screen.

2. On the screen that appears, tap the Radio button at the bottom of the screen.

3. Scroll down and tap a Featured Station; a featured radio station begins to play (see **Figure 15-9**).

4. Use the tools at the bottom of the screen (refer to **Figure 15-10**) to control playback.

 When a song is playing, tap the Share button and then tap Share Station to share a song via AirDrop, Message, Mail, Twitter, or Facebook.

Figure 15-9

Figure 15-10

Playing with Photos

With its gorgeous screen, the iPhone is a natural for taking and viewing photos. It supports most common photo formats, such as JPEG, TIFF, and PNG. You can shoot your photos by using the built-in cameras in iPhone with built-in square or panorama modes. With recent iPhone models, you can edit your images using smart adjustment filters. You can also sync photos from your computer, save images that you find online to your iPhone, or receive them by email, MMS, or iMessage.

The Photo Sharing feature lets you share groups of photos with people using iCloud on an iOS device or on a Mac or Windows computer with iCloud access. Your iCloud Photo Library makes all this storage and sharing easy.

When you have taken or downloaded photos to play with, the Photos app lets you organize photos and view photos in albums, one by one, or in a slideshow. You can also view photos by the years in which they were taken, with images divided into collections by the location or time you took them. You can also AirDrop (iPhone 5 and later), email, message, or tweet a photo to a friend, print it, share it via AirPlay, or post it to Facebook. Finally, you can create time-lapse videos with the Camera app,

Get ready to . . .

allowing you to record a sequence in time, such as a flower opening as the sun warms it or your grandchild stirring from sleep. You can read about all these features in this chapter.

Take Pictures with the iPhone Cameras

1. The cameras in the iPhone are just begging to be used, so no matter which phone model you have, get started! Tap the Camera app icon on the Home screen to open the app.

2. If the camera type at the bottom of the screen (see **Figure 16-1**) is set to Video, slide to the left to choose Photo (the still camera).

Slide to Photo

Figure 16-1

iPhone's front- and rear-facing cameras allow you to capture photos and video (see Chapter 17 for more about the video features) and share them with family and friends. iPhone 6/6s and 6/6s Plus offer an 8-megapixel iSight camera with features such as Phase Detection Autofocus, image stabilization to avoid those fuzzy moving targets, and True Tone Flash, a sensor that tells iPhone when a flash is needed.

3. You can set the Pano (for panorama) and Square options using the slider control above the Capture button. These controls let you create square images like those you see on the popular Instagram site. With Pano selected, tap to begin to take a picture and pan across a view, and then tap Done to capture a panoramic display.

4. Tap the Flash button in the top-left corner of the screen when using the rear camera and tap On if your lighting is dim enough to require a flash, Off if you don't want iPhone to use a flash, or Auto if you want to let iPhone decide for you.

5. To use the High Dynamic Range or HDR feature tap the HDR setting at the top of the screen and tap to turn it on. This feature uses several images, some underexposed and some overexposed, and combines the best ones into one image, sometimes providing a more finely detailed picture.

6. If you want a time delay before the camera snaps the picture, tap the Time Delay button at the top right of the screen and then tap 3s or 10s for a 3- or 10-second delay.

7. Move the camera around until you find a pleasing image. You can do a couple of things at this point to help you take your photo:

- Tap the area of the grid where you want the camera to autofocus.

- Pinch the screen to display a digital zoom control. Drag the circle in the zoom bar to the right or left to zoom in or out on the image.

8. Tap the Capture button at the bottom center of the screen (the big, white button). You've just taken a picture, and it's stored in the Photos app gallery automatically.

 You can also use a Volume button (located on the left side of your iPhone) to capture a picture or start or stop video camera recording.

9. Tap the Switch Camera button in the top-right corner to switch between the front camera and rear camera. You can then take selfies (pictures of yourself), so go ahead and tap the Capture button to take another picture.

10. To view the last photo taken, swipe to the left or tap the thumbnail of the latest image in the bottom-left corner of the screen; the Photos app opens and displays the photo.

11. Tap the Share button (it's the box with an arrow coming out of it, located in the bottom-left corner of the screen) to display a menu that allows you to AirDrop, email, or instant message the photo, assign it to a contact, use it as iPhone wallpaper, tweet it, post it to Facebook, share via iCloud Photo Sharing or Flickr, or print it (see **Figure 16-2**).

12. You can tap images at the top to select more than one. To delete the image, have it displayed and tap the Trash button in the bottom-right corner of the screen.

13. Tap Delete Photo in the confirming menu that appears.

 To go to the camera with the lock screen displayed, swipe the Camera icon up to go directly to the Camera app.

Figure 16-2

 You can use the Photo Sharing feature to automatically sync your photos across various devices. Turn on Photo Sharing by tapping Settings on the Home screen and then tapping Photos & Camera.

Save Photos from the Web

1. The web offers a wealth of images that you can download to your Photo Library. Open Safari and navigate to the web page containing the image you want.

2. Press and hold the image. A menu appears, as shown in **Figure 16-3.**

Tap this option

Figure 16-3

3. Tap Save Image. The image is saved to your Recently Added album in the Photos app, as shown in **Figure 16-4**.

Figure 16-4

For more about how to use Safari to navigate to or search for web content, see Chapter 10.

 A number of sites protect their photos from being copied by applying an invisible overlay. This blank overlay image ensures that you don't actually get the image you're tapping. Even if a site doesn't take these precautions, be sure that you don't save images from the web and use them in ways that violate the rights of the person or entity that owns them.

 If you want to capture your iPhone screen, the process is simple. Press the Sleep/Wake button and Home button simultaneously. The screen capture is saved in PNG format to your Recently Added album. To save a picture sent as an email attachment in Mail, tap the attachment icon and the picture opens. Press the screen until a menu appears and then tap Save.

View an Album

1. The Photos app organizes your pictures into albums, using such criteria as the folder or album on your computer from which you synced the photos or photos captured using the iPhone camera (saved in the Recently Added folder). You may also have albums for images that you synced from other devices through iTunes or shared via Photos. To view your albums, start by tapping the Photos app icon on the Home screen.

2. Tap the Albums button at the bottom of the screen to display your albums, as shown in **Figure 16-5**.

3. Tap an album. The photos in it are displayed.

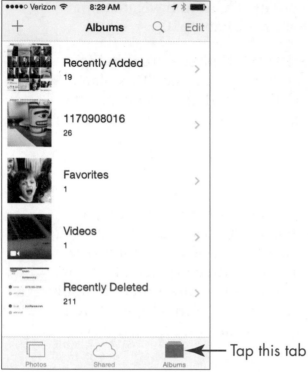

Figure 16-5

View Individual Photos

1. Tap the Photos app icon on the Home screen.

2. Tap Albums (refer to Figure 16-5).

3. Tap an album to open it; then, to view a photo, tap it. The picture expands, as shown in **Figure 16-6.**

4. Flick your finger to the left or right to scroll through the album to look at the individual photos in it.

5. You can tap the Back button and then the Albums button to return to the Album view.

Figure 16-6

> With the new 3D Touch feature, you can preview a photo before you open it. Tap lightly to select the photo. Tap with a medium press to display a preview, and then press harder to open the photo.

> You can place a photo on a person's information record in Contacts. For more about how to do this, see Chapter 5.

> You can associate photos with faces and events. When you do, additional tabs appear at the bottom of the screen when you display an album containing that type of photo.

Edit Photos

1. iPhone Photos isn't Photoshop, but it does provide you with some tools for editing photos. Tap the Photos app on the Home screen to open it.

2. Using methods previously described in this chapter, locate and display a photo you want to edit.

3. Tap the Edit button; the Edit Photo screen shown in **Figure 16-7** appears.

Crop

Filters

Adjustments

Figure 16-7

4. At this point, you can take three possible actions with these tools:

   • **Crop:** To crop the photo to a portion of its original area, tap the Crop button. You can then tap any corner of the image and drag inward or outward to remove areas of the photo. Tap Crop and then Save to apply your changes.

- **Filters:** Apply any of nine filters such as Fade, Mono, or Noir to change the feel of your image. These effects adjust the brightness of your image or apply a black-and-white tone to your color photos. Tap the Filters button in the middle of the tools at the bottom of the screen and scroll to view available filters. Tap one and then tap Apply to apply the effect to your image.

- **Adjustments:** Tap Light, Color, or B&W to access a slew of tools that you can use to tweak contrast, color intensity, shadows, and more.

5. If you're pleased with your edits, tap the Done button, and a copy of the edited photo is saved.

 Each of the editing features has a Cancel button. If you don't like the changes you made, tap this button to stop making changes before you save the image.

Organize Photos

1. If you want to create your own album, display an album.

2. Tap the Select button in the top-right corner and then tap individual photos to select them. Small check marks appear on the selected photos (see **Figure 16-8**).

3. Tap the Add To button and then tap New Album. (*Note:* If you've already created albums, you can choose to add the photo to an existing album at this point.)

4. Enter a name for a new album and then tap Save. If you create a new album, it appears in the Photos main screen with the other albums that are displayed.

 You can also choose the Share or Delete buttons when you've selected photos in Step 2 of this task. This allows you to share or delete multiple photos at a time.

Check marks indicate
selected photos

Figure 16-8

View Photos by Years and Location

1. You can view your photos in logical categories such as by date or a location where they were taken. These so-called smart groupings let you, for example, view all photos taken this year or all the photos from your summer vacation. Tap Photos on the Home screen to open the Photos app.

2. Tap Photos at the bottom of the screen. The display of photos by date appears (see **Figure 16-9**).

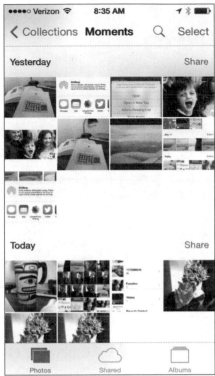

Figure 16-9

3. Tap Collections in the top-left corner; you see collections of photos by location and date (see **Figure 16-10**).

4. Tap a collection and you can view the individual "moments" in that collection broken down day by day.

 To go back to larger groupings, such as from a moment in a collection to the larger collection to the entire last year, just keep tapping the Back button at the top left of the screen (which will be named after the next collection up in the grouping hierarchy, such as Collections or Years).

Figure 16-10

Share Photos with Mail, Twitter, or Facebook

1. You can easily share photos stored on your iPhone by sending them as email attachments, as a text message, by posting them to Facebook, sharing them via iCloud Photo Sharing or Flickr, or as tweets on Twitter. (You have to go to Facebook or Twitter using a browser and set up an account on those services before you can use this feature.) Next, tap the Photos app icon on the Home screen.

2. Tap the Photos or Albums button and locate the photo you want to share.

3. Tap the photo to select it and then tap the Share button. (It looks like a box with an arrow jumping out of it.) The menu shown in **Figure 16-11** appears. Tap to select additional photos, if you like.

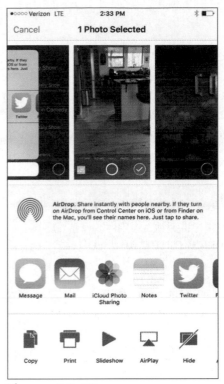

Figure 16-11

4. Tap the Mail, Message, Twitter, iCloud Photo Sharing, Facebook, or Flickr option.

5. In the message form that appears, make any modifications that apply in the To, Cc/Bcc, or Subject fields and then type a message for email, or enter your Facebook posting or Twitter tweet.

6. Tap the Send or Post button, and the message and photo are sent or posted.

 You can also copy and paste a photo into documents such as those created in the Pages word-processor application. To do this, tap a photo in Photos and tap Share. Tap the Copy command. In the destination application, press and hold the screen and tap Paste.

Share a Photo Using AirDrop

AirDrop, available to users of iPhone 5 and later, provides a way to share content such as photos with others who are nearby and who have an AirDrop-enabled device (more recent Macs that can run OS X Yosemite or later). Follow the steps in the previous task to locate a photo you want to share; after you've located that photo, follow these steps:

1. Tap the Share button.

2. If an AirDrop-enabled device is in your immediate vicinity (such as within 30 feet or so), you see the device listed (see **Figure 16-12**). Tap the device name and your photo is sent to the other device.

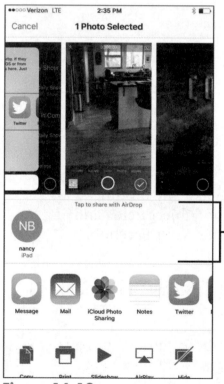

AirDrop-enabled devices within range

Figure 16-12

Note that the other device has to have AirDrop enabled. To enable AirDrop, open the Control Center (swipe up from the bottom of any screen) and tap AirDrop. Choose Contacts Only or Everyone to specify whom you can use AirDrop with.

Share Photos Using iCloud Photo Sharing

1. iCloud Photo Sharing allows you to automatically share photos from the Moments screen. Tap the Share button to the right of a moment and then choose to share the whole moment or selected photos.

2. In the Share screen that opens, tap to select the photos you want to share, and then tap iCloud Photo Sharing.

3. Enter a comment if you like (see **Figure 16-13**), and then tap Post. The photos or moment are posted to your iCloud Photo Library.

Figure 16-13

Work in iCloud Photo Library

1. iCloud Photo Library automatically backs up all your photos and videos to the cloud. Tap Settings, Photos & Camera and then tap the On button for iCloud Photo Library to post all your photos to this library in the cloud. If you want to automatically make photos available to your other devices from iCloud also tap Upload to My Photo Stream to turn the feature on.

2. Tap Home and then tap the Photos app to open it.

3. Go to iCloud.com using your browser, sign in, and click Photos to view all photos and videos stored in the iCloud Library.

 With all these photos available to you, you'll need to be able to search your library for the one you want. Tap the Search button at the top of the Photos screen. A list of so-called "smart" suggestions appears. Enter the date or time of the photo, a location, or an album name such as "Vacation" to locate the photo.

Print Photos

1. If you have a printer that's compatible with Apple's AirPrint technology, you can print photos. With Photos open, locate the photo you want to print and tap it to maximize it.

2. Tap the Share button, and on the menu that appears (refer to Figure 16-11), scroll in the bottom row of buttons to the far right and then tap Print.

3. In the Printer Options dialog that appears (see **Figure 16-14**), tap an available printer in the list or Select Printer. iPhone presents you with a list of any compatible wireless printers on your local network.

← Tap this option

Figure 16-14

4. Tap the plus or minus symbols in the Copy field to set the number of copies to print.

5. Tap the Print button, and your photo is sent to the printer.

Run a Slideshow

1. You can run a slideshow of your images in Photos and even play music and choose transition effects for the show. Tap the Photos app on the Home screen.

2. Display an individual photo in an album that contains more than one photo.

3. Tap the Share button and then tap Slideshow to run the slideshow.

4. Tap the screen and then tap Options to see the Slideshow Options dialog, shown in **Figure 16-15**.

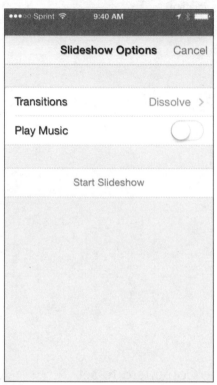

Figure 16-15

5. If you want to play music along with the slideshow, tap the Music and then tap a music selection in the list that appears (see **Figure 16-16**).

6. In the Slideshow Options dialog, tap Theme and then tap the transition effect that you want to use for your slideshow.

7. Tap Done and the slideshow plays with the music and theme you selected. Tap the screen to stop the slideshow at any time.

 To run a slideshow that includes only the photos contained in a particular album, tap the Albums tab, tap an album to open it, and then tap the Slideshow button to make settings and run a slideshow.

Figure 16-16

Delete Photos

1. You might find that it's time to get rid of some of those old photos of the family reunion or the last community center project. If the photos weren't transferred from your computer, but instead were taken, downloaded, or captured as screenshots on the iPhone, you can delete them. Tap the Photos app icon on the Home screen.

2. Tap the Albums or Photos tab and then, if you've opened the Albums tab, tap an album to open it.

3. Locate and tap on a photo that you want to delete and then tap the Trash icon. In the confirming dialog that appears, tap the Delete Photo button to finish the deletion.

 If you delete a photo in Photo Sharing, it is deleted on all devices that you shared it with.

Create Time-Lapse Videos from Photos

1. The Time Lapse feature of Camera appeared with iOS 8. Capturing photos with this feature allows you to create a time-lapse photo show. iPhone captures photos at select intervals, making the capture of a dynamic scene such as a sunset possible. Tap Camera on the Home screen.

2. Swipe the listing at the bottom of the screen until Time Lapse is centered over the Capture button (see **Figure 16-17**).

3. Tap the Capture button. Leave the camera recording as long as you like and then tap the End button. Your new time-lapse images appear in the bottom-left corner. Tap the image and then tap Play.

Figure 16-17

Getting the Most Out of Video Features

Chapter

17

*U*sing the Videos app, you can watch down-loaded movies or TV shows, as well as media that you've synced from iCloud or your Mac or PC.

In addition, iPhone 6s sports both a front and rear video camera that you can use to capture your own videos, and by downloading the iMovie app for iPhone (a more limited version of the longtime mainstay on Mac computers), you add the capability to edit those videos. The 4.7" Retina HD display on iPhone 6s and the 5.5" Retina HD display on iPhone 6s Plus offer even more pixels for better resolution than ever. A 12MP iSight camera can record high-definition video. With these latest models, you also get 4K video, which produces rich detail with 8 million pixels per frame. These two phones are, quite simply, two of the best phones ever for viewing and capturing images, both still and moving.

 A few other features of video in iPhone 6s and 6s Plus include image stabilization to avoid the shakes when recording, more frames shot per second for smoother video, and Cinematic Video Stabilization, which means that your iPhone continually autofocuses as you're recording.

In this chapter, I explain all about shooting and watching video content from a variety of sources. For practice, you might want to refer to Chapter 12 first to find out how to purchase or download one of many available TV shows or movies from the iTunes Store.

Capture Your Own Videos with the Built-In Cameras

The camera lens that comes on iPhone 6s and 6s Plus has perks for photographers, including a large aperture and highly accurate sensor, which make for better images all around. In addition, auto image stabilization makes up for any shakiness in the hands holding the phone, and autofocus has sped up thanks to the fast A9 processor chip. For videographers, you'll appreciate a fast frames-per-second capability as well as a slow-motion feature.

1. To capture a video, tap the Camera app on the Home screen. In iPhone, two video cameras are available for capturing video, one from the front and one from the back of the device. (See more about this topic in the next task.)

2. The Camera app opens (see **Figure 17-1**). Tap and slide the camera-type options above the red Record button to the right until Video rests above the button; this is how you switch from the still camera to the video camera.

3. If you want to switch between the front and back cameras, tap the Switch Camera button in the top-right corner of the screen (refer to Figure 17-1).

4. Tap the red Record button to begin recording the video. (The red dot in the middle of this button turns into a red square when the camera is recording.) When you're finished, tap the Record button again. Your new video is now listed in the bottom-left corner of the screen. Tap the video to play it, share it, or delete it. In the future, you can find and play the video in your Camera Roll when you open the Photos app.

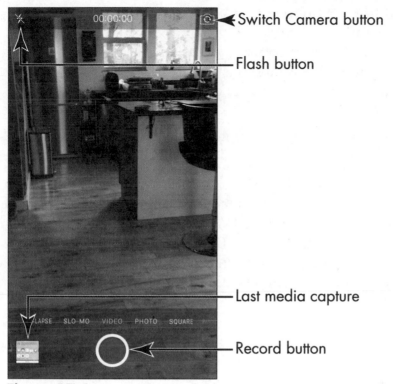

Switch Camera button

Flash button

Last media capture

Record button

Figure 17-1

 Before you start recording, remember where the camera lens is — while holding the iPhone and panning, you can easily put your fingers directly over the lens! Also, you can't pause your recording; when you stop, your video is saved, and when you start recording, you're creating a new video file.

Play Movies or TV Shows with Videos

1. When you first open the Videos app, you may see relatively blank screens with a note that you don't own any videos and a link to the iTunes Store. After you've purchased TV shows and movies or rented movies from the iTunes Store (see Chapter 12 to learn how) or other sources, you'll see tabs of the different kinds of content you own. Tap the Videos app icon on the Home screen to open the application.

If your iPhone is on the same Wi-Fi network as your computer and both are running iTunes, with the iPhone and iTunes set to use the same Home Sharing account, you see the Shared List. With this setup, you can stream videos from iTunes on your computer to your iPhone.

2. On a screen like the one shown in **Figure 17-2**, tap the appropriate category at the bottom of the screen (TV Shows or Movies, depending on the content you've downloaded) and then tap the video you want to watch. Information about the movie or TV show episodes appears, as shown in **Figure 17-3**. Details about TV Shows include Episodes, Details, and Related tabs; Movies contain Details, Chapters, and Related tabs.

Figure 17-2

Figure 17-3

3. For TV Shows, tap the Episodes tab to display episodes that you can tap to play; for Movies, the Play button appears no matter which tab is selected. Tap the Play button (see **Figure 17-4**) and the movie or TV show begins playing. (If you see a small, cloud-shaped icon instead of a Play button, tap it and the content is downloaded from iCloud.) Note that the progress of the playback is displayed on the Progress bar showing how many minutes you've viewed and how many remain. If you don't see the bar, tap the screen once to display it briefly, along with a set of playback tools at the bottom of the screen.

Figure 17-4

4. With the playback tools displayed, take any of these actions:

- Tap the Pause button to pause playback.

- Tap either Go to Previous Chapter or Go to Next Chapter to move to a different location in the video playback. Note that if a video has chapter support, another button appears here for displaying all chapters so that you can move more easily from one to another.

- Tap the circular button on the Volume slider and drag the button left or right to decrease or increase the volume, respectively.

5. To stop the video and return to the information screen, tap the Done button to the left of the Progress bar.

Note that if you've watched a video and stopped it partway, it opens by default to the last location that you were viewing. To start a video from the beginning, tap and drag the circular button (called the *playhead*) on the Progress bar all the way to the left.

 If your controls disappear during playback, just tap the screen and they'll reappear.

 If you download the free iTunes U app, you can access educational video content that you can play back using the Videos app.

Turn On Closed-Captioning

1. iTunes and iPhone offer support for closed-captioning and subtitles. If a movie has either closed-captioning or subtitles, you can turn on the feature in iPhone. Look for the CC logo on media that you download to use this feature; be aware that video you record won't have this capability. Begin by tapping the Settings icon on the Home screen.

2. Tap General ⇨ Accessibility. On the screen that appears, scroll down and tap Subtitles & Captioning.

3. On the menu that displays (see **Figure 17-5**), tap the Closed Captions + SDH switch to turn on the feature. Now when you play a movie with closed-captioning, you can tap the Audio and Subtitles button to the left of the playback controls to manage these features.

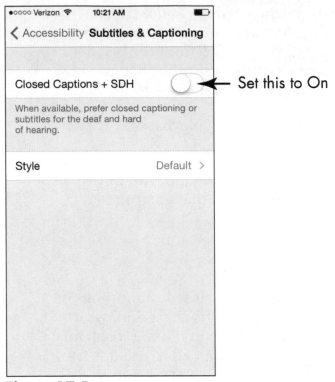

Figure 17-5

Delete a Video from the iPhone

You can buy videos directly from your iPhone, or you can sync via iCloud or iTunes to place content you've bought or created on another device on your iPhone.

When you want to get rid of video content on your iPhone because it's a memory hog, you can delete it by going to the Home screen and tapping Settings ⇨ General ⇨ Storage & iCloud Usage. Tap Manage Storage and then tap Videos to see a list of videos stored on your iPhone. Flick to the left over the video that you want to delete and then tap the Delete button that appears.

You can also delete a video by tapping the round X Delete button on a video thumbnail, or swiping on an episode and then tapping Delete. If you buy a video using iTunes and sync to download it to your iPhone and then delete it from your iPhone, it's still saved in your iTunes Library. You can sync your computer and iPhone again to download the video once more. Remember, however, that rented movies, once deleted, are gone with the wind. Also, video doesn't sync to iCloud as photos and music do.

 iPhone has a much smaller storage capacity than your typical computer, so downloading lots of TV shows or movies can fill its storage area quickly. If you don't want to view an item again, delete it to free space.

Let Others Know about Your Favorite Videos

1. You can share your opinion about a video using AirDrop, Mail, Message, Twitter, or Facebook. Tap the Videos app to open it and then tap the Store button. Find a video you want to share and tap it.

2. In the information screen shown in **Figure 17-6,** tap the Share button (a box with an arrow at the top of it at the top of the screen). Tap AirDrop, Mail, Message, Twitter, or Facebook to use one of these methods of sharing your enthusiasm for the item (see **Figure 17-7**). (You can also share the item as a reminder or note to yourself.)

3. In the corresponding form, enter a recipient in the To field and add to the message, if you like. If you chose to post to your Facebook page, enter your message in the Facebook form.

4. Tap the appropriate Send button to send your recommendation by your preferred method.

Share button

Figure 17-6

Figure 17-7

Playing Games

The iPhone is super for playing games, with its bright screen, portable size, and ability to rotate the screen as you play and track your motions. You can download game apps from the App Store and play them on your device. You can also use the preinstalled Game Center app to help you find and buy games, add friends to play against, share, and track scores.

In this chapter, you get an overview of game playing on your iPhone, including opening a Game Center account, adding a friend, purchasing and downloading games, and playing basic games solo or against friends.

 Of course, you can also download games from the App Store and play them on your iPhone without having to use Game Center. What Game Center provides is a place where you can create a gaming profile, add a list of gaming friends, keep track of and share your scores and perks, and shop for games (and only games) in the App Store, which includes listings of top-rated games and game categories to choose from.

Chapter 18

Get ready to . . .

Open an Account in Game Center

1. Using the Game Center app, you can search for and buy games, add friends with whom you can play those games, and keep records of your scores for posterity. From the Home screen (possibly the second Home screen if you have the smaller iPhone), tap the Game Center icon. If you've never used Game Center, you're asked whether to allow *push notifications.* If you want to receive these notices, which alert you that your friends want to play a game with you, tap OK. You should, however, be aware that push notifications can drain your iPhone's battery.

2. On the Game Center opening screen, you're asked to sign in (see **Figure 18-1**). If you want to use Game Center with another Apple ID, tap Create New Apple ID and follow the onscreen instructions, which ask you to enter your birthdate, agree to terms, choose a security question and so forth; or enter your current account information and tap the Go button. If you're signing in for the first time, you see a series of prompts asking for items like a gaming nickname or whether you want your gaming profile to be public or private.

3. The screen that appears after you've signed in shows games you've downloaded, requests from other players, friends, and so on (see **Figure 18-2**). You can tap any of the floating balloons to get to these categories, or tap a button along the bottom of the screen.

 When you first register for Game Center, if you use an email address other than the one associated with your Apple ID, you may have to create a new Apple ID and verify it by responding to an email message that's sent to your email address. See Chapter 3 for more about creating an Apple ID when opening an iTunes account.

Figure 18-1

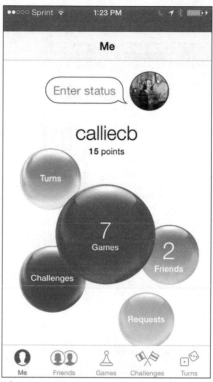

Figure 18-2

Create a Profile

1. When you have an account with which you can sign in to Game Center, you're ready to specify some account settings. On the Home screen, tap Settings.

2. Tap Game Center, and in the dialog that appears (see **Figure 18-3**), if you don't want other players to be able to invite you to play games when Game Center is open, tap the Allow Invites switch to turn off the feature.

3. Tap the account name under Game Center Profile and sign in to the account, if requested to do so.

Allow Invites option

Figure 18-3

4. At this point, depending on what you set up when you first signed into Game Center, you may be prompted to specify some settings. If you want your friends to be able to send you requests for playing games via email, check to see whether the Primary email address listed on this screen is the one you want them to use (see **Figure 18-4**). If not, tap Add Another Email and enter another email address.

5. In the Nickname field, enter the handle that you want to be known by when playing games.

Primary email address

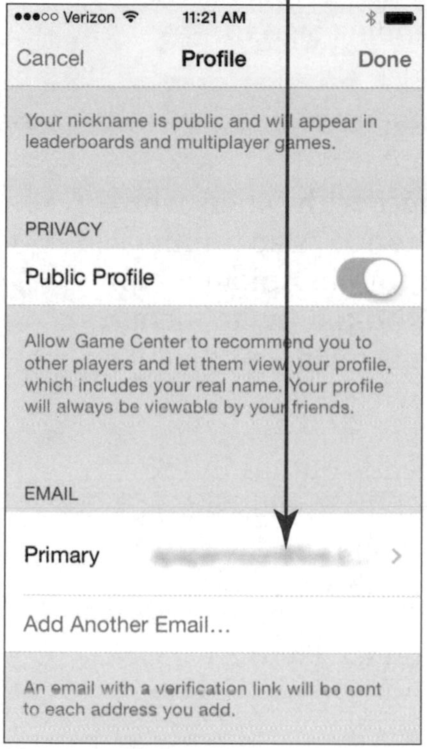

Figure 18-4

6. If you want others to see your profile, including your real name, tap the Public Profile switch to turn on Public Profile (refer to Figure 18-4).

7. Tap Done when you're finished with the settings and then tap Game Center on the Home screen. You return to the Game Center Home screen, already signed in to your account with information displayed about friends, games, and gaming achievements (all at zero, initially).

After you create an account and a profile, whenever you go to Game Center, you log in by entering your email address and password and then tapping Sign In.

Add Friends

1. If you want to play Game Center games with others who have an Apple ID and an iPad, iPod touch, Mac running Mountain Lion, Mavericks, Yosemite, or El Capitan, or an iPhone, add them as friends so that you can invite them to play. From the Game Center Home screen, tap the Friends button at the bottom of the screen.

2. On the Friends page, tap the Add Friends button in the top-right corner (the button is shaped like a plus sign). Note that you also have the option of tapping the Requests button and tapping Add Friends from there.

3. Enter an email address in the To field (see **Figure 18-5**) and edit the invitation, if you like.

4. Tap the Send button. After your friend accepts your invitation, his or her name is listed on the Friends screen.

 Game Center contains a Friend Recommendations feature. Tap the Friends tab and then tap the A-Z button in the top-left corner. A Recommendations section appears below the list of your current friends. These are people who play the same or similar games, so if you like, try adding one or two as friends. You can tap the Points tab to view the points these folks have accumulated so that you can stay in your league.

 You will probably also receive requests from friends who know you're on Game Center. When you get one of these email invitations, be sure that you know the person sending it before you accept; otherwise, you could be enabling a stranger to communicate with you.

Enter address here

Figure 18-5

 Although a few games have versions for both Mac and iOS users, the majority are either Mac-OS X-version only or iOS-version only — something to be aware of when you buy games.

Purchase and Download Games

1. Time to get some games to play! Open Game Center and sign in to your account.

2. Tap the Games button at the bottom of the screen, and under the Recommended category, tap Show More.

3. Scroll through the list of games that appears and tap one that appeals to you to display details about achievements and players (see **Figure 18-6**) and then tap the price button (or Get button for a free game).

Details tab

Figure 18-6

4. Note that you can tap the Store button from here to go to the iTunes Store to view more games. To buy a game, tap the button labeled with either the word *Get* or the price (such as $1.99). Then tap the button again, which is now labeled Buy if it has a price or Install if it's free.

5. A dialog appears, asking for your Apple ID and password. Enter these and tap OK.

6. Another dialog appears, asking you to sign in. Follow the instructions on the next couple of screens to enter your password and verify your payment information if this is the first time you've signed in to your account from this device.

7. When the confirmation dialog appears, tap Buy or Install. The game downloads. Tap the Open button to go to the downloaded game.

 If you've added friends to your account, you can go to the Friends screen and view games that your friends have downloaded. To purchase one of these games, just tap it in your friend's list and, at the top of the screen that appears, tap the button labeled with the game's price.

Master iPhone Game-Playing Basics

It's almost time to start playing games, but first let me give you an idea of iPhone's gaming strengths. For many reasons, iPhone is a good, smaller-screen gaming device because of the following strengths:

➡ **Fantastic-looking screen:** First, the iPhone screen offers bright colors for great gaming. In-Plane Switching (IPS) technology lets you hold your iPhone at almost any angle (it has a 178-degree viewing angle) and still see good color and contrast.

➡ **Faster processor:** The super-fast A9 processor chip in your iPhone 6s or 6s Plus is ideal for gaming.

➡ **Long battery life:** A device's long battery life (24 hours of talk with iPhone 6s and 14 with iPhone 6s Plus) means that you can tap energy from it for many hours of gaming fun.

➡ **Specialized game-playing features:** Some newer games have features that take full advantage of the iPhone's capabilities. For example, *Nova* (from Gameloft) features Multiple Target Acquisition, which lets you to target multiple bad guys in a single move to blow them out of the water with one shot. In *Real Racing Game* (Firemint), for example, you can look in your rearview mirror as you're racing to see what's coming up behind you, a feature made possible by the iPhone's large screen.

➡ **The M9 coprocessor:** iPhone contains a motion-detecting coprocessor that can interpret data from a sensor about your motion when walking or driving. Look for game and fitness app designers to begin to take advantage of that capability in the near future.

➡ **Great sound:** The built-in iPhone speaker is a powerful little item, but if you want an experience that's even more up close and personal, you can plug in a headphone, some speaker systems, or a microphone using the built-in jack.

In addition to the M9 motion coprocessor, most later iPhone models using iOS 8 or later have a built-in motion sensor — the *three-axis accelerometer* — as well as a gyroscope. These features provide lots of fun for people developing apps for the iPhone because they make the automatically rotating screen part of the gaming experience for you to enjoy. For example, a built-in compass reorients itself automatically as you switch your iPhone from landscape to portrait orientation. In some racing games, you can grab the iPhone as though it were a steering wheel and rotate the device to simulate the driving experience.

Play Against Yourself

Many games allow you to play a game all on your own. Each has different rules and goals, so you'll have to study a game's instructions and Help to learn how to play it, but here's some general information about these types of games:

⟶ Often, a game can be played in two modes: with others or in a *solitaire version*, in which you play yourself or the computer.

⟶ Many games you may be familiar with in the offline world, such as *Carcassonne* or *Scrabble*, have online versions. For these, you already know the rules of play, so you simply need to figure out the execution. For example, in the online *Carcassonne* game, you tap to place a tile on the board, tap the placed tile to rotate it, and tap the check mark to complete your turn and reveal another tile.

⟶ All the games you play on your own record your scores in Game Center so that you can track your progress.

Challenge Friends in Game Center

1. After you have added a friend and both of you have downloaded the same games, you can challenge your friends to beat your scores. Tap the Game Center app icon on the Home screen and sign in, if necessary.

2. Tap Friends. The Friends page (see **Figure 18-7**) appears.

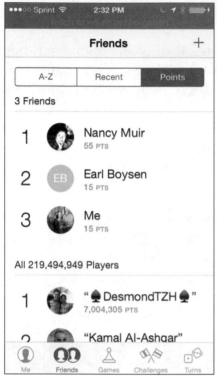

Figure 18-7

3. Tap the name of the friend you want to challenge.

4. Tap the Game bubble and then tap the name of a game you have in common.

5. Tap the Achievements tab for your friend and then tap one of her achievements. On the screen that appears (see **Figure 18-8**), tap Send Challenge.

6. At this point, some games offer you an invitation to fill out with a message and send to the friend. If you do that, wait for your friend to respond, which he can do by tapping Accept or Decline on his device.

Figure 18-8

Finding Your Way with Maps

19

The Maps app has lots of useful functions. You can find directions with suggested alternative routes from one location to another. You can bookmark locations to return to them again. And the Maps app lets you get information about locations, such as phone numbers and web links to businesses. You can even add a location to your Contacts list or share a location link with your buddy using Mail, Messages, Twitter, or Facebook. New with iOS 9 comes the Nearby feature to explore local attractions and businesses, and the Transit view for public transit maps for select cities around the world.

You're about to have some fun exploring Maps in this chapter.

Get ready to . . .

➡ Go to Your Current
    Location 338

➡ Change Views 339

➡ Zoom In and Out 342

➡ Go to Another Location
    or a Favorite 343

➡ Drop a Pin 345

➡ Find Directions 346

➡ View Information about
    a Location 349

➡ Add a Location to a
    New Contact 351

➡ Share Location
    Information 352

➡ Get Turn-by-Turn
    Navigation Help 353

➡ Find Local Places with
    Nearby 354

Go to Your Current Location

1. iPhone can figure out where you are at any time and display your current location. From the Home screen, tap
   the Maps icon. Tap the Current Location button (the
   small arrow in the bottom-left corner; see **Figure 19-1**).

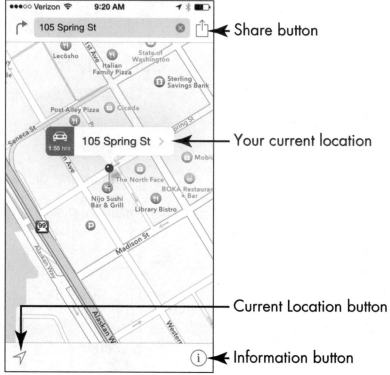

Figure 19-1

2. A map is displayed with your current location indicated
   (refer to Figure 19-1). Depending on your connection,
   Wi-Fi or 3G/4G (sometimes noted as LTE in Maps), a
   pulsating circle may appear around the pin, indicating
   the area surrounding your location is based on cell tower
   triangulation. Your exact location can be anywhere
   within the area of the circle, and the location service is
   likely to be less accurate using a Wi-Fi connection than
   your phone's 3G or 4G connection.

3. Double-tap the screen to zoom in on your location. (Additional methods of zooming in and out are covered in the "Zoom In and Out" task, later in this chapter.)

 As mentioned previously, if you access maps via a Wi-Fi connection, your current location is a rough estimate based on a triangulation method. By using your 3G or 4G data connection, you access the global positioning system (GPS), which can more accurately pinpoint where you are. Still, if you type a starting location and an ending location to get directions, you can get pretty accurate results even with a Wi-Fi–connected iPhone.

Change Views

1. The Maps app offers three views: Standard, Satellite, and Transit. iPhone displays the Standard view (see the top-left image in **Figure 19-2**) by default the first time you open Maps. To change views, with Maps open, tap the Information button in the bottom right of the screen (refer to Figure 19-1) to reveal the Maps menu, shown in **Figure 19-3**.

2. Tap the Satellite tab. The Satellite view (refer to the top-right image in Figure 19-2) appears.

3. Tap the Information button to reveal the menu again and then tap the Transit tab (refer to the bottom image in Figure 19-2). In Transit view, if you have a major city for which Transit information is available, you'll see data about public transit.

 You can also tap Show Labels to show street names superimposed on any map.

4. Finally, you can display a 3D effect on any view by tapping the Show 3D map option in the Maps menu.

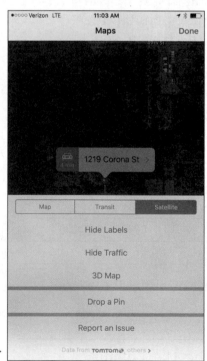

Figure 19-2

Figure 19-3

 On the Maps menu, you can also access a Traffic overlay feature. If you live in a large metropolitan area (this feature doesn't really work in small towns or rural settings), turn on this feature by tapping the Show Traffic option in the Maps menu. To help you navigate your rush-hour commute or trip to the mall, the traffic overlay shows red dashes on roads, indicating accidents or road closures; yellow dashes indicate traffic slowdowns.

 You can drop a pin to mark a location on a map that you can then return to. See the task "Drop a Pin," later in this chapter, for more about this topic.

 To print any displayed map to an AirPrint-compatible wireless printer, just tap the Share button on the Maps main screen and tap Print on the Sharing screen that appears.

Zoom In and Out

1. You'll appreciate the Zoom feature because it gives you the capability to zoom in and out to see more or less detailed maps and to move around a displayed map. With a map displayed, double-tap with a single finger to zoom in (see **Figure 19-4**; the image on the left shows the map before zooming in, and the image on the right shows the map after zooming).

Figure 19-4

2. Double-tap with two fingers to zoom out, revealing less detail.

3. Place two fingers positioned together on the screen and move them apart to zoom in.

4. Place two fingers apart on the screen and then pinch them together to zoom out.

5. Press your finger to the screen and drag the map in any direction to move to an adjacent area.

 It can take a few moments for the map to redraw itself when you enlarge, reduce, or move around it, so be patient. Areas that are being redrawn look like blank grids but are filled in eventually. Also, if you're in Satellite view, zooming in may take some time; wait it out because the blurred image resolves itself.

Go to Another Location or a Favorite

1. With Maps open, tap in the Search field (see **Figure 19-5**); the keyboard opens. If you have displayed directions for a route, you won't see the Search field in the top of the screen; you may have to tap the Clear button on a directions screen to get back to the Search field.

Search field

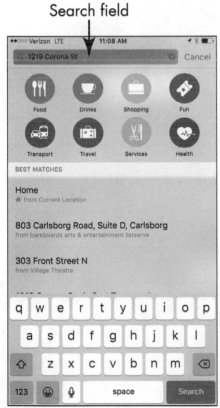

Figure 19-5

2. Type a location, using a street address with city and state, a stored contact name, or a destination such as *Empire State Building* or *Detroit airport*. Maps may make suggestions as you type if it finds any logical matches. Tap the result you prefer. The location appears with a red pin inserted in it and an information bar with the location name with a Directions button to the left and an arrow to the right (see **Figure 19-6**). Tap the arrow, and more information is displayed. In some cases, the Street View icon is also displayed. Note that if several locations match your search term, several pins may be displayed in a suggestions list.

Directions button   Information bar

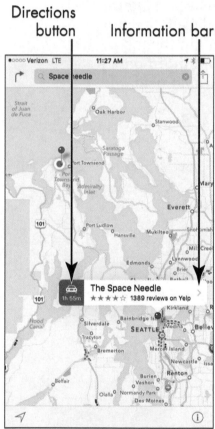

Figure 19-6

When you start a search, icons for nearby businesses appear. This Nearby feature is new in iOS 9. Find out more about using it in the last section of this chapter, "Find Local Places with Nearby."

3. Tap Map in the top-left corner, and you move back to the map where you can tap the screen and drag in any direction to move to a nearby location.

4. Tap the Share button (the symbol to the right of the Search field; refer to Figure 19-6), and then tap Add to Favorites. Tap Save in the screen that appears (modifying the location name first, if you like), and the location is saved to Favorites. Now when you tap in the Maps Search field, Favorites is the first result. Tap on Favorites to view and go to a favorite site.

5. To delete a location from Favorites, with Favorites displayed tap Edit, tap the red circle to the left of any item, and then tap Delete.

 You can use the new 3D Touch feature with an iPhone 6s or 6s Plus to preview the map associated with a location. For example, if there is an address noted in an iMessage text, you can press it with medium force and preview the map of that location or press it harder to display the map.

Drop a Pin

1. Pins are markers: A green pin marks a start location, a red pin marks a search result, and a blue pin (referred to as the *blue marker*) marks your iPhone's current location. If you drop a pin yourself, it appears in a lovely purple. Display a map that contains a spot where you want to drop a pin to help you find directions to or from that site.

2. If you need to, you can zoom in to a more detailed map to see a better view of the location you want to pin.

3. Press and hold your finger on the screen at the location where you want to place the pin. The pin appears, together with an information bar (refer to Figure 19-6).

4. Tap the arrow on the information bar to display details about the pin location (see **Figure 19-7**).

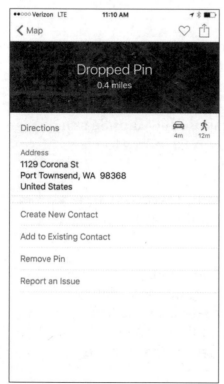

Figure 19-7

 If a location has associated reviews on sites, such as the restaurant and travel review site Yelp (www.yelp.com), you can display details about the location and scroll down to read the reviews.

Find Directions

1. You can get directions in a couple of different ways. With at least one pin on your map in addition to your current location or a dropped pin, tap the Directions button in the top-left corner (an arrow bending to the right). A line appears, showing the route between your current location and the closest pin (see **Figure 19-8**). Tap Clear to return to the Maps main screen.

Line indicating your route

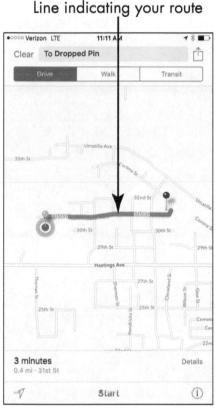

Figure 19-8

2. You can also enter two locations to get directions from one to the other. Clear any previous search and then tap the Directions button in Maps and then tap in the Start field (see **Figure 19-9**). The keyboard appears along with an End field.

3. Enter a different starting location.

4. Tap in the End field and enter a destination location. If you like, you can tap the Walk or Public Transit buttons to get walking or bus/train routes rather than driving

directions. Tap the Route button on the keyboard. The route between the two locations is displayed.

Start field

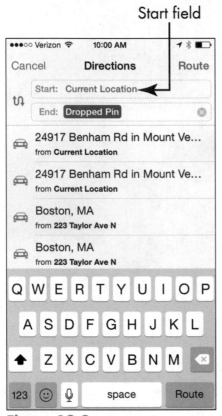

Figure 19-9

5. When a route is displayed, a bar appears along the bottom of the Maps screen (refer to Figure 19-8) with information about the distance and time it takes to travel between the two locations. Here's what you can do at this point:

- Tap the Details button (it's the icon at the bottom of the screen that looks like a numbered list) to display written directions.

- Tap Start (see **Figure 19-10**) to begin turn-by-turn direction narration.

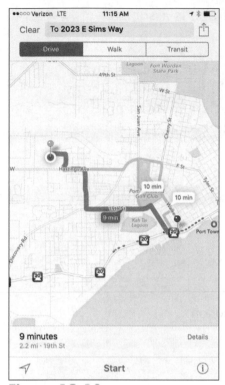

Figure 19-10

6. If there are alternative routes, Maps notes the number of such routes in the Directions informational display and shows the routes on the map. Tap a route number to make it the active route.

View Information about a Location

1. You display the Information dialog for locations to get directions in previous tasks. In this task, you focus on the useful information displayed there. Go to a location and tap the pin.

2. On the information bar that appears above the pinned location, tap the arrow (refer to Figure 19-6).

3. In the Information dialog (refer to Figure 19-7), tap the web address listed in the Homepage field, which you can use to go the location's web page, if one is associated with it.

4. You can also press and hold either the Phone or Address field and use the Copy button (see **Figure 19-11**) to copy the phone number, for example, so that you can place it in a Notes document for future reference.

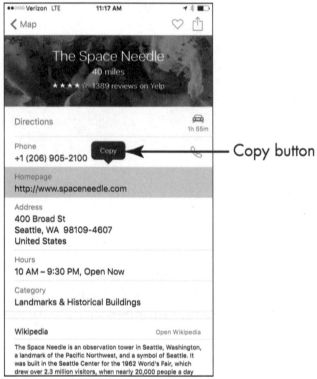

Figure 19-11

5. Tap the Map button in the top-left corner to return to the map view.

 Rather than copy and paste information, you can easily save all information about a location in your Contacts address book. See the next task, "Add a Location to a New Contact," to find out how it's done.

New to iOS 9 is the ability to share a map with the Notes app, which places the current map in a new note. Just tap the Share button and select Notes from the list of options.

Add a Location to a New Contact

1. Tap a pin to display the information bar.

2. Tap the arrow.

3. In the Information dialog that appears, scroll down and then tap Create New Contact or Add to Existing Contact.

4. The New Contact dialog appears (see **Figure 19-12**). (Note that if you choose Add to an Existing Contact here, you can choose a contact from your Contacts list to add the location information to.)

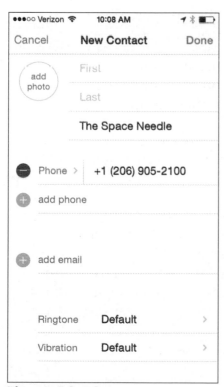

Figure 19-12

5. Whatever information was available about the location has already been entered. Enter any additional information you need, such as a name, phone number, or email address.

6. Tap Done. The information is stored in your Contacts address book.

Share Location Information

1. Tap a pin to display the information bar.

2. Tap the arrow to display more information.

3. In the Information dialog that appears, tap Share in the upper-right corner. In the dialog that appears (see **Figure 19-13**), you can choose to share via AirDrop, text message, Mail, Twitter, or Facebook. New with iOS 9, you also have the ability to share to a Note or Reminder. Tap Mail to see how this option works.

4. On the form that appears, use the onscreen keyboard to enter a recipient's information. (If you're using Facebook or Twitter, you enter recipient information as appropriate to the service you choose to use.)

5. Tap Send. A link to the location information in Maps is sent to your designated recipients.

 If you choose Twitter or Facebook in Step 3, you must have already installed and set up the Twitter or Facebook app and have a Twitter or Facebook account set up using iPhone Settings before sharing Maps content using those services. You also must have an account with these services to use them to share content.

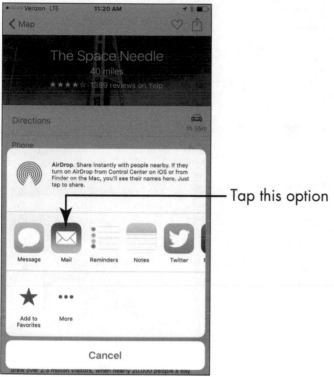

Tap this option

Figure 19-13

Get Turn-by-Turn Navigation Help

1. When you enter directions for a route and display that route (refer to Figure 19-10), you can then begin listening to turn-by-turn navigation instructions that can be helpful as you're driving. Tap the Start button at the bottom of the screen.

2. The narration begins and, in landscape mode, text instructions are displayed (tap Details to display this text from portrait orientation). Continue driving according to the route until the next instruction is spoken.

3. For an overview of your route (as shown in **Figure 19-14**), at any time you can tap the screen and then tap the Overview button that appears in the upper-right corner.

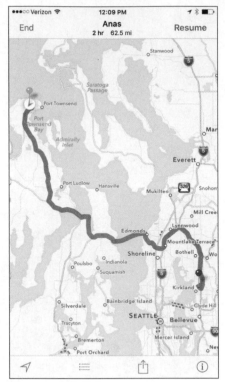

Figure 19-14

 To adjust the volume of the spoken navigation aid, tap Settings on the iPhone Home screen, tap Maps, and then adjust the Navigation Voice Volume settings to No Voice, Low Volume, Normal Volume, or Loud Volume.

 To change route information from miles to kilometers, go to Settings, tap Maps, and tap In Kilometers to change the setting.

Find Local Places with Nearby

1. As you can see in **Figure 19-15,** when you perform a search, a row of buttons is displayed across the top of the results. These take you to Nearby results; that is, businesses and services that are near your current location. Begin a search and tap one of these buttons, such as Fast Food.

2. Results for the Food category are shown in Figure 19-15.
These results offer additional buttons that help you narrow the type of food you're looking for, as well as a list
of nearby restaurants. Tap an item in the list. A map of
all results in that category, including an information bar
for the item you selected, is displayed, as shown in
Figure 19-16.

3. Tap the information bar for the location you selected to
display more information about it.

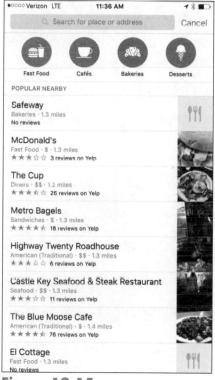

Figure 19-15

Figure 19-16

Part V
Managing Your Life and Your iPhone

Visit www.dummies.com/extras/iphoneforseniors for information about working with the Stocks app.

Getting in Step with Health

Health is an app that arrived with iOS 8. Health is one of the apps you can access from the first Home screen on your iPhone. Essentially, Health is an aggregator for health and fitness data. You can input information about your height, weight, medications, nutrition, sleep quality, and more. You can then view exercise tracking based on that data in the Dashboard view.

In this chapter, I provide an overview of the Health app and how to get information into and out of it. I also give you a glimpse at some of the possible apps and health equipment that are slated to interact with Health to make it even more useful in months and years to come.

Get an Overview of the Health App

This has to be said right up front: Health is not ready for prime time. Although there are some apps and even equipment such as blood-pressure monitors that can connect with Health today, many more are under development.

That means that, at this point, you can mainly input data about your health and fitness manually and view exercise tracking information by displaying charts on the Dashboard or by viewing tables.

Health is divided into categories such as fitness, lab results, medication, nutrition, and sleep. When you tap the Health Data tab at the bottom of the Health Dashboard screen (see **Figure 20-1**), you see the categories listed in **Figure 20-2**. Each of these categories can have subtopics contained within it that you reach by tapping a main topic, such as Fitness.

The Health app also has a medical record feature called Medical ID, which is covered in the next task.

Health Data tab

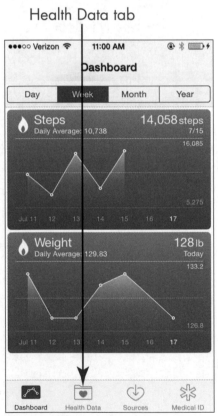

Figure 20-1

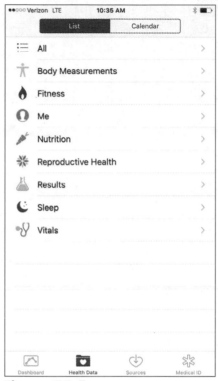

Figure 20-2

Use Medical ID

One of the simplest and easiest to use features is Medical ID, which allows you to store your vital statistics. This could be useful if you're in an accident and emergency medical personnel need to access information about your blood type or allergies to medications, for example.

1. In the Health app, tap the Medical ID tab in the lower-right corner. You see an introduction to Medical ID.

2. Tap Create Medical ID.

3. In the screen that appears, tap Edit to display the screen shown in **Figure 20-3**). For items with a + sign surrounded by a green circle, tap the Add button to add a field.

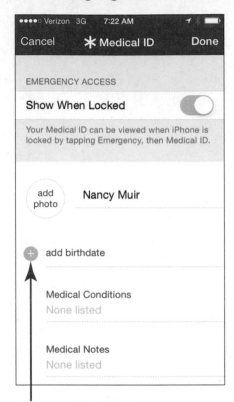

Tap to add a field

Figure 20-3

4. For example, you might tap Add Birthdate. When the screen in **Figure 20-4** appears, use the scrolling columns that appear at the bottom of the screen to set a birth date; for example, use your finger to scroll up and down on the month field till you find your birth month; then do the same thing to the day and year columns until your birth date is set.

5. Tap a field such as Medical Conditions to enter information using the onscreen keyboard that appears.

6. You can tap Edit to add more fields or edit existing fields, or tap Done to save your entries.

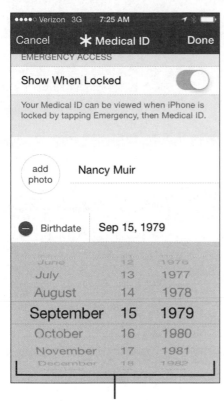

Scroll these columns
Figure 20-4

 On the Medical ID screen of Health is a note saying that if you choose to set the Show When Locked switch to On, emergency medical information will be available on the lock screen.

Discover How to Input Data

1. Because most entry of data in the Health app at this time is manual, knowing how to enter data is important. Tap the Health Data tab.

2. Tap a category such as Fitness.

3. Tap one of the subtopics shown in **Figure 20-5**, such as Flights Climbed.

Tap a subtopic

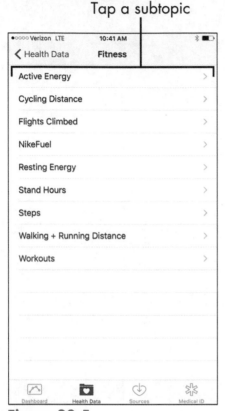

Figure 20-5

4. On the screen shown in **Figure 20-6,** tap Add Data Point.

5. Enter data using the onscreen keypad.

6. Tap Add.

7. Tap Show All Data (refer to Figure 20-6) to see a table of entries, including your most recent entry.

If you go into the Fitness category in Health, you see an item named Steps, a steps counter built into Health that can replace any third-party pedometer app. If you're a walker or runner, be sure the Show On Dashboard item for Steps is turned to On to enable this pedometer feature.

Tap this to see data
you've entered

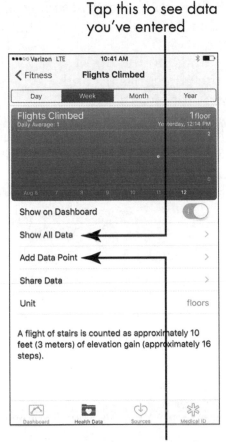

Tap this to enter data

Figure 20-6

Import and Export Data

Developers just began to create or modify apps to work with Health a year or so ago. Some apps from which you can import data are MyFitnessPal, Strava, and LifeSum. Different apps may send or receive data from Health using different interfaces and commands. But, in essence, here's how it works.

When you use an app that supports Health, those apps will request permission to update data. For example, a pedometer or activity tracker app might be able to upload data to Health, saving you the drudgery of manual entry. You can tap the Sources tab in Health to view supporting apps that you've downloaded and installed to your iPhone.

 To find apps that work with Health, go to the App Store. Open Health & Fitness in the Categories list and scroll down until you find the Apps for Health section.

In addition, you'll eventually be able to export data using apps such as Patient from the Mayo Clinic (see **Figure 20-7**) so that you can keep your physician informed about your progress or challenges.

Figure 20-7

Explore Apps Health Can Work With

Health is essentially an information aggregator, and it is continuing to grow in terms of available apps that are designed to interact with it to supply imported data such as calories consumed and steps walked. Here are some of the apps available today that work with the Health app:

➡ **Patient app by Mayo:** This app (refer to Figure 20-7) allows you to manage doctor appointments, get test results, and read the latest medical news. Apple has been working with the Mayo Clinic to add support for the Health app.

➡ **MyChart app by Epic:** This app is very similar to Patient by Mayo, allowing you to handle appointments, get test results, and so on. This app is available in the App Store today but might take a while to become a full-fledged support tool for Health.

➡ **Nike+ apps by Nike:** Several Nike apps, such as Running, take advantage of iPhone and iPad's built-in accelerometer that allows the devices to handle and track movements. Track a variety of activities via Nike+ apps and integrate the data into Health.

➡ **Fitbit by Fitbit, Inc.:** FitBit wristbands measure activity, sleep, and calories. They have an app that works on the iPad and iPhone, which they are likely to connect to Health.

➡ **CARROT Hunger by Grailr, LLC:** This talking calorie counter app helps you monitor the food you eat every day.

➡ **Human by Human:** This great activity and calorie consumption app helps you keep on top of the balance of energy absorbed and expended.

Understand What Equipment Connects with Health

Health is designed to connect with a variety of equipment to import data about your health and fitness. For example, LEConnect currently has treadmills that can send data on your gym accomplishments.

Withings produces a wireless blood pressure monitor and weight scales that support iPhone apps. Omron also produces a blood-pressure monitor that can supply data wirelessly.

Glucose monitors are another likely piece of equipment for porting data to Health, though some health care proponents are concerned about this more hard-core health data and the chance for error when used with an app not produced by a medical manufacturer. In addition, some of these health monitors are subject to federal approval, and self-reporting to a medical provider is under debate because it can become part of the official patient records, so it will be interesting to see how far into this area Apple can go with its Health app.

Set Up the Dashboard

1. Open a category on the Health Data tab and then a topic, such as Carbohydrates under Nutrition.

2. Tap the Show on Dashboard switch to turn it on (see **Figure 20-8**).

3. Tap the Dashboard tab at the bottom of the screen to see the item included with other data graphs.

4. To change the increment of time displayed on Dashboard graphs, tap Day, Week, Month, or Year (see **Figure 20-9**).

 To remove an item from the Dashboard, just tap the Health Data tab, tap the appropriate topic, and then tap the subtopic, such as Height. Tap the Show on Dashboard switch to turn it off.

Tap this switch

Tap one of these

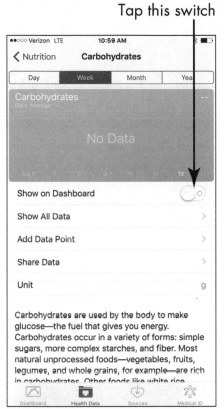

Figure 20-8

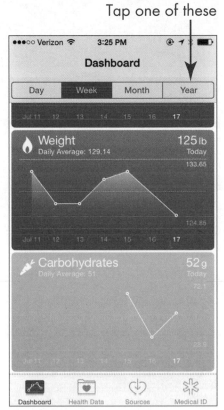

Figure 20-9

Keeping On Schedule with Calendar and Clock

Whether you're retired or still working, you have a busy life full of activities (even busier if you're retired, for some unfathomable reason). You may need a way to keep on top of all those activities and appointments. The Calendar app on your iPhone is a simple, elegant, electronic daybook that helps you do just that.

In addition to being able to enter events and view them in a list or by the day, week, or month, you can set up Calendar to send alerts to remind you of your obligations and search for events by keywords. You can even set up repeating events, such as birthdays, monthly get-togethers with the girls or guys, or weekly babysitting appointments with your grandchild. To help you coordinate calendars on multiple devices, you can also sync events with other calendar accounts. And by taking advantage of the Family Sharing feature, you can create a Family calendar that everybody in your family can view and add events to.

Another preinstalled app that can help you stay on schedule is Clock. Though simple to use, Clock helps you view the time in multiple locations, set alarms, check yourself with a stopwatch feature, and use a timer.

In this chapter, you master the simple procedures for getting around your calendar, creating a Family calendar, entering and editing events, setting up alerts, syncing, and searching. You also learn the simple ins and outs of using Clock.

View Your Calendar

1. Calendar offers several ways to view your schedule. Start by tapping the Calendar app icon on the Home screen to open it. Depending on what you last had open and the orientation in which you're holding your iPhone, you may see today's calendar, List view, the month, week, or an open event, or the Search screen with search results displayed.

2. Tap the Today button at the bottom of the screen to display Today's view (if it's not already displayed) and then tap the List View button to see all scheduled events for that day. The List view, shown in **Figure 21-1,** displays your daily appointments for every day in a list, with times listed on the left. Tap an event in the list to get more event details, or tap the Add button (the + symbol) to add an event.

 If you'd like to display events only from a particular calendar, such as the Birthday or US Holidays calendars, tap the Calendars button at the bottom of the List view and select a calendar to base the list on.

3. Tap the current month in the upper-left corner to display months; in the Month view, the List View button changes to a Combined View button. Tap this to show the month calendar at the top and a scrollable list of events at the bottom, as shown in **Figure 21-2**. Tap the button again to return to the Monthly view.

Tap to add an event   Combined View button

Figure 21-1

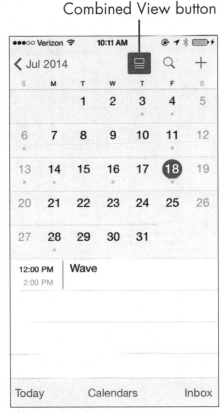

Figure 21-2

4. Tap a date in the Monthly calendar and you'll see that week at the top and the selected day's events below. Note that the Weekly view doesn't have the capability to display combined lists.

5. In the Monthly view, if the month displayed at the top of the screen is August, tap the arrow to its left to get a yearly display (see **Figure 21-3**) and then tap another month to display it. In the Yearly view, you see the calendar for the entire year with a red circle around today.

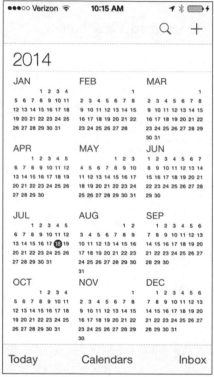

Figure 21-3

6. To move from one month to the next in Monthly view, you can also scroll up or down the screen with your finger.

7. To jump back to today, tap the Today button in the bottom-left corner of Calendar. The month containing the current day is displayed. Tap the Combined View button to hide the month display at the top of the screen.

To view any invitation that you accepted, which placed an event on your calendar, tap Inbox, and a list of invitations is displayed. You can use text within emails such as a date, flight number, or phone number to add an event to Calendar. Tap Done to return to the calendar.

Note that if you're lucky enough to own an iPhone 6s or 6s Plus, because of its wider screen, when you hold it horizontally and you're in the Calendar app, you'll see more information on the screen than you'll see on any other iPhone. For example, in Monthly view, you'll see the entire month on the left and detailed information on events for the selected day.

Add Calendar Events

1. With any view displayed, tap the plus-symbol-shaped Add button (refer to Figure 21-3) to add an event. The Add Event dialog appears.

2. Enter a title for the event and, if you want, a location.

3. Tap the All-day switch to turn it on for an all-day event. Tap the Starts or Ends field; the scrolling setting for day, hour, and minute appears (see **Figure 21-4**).

4. Place your finger on the date, hour, minute, or AM/PM column and move your finger to scroll up or down.

5. If you want to add notes, use your finger to scroll down in the Add Event dialog and tap in the Notes field. Type your note and then tap the Add button to save the event.

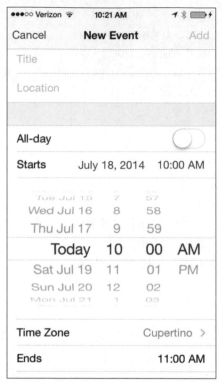

Figure 21-4

 You can edit any event at any time by simply tapping it in any view of your calendar and, when the details are displayed, tap Edit. The Edit dialog appears, offering the same settings as the Add Event dialog. Tap the Done button to save your changes or Cancel to return to your calendar without saving any changes.

Create Repeating Events

1. If you want an event to repeat, such as a weekly or monthly appointment, you can set a repeating event. With any view displayed, tap the Add button to add an event. The New Event dialog (refer to Figure 21-4) appears.

2. Enter a title and location for the event and set the start and end dates and times, as shown in the preceding task, "Add Calendar Events."

3. Scroll down the page if necessary and then tap the Repeat field; the Repeat dialog, shown in **Figure 21-5,** is displayed.

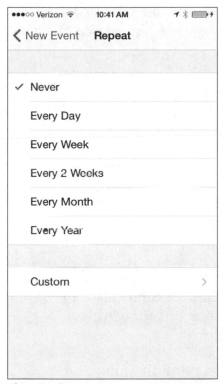

Figure 21-5

4. Tap a preset time interval: Every Day, Week, 2 Weeks, Month, or Year and you return to the New Event dialog. Tap Custom and make the appropriate settings if you want to set any other interval, such as every two months on the 6th of the month.

5. Tap Done. You return to the Calendar.

Other calendar programs may give you more control over repeating events; for example, you might be able to make a setting to repeat an event the fourth Tuesday of every month. If you want a more robust calendar feature, you might consider setting up your appointments in an application such as Outlook or the Mac version of Calendar and syncing them to iPhone. But if you want to create a simple repeating event in iPhone's Calendar app, simply add the first event on a Tuesday and make it repeat every week. Easy, huh?

Add Alerts

1. If you want your iPhone to alert you when an event is coming up, you can use the Alert feature. First, tap the Settings icon on the Home screen and choose Sounds.

2. Scroll down to Calendar Alerts and tap it; then tap any Alert Tone, which causes iPhone to play the tone for you. When you've chosen the alert tone you want, tap Sounds to return to Sounds settings.

Press the Home button and then tap Calendar and create an event in your calendar or open an existing one for editing, as covered in earlier tasks in this chapter.

3. In the New Event (refer to Figure 21-4) or Edit dialog, tap the Alert field. The Event Alert dialog appears, as shown in **Figure 21-6**.

4. Tap any preset interval, from 5 Minutes to 2 Days Before or At Time of Event and tap New Event to return to the New Event dialog. (Remember that you can scroll down in the Event Alert dialog to see more options.)

5. Note that the Alert setting is shown in the New Event or Edit dialog (see **Figure 21-7**).

6. Tap Done in the Edit dialog or Add in the New Event dialog to save all settings.

Alert setting for an event

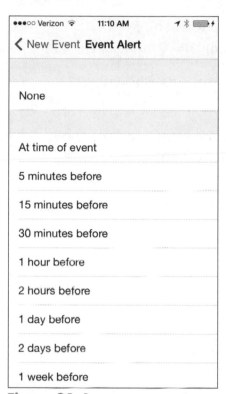

Figure 21-6

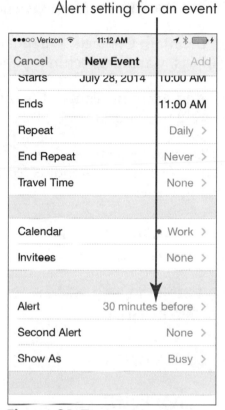

Figure 21-7

 If you work for an organization that uses a Microsoft Exchange account, you can set up your iPhone to receive and respond to invitations from colleagues in your company. When somebody sends an invitation that you accept, it appears on your calendar. Check with your company network administrator (who will jump at the chance to get her hands on your iPhone) or the *iPhone User Guide* to set up this feature if it sounds useful to you. Note that iCloud offers similar functionality to individuals.

Create a Calendar Account

1. If you use a calendar available from an online service such as Yahoo! or Google, you can subscribe to that calendar to read events saved there on your iPhone. Note that you can only read, not edit, these events. Tap the Settings icon on the Home screen to get started.

2. Tap the Mail, Contacts, Calendars option. The Mail, Contacts, Calendars settings pane appears.

3. Tap Add Account. The Add Account options, shown in **Figure 21-8,** appear.

4. Tap an email choice, such as Outlook.com, Gmail, or Yahoo!. (Turn on Calendars for other accounts by tapping Other.)

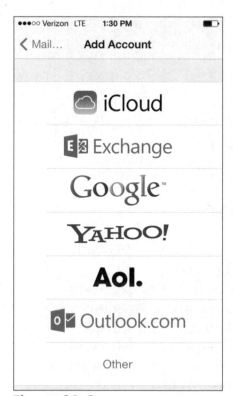

Figure 21-8

5. In the screen that appears (see **Figure 21-9**), enter your email address and email account password.

6. Tap Next. iPhone verifies your address.

7. On the following screen (see **Figure 21-10**), tap the On/Off switch for the Calendars field; your iPhone retrieves data from your calendar at the interval you have set to fetch data. Tap the back arrow in the top-left corner. To review these settings, tap the Fetch New Data option in the Mail, Contacts, Calendars dialog.

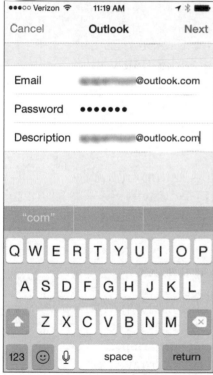

Figure 21-9

Set this to On, as it is here

Figure 21-10

8. In the Fetch New Data dialog that appears, be sure that the Push option's On/Off switch reads On and then scroll down to choose the option you prefer for how frequently data is pushed to your iPhone: every 15 minutes; every 30 minutes; hourly; or manually.

If you store birthdays for people in the Contacts app, by default the Calendar app then displays these when the day comes around so that you won't forget to pass on your congratulations! You can turn off this feature by tapping Calendars in the Calendar app and deselecting Birthday Calendar.

 Though you can have calendar events pushed to you or synced from multiple email accounts, remember that having data pushed to your iPhone may drain your battery more quickly.

Use a Family Calendar

1. If you set up the Family Sharing feature (see Chapter 12 for how to do this), you create a Family calendar that you can use to share family events with up to five other people. After you set up Family Sharing, you have to make sure that the Calendar Sharing feature is on. Tap Settings on the Home screen.

2. Tap iCloud and check that Family Sharing is set up in the second line of the dialog (see **Figure 21-11**). You will see Family rather than Set Up Family Sharing if it has been set up.

3. Tap the switch for Calendars to turn it on if it's not already on.

4. Now tap the Home button and then tap Calendars. Tap the Calendars button at the bottom of the screen. Scroll down, and in the Calendars dialog that appears, make sure that Family is selected. Tap Done.

5. Now when you create a new event in the New Event dialog, tap Calendar and choose Family or Show All Calendars. The details of events contain a notation that an event is from the Family calendar.

Family Sharing is already set up

Figure 21-11

Delete an Event

1. When an upcoming luncheon or meeting is canceled, you should delete the appointment. With Calendar open, tap an event (see **Figure 21-12**).

2. Tap Delete Event at the bottom of the screen.

3. If this is a repeating event, you have the option to delete this instance of the event or this and all future instances of the event (see **Figure 21-13**). Tap the button for the option you prefer. The event is deleted, and you return to Calendar view.

Tap this button

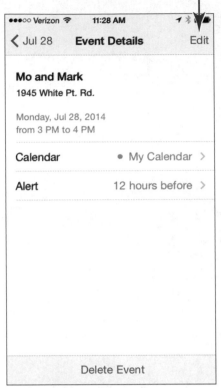

Figure 21-12

Figure 21-13

 If an event is moved but not canceled, you don't have to delete the old one and create a new one. Simply edit the existing event to change the day and time in the Event dialog.

Display Clock

1. Clock is a preinstalled app that resides on the Home screen along with other preinstalled apps such as Videos and Camera. Tap the Clock app to open it. Preset locations are displayed (see **Figure 21-14**).

2. You can add a clock for many (but not all) locations around the world. With Clock displayed, tap the Add button.

3. Tap a city on the list or tap a letter on the right side to display locations that begin with that letter (see **Figure 21-15**) and then tap a city. You can also tap in the Search field and begin to type a city name to find and tap a city. The clock appears in the last slot at the bottom.

Figure 21-14

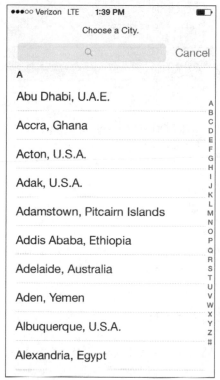

Figure 21-15

Delete a Clock

1. To remove a location, tap the Edit button in the top-left corner of the World Clock screen.

2. Tap the minus symbol next to a location and then tap Delete (see **Figure 21-16**).

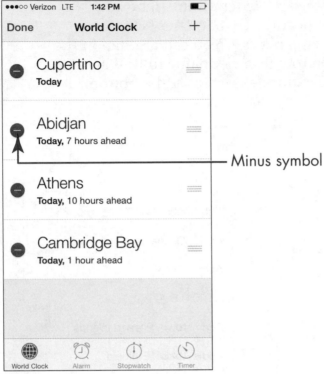

— Minus symbol

Figure 21-16

Set an Alarm

1. With the Clock app displayed, tap the Alarm tab.

2. Tap the Add button. In the Add Alarm dialog shown in **Figure 21-17,** take any of the following actions, tapping Back after you make each setting to return to the Add Alarm dialog:

   • Tap Repeat if you want the alarm to repeat at a regular interval, such as every Monday or every Sunday.

   • Tap Sound to choose the tune the alarm will play.

   • Tap the On/Off switch for Snooze if you want to use the Snooze feature.

   • Tap Label if you want to name the alarm with a name such as "Take Pill" or "Call Helen."

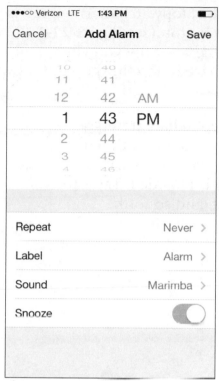

Figure 21-17

3. Place your finger on any of the three columns of sliding numbers at the top of the dialog and scroll to set the time you want the alarm to occur; then tap Save. The alarm appears on the calendar on the Alarm tab.

 To delete an alarm, tap the Alarm tab and tap Edit. All alarms appear. Tap the red circle with a minus in it and then tap the Delete button.

Use Stopwatch and Timer

Sometimes life seems like a countdown or a ticking clock counting the minutes you've spent on a certain activity. You can use the Timer and Stopwatch tabs of the Clock app to do a countdown to a specific time, such as the moment when your chocolate chip cookies are done cooking or to time an activity such as a walk.

These two work very similarly: Tap the Stopwatch or Timer tab from Clock's screen and then tap the Start button (see **Figure 21-18**). When you set the Timer, iPhone uses a sound to notify you when time's up. When you start the Stopwatch, you have to tap the Stop button when the activity is done.

 Stopwatch allows you to log intermediate timings, such as a lap in the pool or the periods of a timed game. With Stopwatch running, just tap the Lap button and the first interval of time is recorded. Tap Lap again to record a second interval, and so forth.

Figure 21-18

Working with Reminders and Notifications

The Reminders app and Notification Center features warm the hearts of those who need help remembering all the details of their lives.

Reminders is a kind of to-do list that lets you create tasks and set reminders so that you don't forget important commitments.

You can even be reminded to do things when you arrive at or leave a location. For example, you can set a reminder so that, when your iPhone detects that you've left the location of your golf game, an alert reminds you to pick up your grandchildren, or when you arrive at your cabin, iPhone reminds you to turn on the water . . . you get the idea.

Notification Center allows you to review all the things you should be aware of in one place, such as mail messages, text messages, calendar appointments, and alerts.

If you occasionally need to escape all your obligations, try the Do Not Disturb feature. Turn this feature on, and you won't be bothered with alerts until you turn it off again.

Get ready to . . .

In this chapter, you discover how to set up and view tasks in Reminders and how Notification Center can centralize all your alerts in one easy-to-find place.

Create a Reminder

1. Creating an event in Reminders is pretty darn simple. Tap Reminders on the Home screen.

2. On the screen that appears, tap Reminders, then tap a blank slot with a plus sign to the left of it in the displayed list to add a task (see **Figure 22-1**). The onscreen keyboard appears.

Tap here to add a task

Figure 22-1

3. Enter a task name or description using the onscreen keyboard and then tap Done.

 See the next task to discover how to add more specifics about an event for which you've created a reminder.

Edit Reminder Details

1. Tap a reminder and then tap the Details button (an *i* in a circle) that appears to the right of it to open the Details dialog shown in **Figure 22-2**. (Note that I deal with reminder settings in the following task.)

Figure 22-2

2. Tap a Priority: None, Low (!), Medium (!!), or High (!!!) from the choices that appear.

3. Tap Notes and enter any notes about the event using the onscreen keyboard (see **Figure 22-3**).

Enter notes here

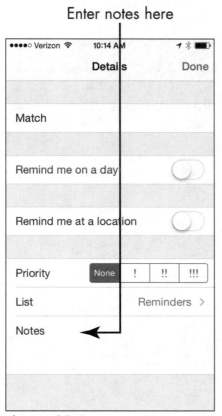

Figure 22-3

4. Tap List and then tap which list you want the reminder saved to, such as your calendar, iCloud, Exchange, or a category of reminders that you've created. Tap Details to return to the Details screen.

5. Tap Done to save the task.

With this version of the app, priority settings now display the associated number of exclamation points on a task in a list to remind you of its importance.

Schedule a Reminder by Time or Location

1. One of the major purposes of Reminders is to remind you of upcoming tasks. To set a reminder, tap a task and then tap the Details button that appears to the right of the task.

2. In the dialog that appears (refer to Figure 22-2), tap Remind Me on a Day to turn the feature on.

3. Tap the Alarm field that appears below this setting (see **Figure 22-4**) to display date settings.

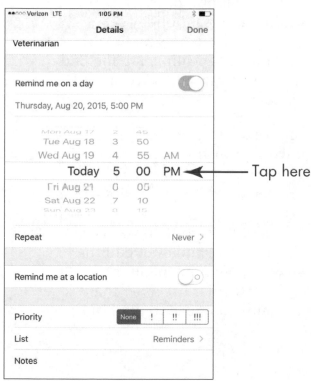

Figure 22-4

4. Tap and flick the day, hour, and minutes fields to scroll to the date and time for the reminder.

5. Tap Remind Me at a Location and then tap the Location field. If prompted, tap Allow to let Reminders use your current location.

6. Use the field labeled Current Location or Home to find your location or enter a location in the Search field. Tap Details to return to the task detail screen.

7. Tap Done to save the settings for the reminder.

 If you want a task to repeat with associated reminders, tap the Repeat field in the Details dialog, and from the dialog that appears, tap Every Day, Every Week, Every 2 Weeks, Every Month, or Every Year (for those annual meetings or great holiday get-togethers with the gang). Tap Done to save details for the task. To stop the task from repeating, tap the End Repeat field, tap End Repeat Date, and select a date from the scrolling calendar.

 You have to be in range of a GPS signal for the location reminder to work properly.

Create a List

1. You can create your own lists of tasks to help you keep different parts of your life organized and even edit the tasks on the list in List view. Tap Reminders on the Home screen to open it. If a particular list other than Reminders is open, tap its name to return to the List view.

2. Tap New List (the + symbol) to display the New List form shown in **Figure 22-5**.

Enter a name for the list here

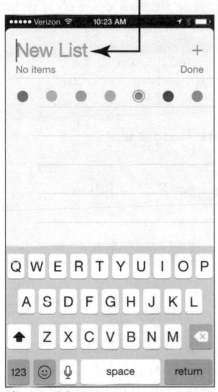

Figure 22-5

3. Tap List and then enter a name for the list.

4. Tap a color; the list name will appear in that color in List view.

5. Tap Done to save the list. Tap a blank line to enter a task, or tap the list name to return to the List view.

Sync with Other Devices and Calendars

To make all these settings work, you should set up your default Calendar in the Mail, Contacts, Calendar settings and set up your iCloud account under Accounts to enable Reminders. (Your default Calendar account is also your default Reminders account.)

1. To determine which tasks are brought over from other calendars such as Outlook, tap the Settings button on the Home screen.

2. Tap iCloud. In the dialog that appears, be sure that Reminders is set to On.

3. Tap Settings to return to the main settings list, and then tap Reminders.

4. Tap the Sync button and then choose how far back to sync Reminders.

Mark as Complete or Delete a Reminder

1. You may want to mark a task as completed or just delete it entirely. With Reminders open and a list of tasks displayed, tap the check box to the left of a task to mark it as complete. When you tap Show Completed, the task now appears as completed and when you next open Reminders, it will have been removed from the Reminders category.

2. To delete more than one reminder, with the list of tasks displayed, tap Edit, and in the screen shown in **Figure 22-6,** tap the red minus icon to the left of any task and tap Delete; or tap Delete List at the bottom of the screen and tap Delete in the confirming dialog to delete all the events on the list.

3. Tap Done.

Red minus icon

Figure 22-6

Set Notification Types

Notification Center is a list of various alerts and scheduled events; it even provides information such as stock quotes that you can display by swiping down from the top of your iPhone screen. Notification Center is on by default, but you don't have to include every type of notification there if you don't want to; for example, you may never want to be notified of incoming messages but always want to have reminders listed here — it's up to you. Some Notification Center settings let you control what types of notifications are included:

1. Tap Settings and then tap Notifications.

2. In the settings that appear (see **Figure 22-7**), you see a list of items to be included in Notification Center and a notation of items that are turned off. For example, Messages and Reminders may be included, but alerts in game apps may not.

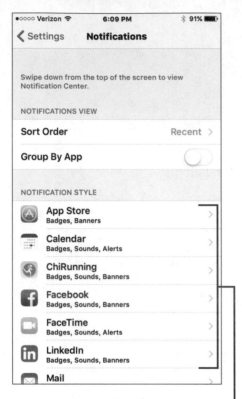

Items in Notification Center

Figure 22-7

3. Tap any item, and in the settings that appear, set an item's switch (see **Figure 22-8**) to On or Off, to include or exclude it from Notification Center.

4. Tap an Alert Style to choose to have no alert, view a banner across the top of the screen, or have a boxed alert appear. If you choose Banner, it will appear and then disappear automatically. If you choose Alert, you have to take an action to dismiss the alert when it appears.

5. If you want to be able to view alerts when the lock screen is displayed, turn on the Show on Lock Screen setting.

6. Tap the Notifications button to return to the main Notifications settings screen. When you've finished making settings, press the Home button.

Include in/Exclude
from Notification Center

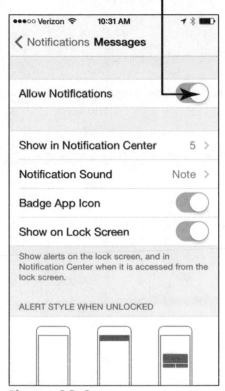

Figure 22-8

 You can drag across or tap an alert displayed in
Notification Center to go to its source, such as the
Reminders app, to see more details about it.

View Notification Center

After you've made settings for what should appear in Notification
Center, you'll regularly want to take a look at those alerts and
reminders.

1. From any screen, tap at the top of the screen and drag
down to display Notification Center (see **Figure 22-9**).

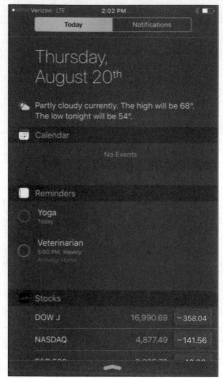

Figure 22-9

2. Note that items are divided into lists by type — for example, you see items categorized as Reminders, Mail, Calendar, and so on.

3. To close Notification Center, swipe upward from the bottom of the screen.

 To determine what is displayed in Notification Center, see the previous task.

 You can display Stocks in Notification Center by tapping Settings from the Home screen, tapping Notifications, and making sure that Stocks is set to On.

View Notifications from the Lock Screen

You will receive notifications on your lock screen when a message has been received or you've missed a phone call, for example. You have two possible ways to respond to notifications:

➥ You don't have to unlock your phone; just tap and drag down from the Status bar to view Notification Center.

➥ Tap an item, and you're taken to the originating app, where you can take the appropriate action: Create and send a return message, initiate a phone call, or whatever.

Check Out Today and Notifications Tabs

There are two tabs in Notification Center for you to play with: Today and Notifications.

1. Swipe down from the top of the screen to display Notifications.

2. Tap Today to show all information about today, such as Reminders, weather, stock prices, Calendar items, and other items you've selected to display in Notification Center (see the previous task).

 You select what appears in the Today tab by tapping the Edit button at the bottom of the Today screen and then selecting which items you want to see: Today Summary, Traffic Conditions, Calendar, Stocks, Reminders, or Tomorrow Summary. Tap Done to return to the Notifications screen.

3. Tap the Notifications tab to see all notifications that you set up in the Settings app for Notification Center. You'll see only notifications that you haven't responded to or deleted in the Notifications tab or that you haven't viewed in their originating app.

Go to an App from Notification Center

You can easily jump from Notification Center to any app that caused an alert or reminder to appear.

1. Swipe down from the top of the screen to display Notification Center.

2. Tap any item in a category such as Reminders or Stocks; it opens in its originating app. If you tap a message such as an email, you can then reply to the message using the procedure described in Chapter 11.

Get Some Rest with Do Not Disturb

1. Do Not Disturb is a simple but useful setting you can use to stop any alerts, phone calls, text messages, and FaceTime calls from appearing or making a sound. You can make settings to allow calls from certain people or several repeat calls from the same person in a short time period to come through. (The assumption here is that such repeat calls may signal an emergency situation or urgent need to get through to you.) Tap Settings and then tap Do Not Disturb.

2. Set the Manual switch to On to turn the feature on.

3. In the other settings shown in **Figure 22-10,** do any of the following:

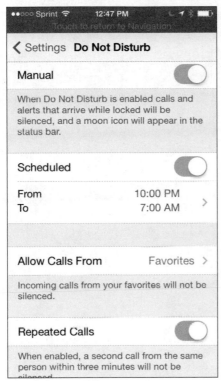

Figure 22-10

- Tap Scheduled to allow alerts during a specified time period to appear.

- Tap Allow Calls From and then from the next screen select Everyone, No One, Favorites, or Groups such as All Contacts.

- Tap Repeated Calls to allow a second call from the same person in a three-minute time period to come through.

4. Press the Home button to return to the Home screen.

Making Notes

*N*otes is the preinstalled app that you can use to do everything from jotting down notes at meetings to keeping to-do lists. It isn't a robust word processor (such as Apple Pages or Microsoft Word) by any means, but for taking notes on the fly, jotting down shopping lists, or writing a few pages of your novel-in-progress while you sit and sip a cup of tea on your deck, it's a useful option.

In this chapter, you see how to enter and edit text in Notes and how to manage those notes by navigating among them, searching for content, or sharing or deleting them. I also help you to explore the new shortcut menu that allows you to create bulleted checklists, add pictures to notes, add drawings to notes, and apply styles to text in a note.

Open a Blank Note

1. To get started with Notes, tap the Notes app icon on the Home screen. If you've never used Notes, it opens with a blank notes list displayed. (If you have used Notes, it opens to the last note you were working on. If that's the case, you might want to jump to the next task to display a new, blank note.) You see the view shown in **Figure 23-1**.

2. Tap the New button in the bottom-right corner of the open note. The onscreen keyboard, shown in **Figure** 23-2, appears.

3. Tap keys on the keyboard to enter text or, with Siri enabled, tap the Dictation key (the one with the microphone on it) to speak your text. If you want to enter numbers or symbols, tap the key labeled *123* on the keyboard (refer to Figure 23-2). The numeric keyboard, shown in **Figure** 23-3, appears. Whenever you want to return to the alphabetic keyboard, tap the key labeled *ABC*.

Shift key   Delete key

Figure 23-1

123 key   Return key

Figure 23-2

4. To capitalize a letter, tap the Shift key that looks like a bold, upward-facing arrow (refer to Figure 23-2) and then tap the letter. Tap the Shift key once again to turn the feature off.

5. When you want to start a new paragraph or a new item in a list, tap the Return key (refer to Figure 23-2).

6. To edit text, tap to the right of the text you want to edit and either use the Delete key (refer to Figure 23-2) to delete text to the left of the cursor or enter new text. No need to save a note — it's kept automatically until you delete it

 When you have the numerical keyboard displayed (refer to Figure 23-3), you can tap the key labeled #+= to access more symbols, such as the percentage sign or the euro symbol, or additional bracket styles.

ABC key

Figure 23-3

You can activate the Enable Caps Lock feature in the General Keyboard Settings so that you can then turn Caps Lock on by double-tapping the Shift key (this upward-pointing arrow is available only in the letter keyboard).

Create a New Note

1. With one note open, to create a new note, tap the Done button (refer to Figure 23-3) and then tap New.

2. A new, blank note appears (refer to Figure 23-1). Enter and edit text as described in the previous task.

 Notes can be shared among Apple devices via iCloud. In Settings, both devices must have Notes turned on under iCloud. New notes are shared instantaneously if both devices are connected to the Internet.

 Tap an individual note to display it. When you're displaying a note, you can tap the Back button to see a list of all notes you've created.

 You can press a spot on your note and, from the menu that appears, choose Select or Select All. Then you can tap the button labeled BIU to apply bold, italic, or underline formatting.

Use Copy and Paste

1. The Notes app includes two essential editing tools that you're probably familiar with from using word processors: Copy and Paste. With a note displayed, press and hold your finger on a word.

2. Tap Select or Select All.

3. On the toolbar that appears (see **Figure 23-4**), tap the Copy button.

Tap this button

Figure 23-4

4. Tap in the document where you want the copied text to go and then press and hold your finger on the screen.

5. On the toolbar that appears (see **Figure 23-5**), tap the Paste button. The copied text appears (see **Figure 23-6**).

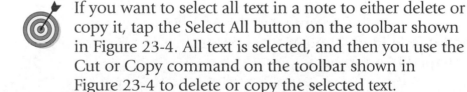 If you want to select all text in a note to either delete or copy it, tap the Select All button on the toolbar shown in Figure 23-4. All text is selected, and then you use the Cut or Copy command on the toolbar shown in Figure 23-4 to delete or copy the selected text.

To extend a selection to adjacent words, press one of the little handles that extend from an edge of the selection and drag to the left, right, up, or down.

Tap this

Copied text

Figure 23-5

Figure 23-6

 To delete text, you can also choose text using the Select or Select All command and then tap the Delete key on the onscreen keyboard.

Insert a Picture

1. To insert a photo into a note, tap the Add key above the keyboard, and in the toolbar that appears, tap the Picture icon shaped like a camera.

2. Tap Photo Library (see **Figure 23-7**) to insert a picture you've already taken and choose the photo you want to insert.

Figure 23-7

3. Tap Choose and the photo is inserted into your note.

 If you want to take a photo or video, tap Take Photo or Video in Step 2 and take a new photo or video. Tap Use Photo to insert it in your note.

Add a Drawing

1. With the latest version of Notes, you can create a drawing to add to your note. With a note open, tap the Add button above the keyboard to display the shortcut toolbar.

2. Tap the Drawing tool button (a squiggle near the right side of the toolbar). The drawing tools shown in **Figure 23-8** appear.

3. Tap a drawing tool (Pen, Marker, or Pencil).

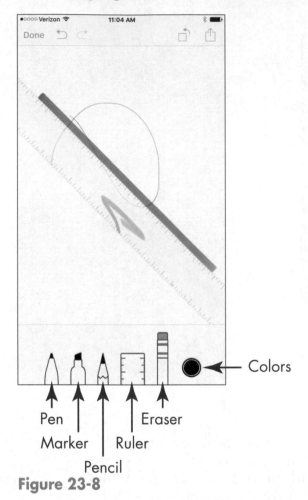

Colors

Pen
Marker
Pencil
Ruler
Eraser

Figure 23-8

4. Tap the Color button; the color palette shown in **Figure 23-9** appears.

5. Tap a color and then draw on the screen using your finger.

6. When you've finished drawing, tap Done.

 Tapping the Ruler tool places a ruler-shaped item on screen that you can use to help you to draw straight lines.

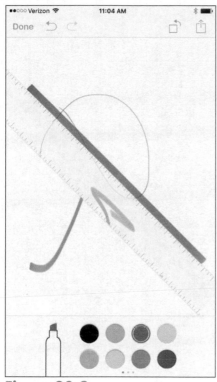

Figure 23-9

Apply a Text Style

Text styles, including Title, Heading, Body, Bulleted List, Dashed List, and Numbered List, are available on the new shortcut toolbar. With a note open and the shortcut toolbar displayed, press on the text and choose Select or Select All.

Tap the Text Style tool on the shortcut bar (labelled with Aa) and then tap to choose a style on the list that's shown in **Figure 23-10**. Tap Done and the style is applied.

Figure 23-10

Create a Checklist

1. The new Checklist formatting feature in Notes allows you to add circular buttons in front of text and then tap those buttons to check off completed items on a checklist. With a note open and the shortcut toolbar displayed, tap the Checklist button.

2. Enter text and press Return on the keyboard. A second checklist bullet appears.

3. When you're done entering Checklist items, tap the Checklist button again to turn the feature off.

 You can apply the Checklist formatting to existing text if you press on the text, tap Select or Select All, and then tap the Checklist button.

Add a Shared Item to a Note

 In iOS 9, you can share items to a note. For example, if you are displaying a map in Maps or a photo in Photos, you can tap the Share button and then choose Notes.

When you do, in the dialog that appears (see **Figure 23-11**), you can either add text to the note and save it or select an existing note to add the item to.

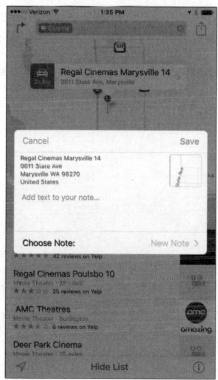

Figure 23-11

Display the Notes List

1. Tap the Notes app icon on the Home screen to open Notes. If an individual note is displayed, tap the Back button to go to the Notes list.

2. The Notes list appears, as shown in **Figure 23-12**. This
list is organized chronologically (the date isn't indicated
if you created the note today).

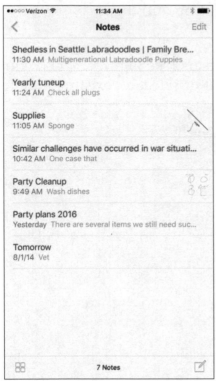

●●○○○ Verizon 🤳   11:34 AM   ∗ ▬

‹   **Notes**   Edit

Shedless in Seattle Labradoodles | Family Bre...
11:30 AM Multigenerational Labradoodle Puppies

Yearly tuneup
11:24 AM Check all plugs

Supplies
11:05 AM Sponge

Similar challenges have occurred in war situati...
10:42 AM One case that

Party Cleanup
9:49 AM Wash dishes

Party plans 2016
Yesterday There are several items we still need suc...

Tomorrow
8/1/14 Vet

⊞   7 Notes   ☑

Figure 23-12

3. Tap any note on the list to display it.

 Notes names your note, using the first line of text. If
you want to rename a note, first display the note, tap
at the start of the first line of text, and then enter a
new title and press Return on the keyboard; the new
first line is now reflected as the name of your note in
the Notes list.

Move Among Notes

1. Tap the Notes app icon on the Home screen to open Notes.

2. With the Notes list displayed (see the previous task), tap a note to open it.

3. To move among notes, tap the Notes button in the top-left corner and then tap another note in the list to open it.

 Because Notes lets you enter multiple notes with the same title — which can cause confusion — name your notes uniquely!

Search for a Note

1. You can search to locate a note that contains certain text. The Search feature lists only the notes that contain your search criteria, and it highlights only the first instance of the word or words you enter when you open a note. Tap the Notes app icon on the Home screen to open Notes.

2. Tap the Notes button in the top-left corner to display the notes list if it isn't already displayed.

3. Press your finger on the middle of the screen and swipe down. The Search field appears above the Notes list, as shown in **Figure 23-13**.

4. Tap in the Search field. The onscreen keyboard appears (see **Figure 23-14**).

5. Begin to enter the search term. All notes that contain matching words appear on the list, as shown in **Figure 23-14**.

Figure 23-13

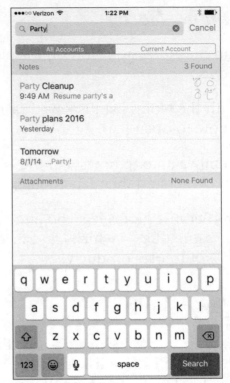

Figure 23-14

6. Tap a note to display it with the first instance of the search term highlighted; locate other instances of the matching word the old-fashioned way — by skimming to find it.

Share a Note

1. If you want to share what you wrote with a friend or colleague, you can easily use AirDrop (iPhone 5 or later), Mail, or Message to send the contents of a note. With a note displayed, tap the Share button at the top right of the screen and a popover appears, as shown in **Figure 23-15**.

2. Tap Mail or Message. In the email or message form that appears, type one or more addresses in the appropriate fields. At least one address must appear in the To field.

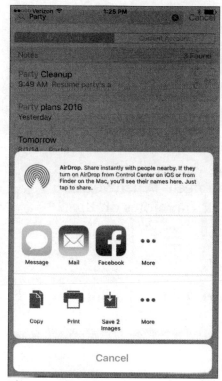

Figure 23-15

3. If you need to make changes to the subject or message, tap in either area and make the changes.

4. Tap the Send button, and your email is sent.

5. To send via AirDrop to an AirDrop-enabled device (including Macs running OS X Yosemite or later with an AirDrop Finder window open) nearby, tap AirDrop in Step 2 and then tap the detected device to which you want to send the note.

 If you want to print a note, in Step 2, choose Print rather than Mail. Complete the Printer Options dialog by designating an AirPrint-enabled wireless printer (or shared printer on a network that you can access using AirPrint) and how many copies to print; then tap Print.

To leave a message before sending it but save a draft so that you can finish and send it later, tap Cancel and then tap Save Draft. The next time you tap the email button with the same note displayed in Notes, your draft appears.

Delete a Note

1. There's no sense in letting your Notes list get cluttered, making it harder to find the ones you need. When you're done with a note, it's time to delete it. Tap Notes on the Home screen to open Notes.

2. Tap a note in the Notes list to open it.

3. Tap the Trash button, shown in **Figure 23-16.** The note is deleted.

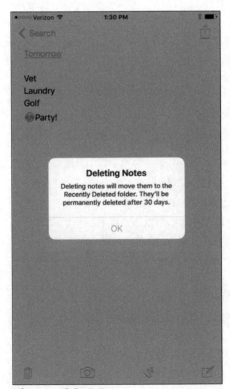

Figure 23-16

An alternative method to delete a note is to swipe to the left on a note in the Notes list and then tap the Delete button that appears.

 Notes is a nice little application, but it's limited. It offers no formatting tools beyond preset styles, Bold, Italic, and Underline, for example. So if you've made some notes and want to graduate to building a more robust document in a word processor, you have a couple of options. One way is to buy the Pages word-processor app for iPad, which costs about $10 and is free with a new iOS device, and copy your note (using the copy-and-paste feature discussed earlier in this chapter). Alternatively, you can send the note to yourself in an email message or sync it to your computer. Open the email or note and copy and paste its text into a full-fledged word processor and you're good to go.

Getting the News You Need

With iOS 9 comes the News app. This so-called news aggregator gathers news stories that either match your news reading habits or match the channels and topics you've selected. You can choose which news sites are your favorites, search for news on a particular topic, and save news stories to read later. In this chapter, you get an overview of all these features.

Read Your News

1. To get started with the News app, tap the app to open it. The first time you open it you will be asked a few questions to set up the app, choosing your favorite news sources and whether to deliver news to your inbox, for example.

2. The For You tab of news stories shown in **Figure 24-1** appears by default, though whichever tab you last chose will appear next time you open the app.

3. Scroll down the page to see the news stories of the day.

4. Tap an item in the You Might Like list (see **Figure 24-2**) for more items that might be of interest to you.

Figure 24-1

Figure 24-2

 When you're reading a story you like, you can tap the Share button at the bottom of the screen to share via Mail, Message, Twitter, or Facebook.

Select Favorites

1. Favorites allows you to select the topics and channels you prefer to include in Your News. With the News app open, tap the Favorites button at the bottom of the screen. The screen shown in **Figure 24-3** appears.

2. Tap Edit.

3. Tap an item to delete it from Favorites and then tap Done (see **Figure 24-4**).

4. Tap an item to view it.

You can add an item to Favorites by tapping the Explore button and then selecting a channel.

Figure 24-3

Figure 24-4

Explore Channels and Topics

1. Using the Explore feature, you can select channels to add to Favorites. With the News app open, tap Explore at the bottom of the screen. The options shown in **Figure 24-5** appear.

Figure 24-5

2. Tap a Suggested Topic to explore it.

3. Tap the Back button, and then tap an item in the Browse list (see **Figure 24-6**) to display channels related to a topic. Tap a channel to add it to Favorites.

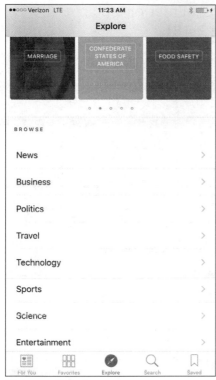

Figure 24-6

 You can preview stories before opening them, which saves some download time. In Settings, tap News and then be sure the Show Story Previews switch is set to On (which it is by default).

Search for News

1. If you have a particular news story you'd like to follow, you can search for it from within News. With the app open, tap the Search button at the bottom of the screen. You're presented with a Search field as well as some Suggestions (see **Figure 24-7**).

2. Enter a search term or phrase and press Enter or tap an item in the search results (see **Figure 24-8**).

 If you don't find what you want in the results, tap the Show More Topics or Show More Channels links in the results list.

Figure 24-7

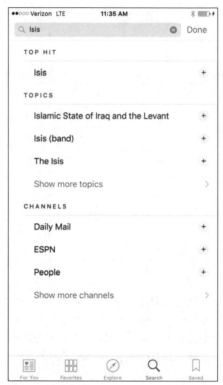

Figure 24-8

Save News Stories

1. It's handy to be able to save news stories to read offline at any time. In the News app, open a news story using any of the methods described in this chapter.

2. Tap the Save button in the bottom-right corner.

3. Tap the Back button to return to the News app and then tap the Saved button. Your saved stories are displayed (see **Figure 24-9**).

Figure 24-9

Troubleshooting and Maintaining Your iPhone

Chapter 25

*i*Phones don't grow on trees — they cost a pretty penny, especially with phone equipment subsidies and two-year contracts disappearing. That's why you should learn how to take care of your iPhone and troubleshoot any problems it might have so that you get the most out of it.

In this chapter, I provide some advice about the care and maintenance of your iPhone, as well as tips about how to solve common problems, update iPhone system software, and even reset the iPhone if something goes seriously wrong. In case you lose your iPhone, I even tell you about a feature that helps you find it, activate it remotely, or even disable it if it has fallen into the wrong hands. Finally, you get information about backing up your iPhone settings and content using iCloud and the new fingerprint reader feature, Touch ID.

Get ready to . . .

Keep the iPhone Screen Clean

If you've been playing with your iPhone, you know (despite Apple's claim that the iPhone has a fingerprint-resistant screen) that it's a fingerprint magnet. Here are some tips for cleaning your iPhone screen:

➡ **Use a dry, soft cloth.** You can get most fingerprints off with a dry, soft cloth such as the one you use to clean your eyeglasses or a cleaning tissue that's lint and chemical free. Or try products used to clean lenses in labs, such as Kimwipes or Kaydry, which you can get from several major retailers such as Amazon.

➡ **Use a slightly dampened soft cloth.** To get the surface even cleaner, very slightly dampen the soft cloth. Again, make sure that whatever cloth material you use is free of lint.

➡ **Remove the cables.** Turn off your iPhone and unplug any cables from it before cleaning the screen with a moistened cloth.

➡ **Avoid too much moisture.** Avoid getting too much moisture around the edges of the screen, where it can seep into the unit.

➡ **Don't use your fingers!** That's right, by using a stylus rather than your finger, you entirely avoid smearing oil from your skin or cheese from your pizza on the screen.

➡ **Never use household cleaners.** They can degrade the coating that keeps the iPhone screen from absorbing oil from your fingers.

 Do *not* use premoistened lens-cleaning tissues to clean your iPhone screen. Most brands of wipes contain alcohol, which can damage the screen's coating.

Protect Your Gadget with a Case

Your screen isn't the only element on the iPhone that can be damaged, so consider getting a case for it so that you can carry it around the house or around town safely. Besides providing a bit of padding if you drop the device, a case makes the iPhone less slippery in your hands, offering a better grip when working with it.

Several types of cases are available, but be sure to get one that will fit your model of iPhone because their dimensions differ, and some models have slightly different thicknesses. You can choose covers from manufacturers such as Griffin (www.griffintechnology.com) that come in materials ranging from leather to silicone.

Cases range from a few dollars to $70 or more for leather (with some outrageously expensive designer cases costing upward of $500). Some provide a cover for the screen and back, and others protect only the back and sides. If you carry your iPhone around much, consider a case with a screen cover to provide better protection for the screen or use a screen overlay, such as InvisibleShield from Zagg (www.zagg.com). If you're the literary type, try the BookBook case that looks like a well-worn leather book.

Extend Your iPhone's Battery Life

The much-touted battery life of the iPhone is a wonderful feature, but you can do some things to extend it even further. Here are a few tips to consider:

 → **Keep tabs on remaining battery life.** You can estimate the amount of remaining battery life by looking at the Battery icon on the far-right end of the Status bar, at the top of your screen.

→ **Use standard accessories to charge your iPhone most effectively.** When connected to a recent-model Mac or Windows computer for charging, the iPhone can slowly charge; however, the most effective way to charge your iPhone is to plug it into a wall outlet using the Lightning to USB Cable and the 10W USB power adapter that come with your iPhone.

➡ **Use a case with an external battery pack.** These cases are very handy when you're traveling or unable to reach an electrical outlet easily.

➡ **The fastest way to charge iPhone is to turn it off while charging it.**

➡ **The Battery icon on the Status bar indicates when the charging is complete.**

 Your iPhone battery is sealed in the unit, so you can't replace it yourself the way you can with many laptops or other cellphones. If the battery is out of warranty, you have to fork over about $79 to have Apple install a new one with AppleCare coverage. See the "Get Support" task, later in this chapter, to find out where to get a replacement battery.

 Apple offers AppleCare+. For $99, you get two years of coverage, which even covers you if you drop or spill liquids on your iPhone (Apple covers up to two incidents of accidental damage). If your iPhone has to be replaced, it will cost you only $49, rather than the $250 it used to cost with garden-variety AppleCare. You can purchase AppleCare+ when you buy your iPhone or within 60 days of the date of purchase. See www.apple.com/support/products/iphone.html for more details.

Find Out What to Do with a Nonresponsive iPhone

If your iPhone goes dead on you, it's most likely a power issue, so the first thing to do is to plug the Lightning to USB Cable into the 10W USB power adapter, plug the 10W USB power adapter into a wall outlet, plug the other end of the cable into your iPhone, and charge the battery.

Another thing to try — if you believe that an app is hanging up the iPhone — is to press the Sleep/Wake button for a couple of seconds, and then press and hold the Home button. The app you were using should close.

You can always try the tried-and-true reboot procedure: On the iPhone, you press the Sleep/Wake button on right until the red slider appears. Drag the slider to the right to turn off your iPhone. After a few moments, press the Sleep/Wake button to boot up the little guy again.

If the situation seems drastic and none of these ideas works, try to reset your iPhone. To do this, press the Sleep/Wake button and the Home button at the same time until the Apple logo appears onscreen.

 If your phone has this problem often, try closing out some active apps that may be running in the background and using up too much memory. To do this, press the Home button twice and then from the screen showing active apps, tap and drag an app upward. Also check to see that you haven't loaded up your phone with too much content, such as videos, which could be slowing down the phone's performance.

Update the iOS Software

1. Apple occasionally updates the iPhone system software to fix problems or offer enhanced features. You should occasionally check for an updated version (say, every month). You can do so by hooking up your iPhone to a recognized computer (that is, a computer that you've used to sign into your Apple account before) with iTunes installed, but it's even easier to just update from your iPhone Settings, though it's a tad slower. Tap Settings from the Home screen.

2. Tap General and then tap Software Update (see **Figure 25-1**).

●○○○○ Verizon LTE   10:32 AM   ✳ ■◗

‹ Settings   **General**

About	›
Software Update	›	⟵ Tap this option
Siri	›
Spotlight Search	›
Handoff & Suggested Apps	›
CarPlay	›
Accessibility	›
Storage & iCloud Usage	›
Background App Refresh	›
Auto-Lock	2 Minutes ›
Restrictions	Off ›

Figure 25-1

3. A message tells you whether your software is up-to-date; if it's not, the phone is updated to the latest software version.

 If you're having problems with your iPhone, you can use the Update feature to try to restore the current version of the software. Follow the preceding set of steps and then tap the Restore button instead of the Software Update button in Step 2.

Restore the Sound

On the morning I wrote this chapter, as my husband puttered with our iPhone, its sound suddenly (and ironically) stopped working. We gave ourselves a quick course in sound recovery, so now I can share some tips with you. Make sure that

➡ **You haven't touched the volume control buttons on the side of your iPhone.** They're on the left side of the phone. Be sure not to touch the volume decrease button and inadvertently lower the sound to a point where you can't hear it.

➡ **You haven't flipped the Silent switch.** Moving the switch located on the left side above the volume buttons mutes sound on the iPhone. Note that this switch can be moved if you drop your iPhone — so don't do that!

➡ **The speaker isn't covered up.** It may be covered in a way that muffles the sound.

➡ **A headset isn't plugged in.** Sound doesn't play over the speaker and the headset at the same time.

➡ **The volume limit is set to Off.** You can set up the volume limit for the Music app to control how loudly your music can play (which is useful if you have teenagers around). Tap Settings on the Home screen and then, on the screen that displays, tap Music and then tap Volume Limit and use the slider that appears (see **Figure 25-2**) to set the volume limit.

 When all else fails, reboot. This strategy worked for us — just press the Sleep/Wake button until the red slider appears. Press and drag the slider to the right. After the iPhone turns off, press the Sleep/Wake button again until the Apple logo appears, and you may find yourself back in business, sound-wise.

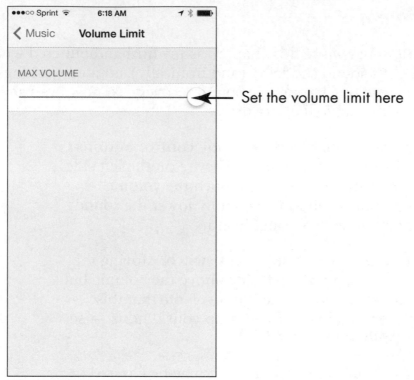

Set the volume limit here

Figure 25-2

Get Support

Every single new iPhone comes with a year's coverage for repair of the hardware and 90 days of free technical support. Apple is known for its helpful customer support, so if you're stuck, I definitely recommend that you try it. Here are a few options that you can explore for getting help:

➠ **The Apple Store:** Go to your local Apple Store (if one is handy) to see what the folks there might know about your problem. Call first and make an appointment at the Genius Bar to be sure to get prompt service.

➠ **The Apple support website:** It's at www.apple. com/support/iphone. You can find online manuals, discussion forums, and downloads, and you can use the Apple Expert feature to contact a live support person by phone.

➡ **The *iPhone User Guide*:** You can download the free manual that is available through iBooks from the iBooks Store.

➡ **The Apple battery replacement service:** If you need repair or service for your battery, visit www.apple.com/batteries/replacements.html. Note that your warranty provides free battery replacement if the battery level dips below 50 percent and won't go any higher during the first year you own it. If you purchase the AppleCare+ service agreement, this is extended to two years.

Apple recommends that you have your iPhone battery replaced only by an Apple Authorized Service Provider.

Find a Missing iPhone

You can take advantage of the Find My iPhone feature to pinpoint the location of your iPhone. This feature is extremely handy if you forget where you left your iPhone or someone steals it. Find My iPhone not only lets you track down the critter but also lets you wipe out the data contained in it if you have no way to get the iPhone back.

If you're using Family Sharing, someone in your family can find your device and play a sound. This works even if the ringer on the iPhone is turned off. See Chapter 12 for more about Family Sharing.

Follow these steps to set up the Find My iPhone feature:

1. Tap Settings on the Home screen.

2. In Settings, in the left pane tap iCloud.

3. In the iCloud settings, tap Find My iPhone and then tap the On/Off switch for Find My iPhone to turn the feature on (see **Figure 25-3**).

Figure 25-3

4. From now on, if your iPhone is lost or stolen, you can go to `https://www.iCloud.com` from your computer, iPad, or another iPhone and enter your Apple ID and password.

5. In your computer's browser, the iCloud screen appears. Click the Find My iPhone button to display a map of its location and some helpful tools (see **Figure 25-4**).

6. Click the circle representing your phone, and then click the Information button (the small *i*). In the toolbar that appears, to wipe information from the iPhone, click the Erase iPhone button. To lock the iPhone from access by others, click the Lost Mode button. Tap Play Sound to have your phone play a sound that might help you locate it if you're in its vicinity.

Figure 25-4

 Erase iPhone will delete all data from your iPhone, including contact information and content such as music. However, even after you've erased your iPhone, it will display your phone number on the Lock screen along with a message so that any Good Samaritan who finds it can contact you. If you've created an iTunes or iCloud backup, you can restore your phone's contents from those sources.

 The Lost Mode feature allows you to send whomever has your iPhone a note saying how to return it to you. If you choose to play a sound, it plays for two minutes, helping you track down your phone in case you left it on top of the refrigerator or somebody holding your iPhone is within earshot.

Back Up to iCloud

You used to be able to back up your iPhone content using only iTunes, but since Apple's introduction of iCloud with iOS 5, you can back up via a Wi-Fi network to your iCloud storage. You get 5GB of storage (not including iTunes-bought music, iTunes Match and Photo Sharing content, video, apps, and e-books) for free or you can pay for increased storage (an additional 10GB for $20 per year, 20GB for $40 per year, or 50GB for $100 per year).

1. To perform a backup to iCloud, first set up an iCloud account (see Chapter 3 for details on creating an iCloud account) and then tap Settings from the Home screen.

2. In Settings, tap iCloud and then tap Backup (see **Figure 25-5**).

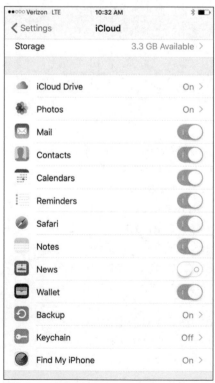

Figure 25-5

3. In the pane that appears (see **Figure** 25-6), tap the iCloud Backup switch to enable automatic backups. To perform a manual backup, tap Back Up Now. A progress bar shows how your backup is moving along.

Set this to On

Figure 25-6

 If you get your iPhone back after it wanders and you've erased it, just enter your Apple ID and password and you can reactivate it.

You can also back up your iPhone using iTunes. This method actually saves more types of content than an iCloud backup, and if you have encryption turned on in iTunes, it can save your passwords as well. However, this method does require that you connect to a computer to perform the backup. Unfortunately, you can't back up to both iTunes and iCloud. However, if you do back up and get a new iPhone down the line, you can restore all your data to the new phone easily.

Index

moving, 384
repeating, 376–377
sounds played when occur, 130
exclamation points, in Reminders
   app, 393
expanding photos, 91
Explore feature, News app, 426–427
Explore option, App Store, 248
exporting data, Health App, 365–366
Extras folder, 251

• F •

Facebook app
  adding info from to Contacts app,
   92–93
  sharing location information using,
   352–353
  sharing new stories using, 424
  sharing photos using, 303–304
  sharing videos using, 321–322
  using Siri with, 154
FaceTime app
  accepting calls, 162
  calling Favorites using, 78
  camera used with, 21
  ending calls, 163
  muting sound during, 163
  overview, 51, 158–159
  rear-facing camera use with, 164
  recent calls in, 162
  requirements for, 158
  using Wi-Fi or 3G/4G with, 159–162
facts, asking for from Siri, 152–153
Family Purchases folder, 256
Family Sharing feature
  Calendar app, 382–383
  finding lost phone using, 439
  using with iTunes Store app, 242–244

Favorites
  Maps app, 345
  News app, 424–425
  Phone app, 76–78
Fetch New Data dialog, 381
Filters tool, Photos app, 300
Find My Friends app, 156
Find My iPhone feature, 63, 65,
   439–441
Fitbit app, 367
Fitness category, Health App,
   363–364
flagging email, 220–221
flash, on camera, 293
flicking, 31
Flickr, 154
folders
  deleting, 255
  organizing apps in, 254
  in Safari app, 194–195
foldout card, 17
follow-up, flagging email for,
   220–221
fonts
  bold, 127
  iBooks app, 269–270
  larger, 127
frames per second, 9
friends, app for finding, 156

• G •

Game Center app
  adding friends, 328–329
  challenging friends, 333–335
  creating profile, 325–328
  game-playing basics, 331–332
  logging in, 328
  notifications from, 324

About the Author

Nancy C. Muir is the owner of a writing and consulting company that specializes in business and technology topics. She has authored more than 100 books, including *Computers For Seniors For Dummies* and *iPad For Seniors For Dummies*. Nancy holds a certificate in Distance Learning Design and has taught Internet safety at the college level.

Dedication

To my husband Earl for going above and beyond in supporting me while writing these books. Honey, you're the best.

Author's Acknowledgments

Thanks to Amy Fandrei, my loyal and supportive acquisitions editor. Also my gratitude to Brian Walls, book juggler supreme. Thanks to Lisa Bucki for tech editing the book to keep me on track. Thanks to Finn and Louise at The Apple Store in Edinburgh for helping me grab images for the book while I was roaming in Scotland.

Publisher's Acknowledgments

Acquisitions Editor: Amy Fandrei
Project Editor: Brian H. Walls
Technical Editor: Lisa Bucki
Proofreader: Debbye Butler

Sr. Editorial Assistant: Cherie Case
Production Editor: Shaik Siddique
Cover Image: ©Bloomua/Shutterstock

Apple & Mac

iPad For Dummies,
6th Edition
978-1-118-72306-7

iPhone For Dummies,
7th Edition
978-1-118-69083-3

Macs All-in-One
For Dummies, 4th Edition
978-1-118-82210-4

OS X Mavericks
For Dummies
978-1-118-69188-5

Blogging & Social Media

Facebook For Dummies,
5th Edition
978-1-118-63312-0

Social Media Engagement
For Dummies
978-1-118-53019-1

WordPress For Dummies,
6th Edition
978-1-118-79161-5

Business

Stock Investing
For Dummies, 4th Edition
978-1-118-37678-2

Investing For Dummies,
6th Edition
978-0-470-90545-6

Personal Finance

Personal Finance
For Dummies, 7th Edition
978-1-118-11785-9

QuickBooks 2014
For Dummies
978-1-118-72005-9

Small Business Marketing
Kit For Dummies,
3rd Edition
978-1-118-31183-7

Careers

Job Interviews
For Dummies, 4th Edition
978-1-118-11290-8

Job Searching with Social
Media For Dummies,
2nd Edition
978-1-118-67856-5

Personal Branding
For Dummies
978-1-118-11792-7

Resumes For Dummies,
6th Edition
978-0-470-87361-8

Starting an Etsy Business
For Dummies, 2nd Edition
978-1-118-59024-9

Diet & Nutrition

Belly Fat Diet For Dummies
978-1-118-34585-6

Mediterranean Diet
For Dummies
978-1-118-71525-3

Nutrition For Dummies,
5th Edition
978-0-470-93231-5

Digital Photography

Digital SLR Photography
All-in-One For Dummies,
2nd Edition
978-1-118-59082-9

Digital SLR Video &
Filmmaking For Dummies
978-1-118-36598-4

Photoshop Elements 12
For Dummies
978-1-118-72714-0

Gardening

Herb Gardening
For Dummies, 2nd Edition
978-0-470-61778-6

Gardening with Free Range
Chickens For Dummies
978-1-118-54754-0

Health

Boosting Your Immunity
For Dummies
978-1-118-40200-9

Diabetes For Dummies,
4th Edition
978-1-118-29447-5

Living Paleo For Dummies
978-1-118-29405-5

Big Data

Big Data For Dummies
978-1-118-50422-2

Data Visualization
For Dummies
978-1-118-50289-1

Hadoop For Dummies
978-1-118-60755-8

Language &
Foreign Language

500 Spanish Verbs
For Dummies
978-1-118-02382-2

English Grammar
For Dummies, 2nd Edition
978-0-470-54664-2

French All-in-One
For Dummies
978-1-118-22815-9

German Essentials
For Dummies
978-1-118-18422-6

Italian For Dummies,
2nd Edition
978-1-118-00465-4

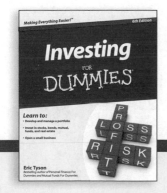 *Available in print and e-book formats.*

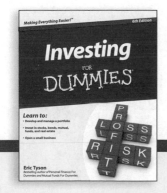
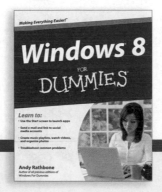

Available wherever books are sold. **For more information or to order direct visit www.dummies.com**

Math & Science

Algebra I For Dummies,
2nd Edition
978-0-470-55964-2

Anatomy and Physiology
For Dummies, 2nd Edition
978-0-470-92326-9

Astronomy For Dummies,
3rd Edition
978-1-118-37697-3

Biology For Dummies,
2nd Edition
978-0-470-59875-7

Chemistry For Dummies,
2nd Edition
978-1-118-00730-3

1001 Algebra II Practice
Problems For Dummies
978-1-118-44662-1

Microsoft Office

Excel 2013 For Dummies
978-1-118-51012-4

Office 2013 All-in-One
For Dummies
978-1-118-51636-2

PowerPoint 2013
For Dummies
978-1-118-50253-2

Word 2013 For Dummies
978-1-118-49123-2

Music

Blues Harmonica
For Dummies
978-1-118-25269-7

Guitar For Dummies,
3rd Edition
978-1-118-11554-1

iPod & iTunes
For Dummies, 10th Edition
978-1-118-50864-0

Programming

Beginning Programming
with C For Dummies
978-1-118-73763-7

Excel VBA Programming
For Dummies, 3rd Edition
978-1-118-49037-2

Java For Dummies,
6th Edition
978-1-118-40780-6

Religion & Inspiration

The Bible For Dummies
978-0-7645-5296-0

Buddhism For Dummies,
2nd Edition
978-1-118-02379-2

Catholicism For Dummies,
2nd Edition
978-1-118-07778-8

Self-Help & Relationships

Beating Sugar Addiction
For Dummies
978-1-118-54645-1

Meditation For Dummies,
3rd Edition
978-1-118-29144-3

Seniors

Laptops For Seniors
For Dummies, 3rd Edition
978-1-118-71105-7

Computers For Seniors
For Dummies, 3rd Edition
978-1-118-11553-4

iPad For Seniors
For Dummies, 6th Edition
978-1-118-72826-0

Social Security
For Dummies
978-1-118-20573-0

Smartphones & Tablets

Android Phones
For Dummies, 2nd Edition
978-1-118-72030-1

Nexus Tablets
For Dummies
978-1-118-77243-0

Samsung Galaxy S 4
For Dummies
978-1-118-64222-1

Samsung Galaxy Tabs
For Dummies
978-1-118-77294-2

Test Prep

ACT For Dummies,
5th Edition
978-1-118-01259-8

ASVAB For Dummies,
3rd Edition
978-0-470-63760-9

GRE For Dummies,
7th Edition
978-0-470-88921-3

Officer Candidate Tests
For Dummies
978-0-470-59876-4

Physician's Assistant Exam
For Dummies
978-1-118-11556-5

Series 7 Exam For Dummies
978-0-470-09932-2

Windows 8

Windows 8.1 All-in-One
For Dummies
978-1-118-82087-2

Windows 8.1 For Dummies
978-1-118-82121-3

Windows 8.1 For Dummies,
Book + DVD Bundle
978-1-118-82107-7

e Available in print and e-book formats.

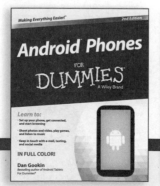

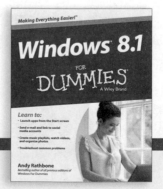

Available wherever books are sold. **For more information or to order direct visit www.dummies.com**